Global Knowledge
International Development

The 'knowledge agenda' has become a central part of the discourse of developing societies as well as advanced economies. Governments and international organisations devote considerable financial resources to both in-house and contracted research. This volume provides a coherent examination of policy thinking and institutional practice on the questions of how, why and to what extent research informs policy in the field of international development.

Drawn from think tanks, academia and development agencies, the contributors provide case histories of how research projects have informed local, national and global policy. They also investigate how development agencies have promoted the development potential of research, and outline various methods and techniques of policy entrepreneurship. Providing an analysis of thinking and practice in this topic, the book explores three key elements:

- The role of knowledge and ideas in development policy
- Case studies of projects bridging research and policy-making at the International Development Research Centre (IDRC) in Canada, the Overseas Development Institute (ODI) and the Washington, DC-based International Food Policy Research Institute (IFPRI)
- The intersection of research and policy communities with case studies on Africa, South Asia and Hungary

Global Knowledge Networks and International Development will interest students, researchers and policy-makers concerned with global policy, global governance and development.

Diane Stone is Marie Curie Chair and Head of the Public Policy Programme at the Central European University, Hungary. **Simon Maxwell** is Director of the Overseas Development Institute, the UK's leading independent think tank on international development and humanitarian policy.

Global Knowledge Networks and International Development

Bridges across boundaries

Edited by Diane Stone and Simon Maxwell

LONDON AND NEW YORK

First published 2005
by Routledge
2 Park Square, Milton Park, Abingdon, Oxon OX14 4RN

Simultaneously published in the USA and Canada
by Routledge
270 Madison Ave, New York, NY 10016

Transferred to Digital Printing 2006

Routledge is an imprint of the Taylor & Francis Group

© 2005 Diane Stone and Simon Maxwell

Reprinted 2008

Typeset in Times New Roman by
GreenGate Publishing Services, Tonbridge, Kent
Printed and bound in Great Britain by
MPG Digital Solutions, Bodmin, Cornwall

All rights reserved. No part of this book may be reprinted or reproduced or
utilised in any form or by any electronic, mechanical, or other means, now
known or hereafter invented, including photocopying and recording, or in
any information storage or retrieval system, without permission in writing
from the publishers.

British Library Cataloguing in Publication Data
A catalogue record for this book is available from the British Library

Library of Congress Cataloging in Publication Data
Global knowledge networks and international development : bridges
across boundaries / edited by Diane Stone and Simon Maxwell.
      p.cm.
   Includes bibliographical references and index.
   ISBN 0-415-43373-8
   ISBN 978-0-415-43373-0

     1. Economic development—Research. 2. Communication in
economic development. 3. Information policy. 4. Communication,
International. I. Stone, Diane, 1964– II. Maxwell, Simon.

HD77.G56 2005
338.9'26—dc22

                           2004011752

Contents

Illustrations

Figures

Tables

Contributors

Fred Carden, PhD, is Director of the Evaluation Unit at the International Development Research Centre. He holds a PhD from the University of Montreal and a master's degree in environmental studies from York University. He has taught and carried out research at York University, the Cooperative College of Tanzania, the Bandung Institute of Technology (Indonesia) and the University of Indonesia. He has published in evaluation theory and methods as well as in development cooperation.

Sarah Clarke was a Specialist in International Development and Economics at the Global Development Network from 2001 to 2002. She received her master's degree from the London School of Economics in International Political Economy. She has also worked with a variety of non-governmental organisations focusing on international development issues, primarily in South and Southeast Asia. Currently, Sarah lives and works in New York City where she serves as Associate Representative to the United Nations for the Quaker United Nations Office. Her current work centres on peace-building efforts and prevention of violent conflict.

Julius Court is a Research Fellow in the Research and Policy in Development Programme at the Overseas Development Institute. He has experience as a researcher and in think tank management. Current research focuses on issues of bridging research and policy as well as governance and development. He worked as an Executive Officer in the Office of the Rector at the United Nations University in Tokyo, Japan. Before joining United Nations University, he was a researcher at the School of Oriental and African Studies, University of London. His recent publications include: *Making Sense of Governance* (forthcoming, 2004) and *Asia and Africa in the Global Economy* (2003). He is currently on the Council of the UK Development Studies Association.

James L. Garrett is a Research Fellow in the Food Consumption and Nutrition Division of the International Food Policy Research Institute. He holds undergraduate and master's degrees in political science and public policy analysis, and a PhD in agricultural economics. He has worked on impact assessment issues at the International Food Policy Research Institute since 1997, including developing a conceptual framework and case studies on the use of research information in the policy process. He is also a member of the International Food Policy Research Institute's Working Group on Impact Assessment. In addition, he co-leads a research programme at the International Food Policy Research Institute on urban livelihoods and urban food and nutrition security.

Kenneth King is the Director of the Centre of African Studies and Professor of International and Comparative Education at the University of Edinburgh. His research interests over the years have focused on aid policy towards all subsectors of education, including higher education; technical and vocational education and training; science and technology education; and education and training in micro-enterprises and the informal sector. He has carried out research and advisory work in Africa for more than 20 years, including in Kenya, Tanzania, Zimbabwe, Botswana, South Africa, Sierra Leone, Ghana, Nigeria, Zaire and Ethiopia. He has edited and published numerous books. Most recently, in 1998, he published for DFID *A Synthesis Evaluation of Higher Education* (DFID, London), and in 1999 *Changing International Aid to Education: Global Patterns, Local Contexts* (NORRAG/UNESCO, Paris: edited by King and Buchert), *Changing Education and Training in South Africa,* University of Cape Town Press (edited by Wally Morrow and Kenneth King), and *Enterprise in Africa: Between Poverty and Growth,* Intermediate Technology Publications (edited by King and McGrath). Also in 2004 he published with S. McGrath *Knowledge for Development? Comparing British, Japanese, Swedish and World Bank Aid* (Zed Press, London).

Andrea Krizsán has been a Research Fellow at the Centre for Policy Studies of the Central European University, Budapest, since 2002. She works as researcher on projects related to gender mainstreaming, disability discrimination, minority ombudsman institutions and ethnic monitoring. She is the group mentor for the Equal Opportunity Policy group of the International Policy Fellowship Program of the Open Society Institute. Her PhD, undertaken in the Political Science Department of the Central European University, was about anti-discrimination policy and the role of specialised agencies in enforcing such policies.

Sandra J. MacLean, PhD, is an Assistant Professor of Political Science at Simon Fraser University, British Columbia, Canada. Her current research, which focuses particularly on the Southern African region, is concerned with (global) governance in areas of human security, health and development. Among her most recent publications are co-edited volumes, *Crises of Governance in Asia and Africa* (Ashgate, 2001) and *Advancing African Security and Development* (Centre for Foreign Policy Studies, 2002). Her work has also appeared as authored or co-authored articles in several journals including *Third World Quarterly, Global Networks, Canadian Foreign Policy, Canadian Journal of*

Development Studies, *New Political Economy* and *Journal of Contemporary African Studies* and as chapters in several edited volumes.

Simon Maxwell has been Director of the Overseas Development Institute since 1997. Before that he worked overseas for ten years, in Kenya, India and Bolivia, and for about fifteen years at the Institute of Development Studies, University of Sussex, latterly as Programme Manager for Poverty, Food Security and the Environment. The Overseas Development Institute describes itself as Britain's leading independent think tank on international development and humanitarian policy – this statement of purpose has led Simon Maxwell to think, write and lecture on policy processes and the role of research-based think tanks, both nationally and across national borders.

Pamela K. Mbabazi, PhD, is a senior lecturer in Development Planning, and Dean, Faculty of Development Studies at Mbarara University in Uganda. She was educated in Uganda, Ghana, Germany and the UK. She teaches Planning and Rural Development and is currently setting up a Centre for Conflict and Peace Studies at Mbarara University. She has recently received a Rockefeller grant for work on, 'Livelihoods and Coping strategies for People in Conflict Situations in Northern Uganda' and is co-author of a contribution to David Lewis and Tina Wallace (eds) *New Roles and Relevance: Development NGOs and the Challenge of Change* (Kumarian, 2000).

Desmond McNeill, BA, PhD (economics) is a Research Professor, and earlier Director, at the Centre for Development and the Environment, University of Oslo, Norway. He has published on a wide range of topics, including foreign aid policy, interdisciplinary research, and the relationship between research and policy. He has worked as adviser or consultant in more than 15 develop-ing countries, mostly in Africa and Asia, for various aid agencies. His publications include (with M. Bøås, eds) *Global Institutions and Development: Framing the World?* (Routledge, 2003); (with M. Bøås) *Multilateral Institutions: A Critical Introduction* (Pluto Press, 2003); (with A. Holland, K. Lee, eds) *Global Sustainable Development in the 21st Century* (Edinburgh University Press, 2000).

Stephanie Neilson is the Evaluation Officer with the Evaluation Unit and has been with IDRC since 2000. She has carried out research and worked in Southern Africa and South Asia. She holds an MSc in Rural Planning and Development from the University of Guelph and a BA in International Development, University of Guelph. Her current work includes examining the influence of donor-supported research on public policy. Her other areas of interest include organisational development, gender violence, and planning and evaluation tools and methods.

Shirin M. Rai is Professor of Politics and International Studies at the University of Warwick. Her research interests are in the area of feminist politics, democ-ratisation, globalisation and development studies. She has written extensively on issues of gender, governance and democratisation. Author of several books, the most recent being *Gender and the Political Economy of Development* (Polity Press, 2002); (co-ed.) *Rethinking Empowerment: Gender and Development in a Global/Local World* (Routledge, 2002); and (ed.) *Mainstreaming Gender, Democratizing the State?* (Manchester University Press, 2003).

James G. Ryan is currently a Visiting Fellow in the Economics Division of the Research School of Pacific and Asian Studies at the Australian National University in Canberra, A.C.T. He is an agricultural economist who has published widely on the economics of agricultural research and technological change in developing countries, including implications for employment and human nutrition and on the formulation of strategies and priorities in agricultural research and development. He was Leader of the Economics Program at the International Crops Research Institute for the Semi-Arid Tropics in Hyderabad India (1974–83), Deputy Director of the Australian Centre for International Agricultural Research in Canberra Australia (1983–91), and Director General of the International Crops Research Institute for the Semi-Arid Tropics (1991–7). Current interests and recent assignments include the assessment of the economic impacts of agricultural and economic policy research, future strategies and priorities for international livestock research, the prospective challenges and opportunities for agricultural research and development in the semi-arid tropics, and strategies for harnessing science and technology for improving agricultural productivity and food security in Africa.

Timothy M. Shaw is Professor of Commonwealth Governance and Development and Director of the Institute of Commonwealth Studies, University College London. He researches and writes on African and other Third World governance, international relations/political economy and development, and security studies/policies, currently focusing on new forms of conflict and response, including think tanks and tracks 2 and 3 diplomacy. Dr Shaw was until recently Professor of Political Science and International Development Studies and Director of the Centre for Foreign Policy Studies at Dalhousie University in Nova Scotia, and holds Ford Foundation and SSHRC collaborative grants. He continues to serve as Visiting Professor at the universities of Mbarara, Stellenbosch and Western Cape (South Africa). His most recent co-edited collections include: (with Fredrik Soderbaum) *Theories of New Regionalism: A Palgrave Reader* (Palgrave–Macmillan, 2003); *Africa's Challenge to International Relations Theory* (Palgrave, 2001); and *Crises of Governance in Asia and Africa* (Ashgate, 2001) and his most recent articles appeared in *Canadian Journal of Development Studies, Commonwealth and Comparative Politics, Journal of International Development, Round Table, African Journal of Political Science, Canadian Foreign Policy, New Political Economy* as well as *Third World Quarterly*.

Lyn Squire. After completing his PhD at Cambridge University, Lyn Squire joined the World Bank in 1972 through the Young Professionals Program. Since then he has held several assignments in both the Operational Complex and Research. Among other accomplishments, Dr Squire established the Economic Research Forum in Cairo, when he was Chief Economist for the Middle East and North Africa, and was the Staff Director for the 1990 World Development Report on Poverty. For four years Dr Squire served as Director of the World Bank's Research Department. The author of many articles and several books, Dr Squire's current research interests are aid effectiveness, inequality, and project evaluation. Dr Squire retired from the World Bank in July 2001 and currently serves as Director of the Global Development Network, a worldwide association of research and policy institutes whose goal is to generate, share, and apply multidisciplinary knowledge for the purpose of development.

Diane Stone is Marie Curie Chair and Head, Master of Public Policy Programme in the Centre for Policy Studies at the Central European University. She is on leave of absence from her position as Reader in Politics and International Studies at Warwick University. She teaches in the area of comparative public policy, globalisation and governance. During 1999 she worked in the World Bank Institute in Washington, DC, involved in the creation of the Global Development Network (http://www.gdnet.org) and is now a member of its governing body. She is a member of the Governing Council of the Overseas Development Institute – a London-based think tank. Her first book was *Capturing the Political Imagination: Think Tanks and the Policy Process* (London: Frank Cass, 1996). Edited volumes include: *Think Tank Traditions: Policy Research and the Politics of Ideas Across Nations* (Manchester University Press, 2004); as well as *Banking on Knowledge: The Genesis of the Global Development Network* (Routledge, 2000). She is working on a research monograph tracking the transnationalisation of knowledge elites.

John Young joined the Overseas Development Institute in May 2001 after five years in Indonesia managing an action-research project to promote more decentralised and client-oriented public services. Before that he was the Intermediate Technology Development Group's Country Director in Kenya, responsible for managing the group's practical project and research work on a wide range of technologies to ensure that lessons were effectively communicated to government and non-government policy makers. Since joining the Overseas Development Institute he has been involved in projects on decentralisation and rural services, information and information systems, strengthening southern research capacity and bridging research and policy. He now runs the Research and Policy in Development Programme which aims to improve the use of research in development policy and practice through improved knowledge about research-policy links; improved knowledge management and learning systems; improved communication; and improved awareness of the importance of research.

Violetta Zentai, PhD, Rutgers University 2001 has been the acting director at the Centre for Policy Studies since 2001 and the director since September 2003. In addition to her work at the centre, she continues a variety of other related occupations including part-time programme manager for the Local Government and Public Service Reform Initiatives with the Open Society Institute in Budapest and visiting lecturer at Janus Pannonius University, Pécs. She also taught at Eötvös Lóránd University, the Budapest University of Economic Sciences and Public Administration, and the Invisible College, Budapest. Violetta is also Chair of Board and spokesperson for MONA (Foundation for the Women of Hungary) and an editor for *Café Bábel*, an interdisciplinary critical quarterly in Hungarian. Her research projects investigate democratic governance and decentralisation, gender equality, and cultures of capitalism in post-socialist transformations. Her recent publications include: (with Krizsán, A., eds) *Reshaping Globalization. Multilateral Dialogues and New Policy Initiatives* (Central European University Press, 2003); (with Peteri, G.) 'Lessons on Successful Reform Management' in G. Peteri (ed.) *Mastering Decentralization and Public Administration Reform in CEE* (LGI, 2002).

Preface

A transnational 'community of practice' has emerged over the past decade, interested in the most effective use of research, data and analysis in the formation of policy. The contributors to this volume are part of the community. Drawn from think tanks, universities and development agencies, they share not only an interest in research and its intellectual attractions, but also a passion for putting research to its best use.

The papers are innovative in this respect. They provide a coherent examination of policy thinking and institutional practice across national boundaries, on the questions of how, why and to what extent research informs policy in the field of international development. Making strong links between research and policy is far from straightforward when the links cross boundaries: there are problems of culture and understanding involved, but also problems of power and participation. The papers do not shy away from these problems. Collectively, they seek to advance understanding of research, not simply as a global public good, but as a policy tool of international organisations, development agencies and civil society.

Our thanks go first to the authors of the papers, who have shared their thinking and experience, and done so both analytically and readably. We are particularly pleased that they all, without exception, combine both theory and practice: these are bridge-builders on their own account.

We would also like to express particular thanks to Lyn Squire and his colleagues at the GDN, who have provided opportunities for us to develop our ideas. Their enterprise embodies the kind of global knowledge network we seek to build. Our thanks also to Susanna Moorehead at the UK DFID for her understanding of this issue and her early buy-in to the process making this book possible.

Domestically, we would like to thank David Sunderland and Erwin Juenemann at the ODI and Tamas Dombas at the Centre for Policy Studies for their work on the text. At Routledge, Grace McInnes has provided timely support and advice. Finally, the Centre for the Study of Globalisation and Regionalisation series editor, Richard Higgott, has given us considerable latitude to explore these innovative new themes in the study of globalisation and development. We, of course, remain responsible for errors, omissions, misrepresentations, elisions and exaggerations.

Diane Stone and Simon Maxwell
March 2004

Acknowledgements

The editors and publisher would like to thank Blackwell Publishing for their permission to reprint 'Governance for reconstruction in Africa: Challenges for policy communities and coalitions' by Pamela K. Mbabazi, Sandra J. MacLean and Timothy M. Shaw. This originally appeared in *Global Networks*, Volume 2: Issue 1, January 2002.

Blackwell publishing are also thanked for permission to print an amended version of 'Networking Across Borders: The South Asian Reseach Network on Gender, Law and Governance'. This originally appeared in *Global Networks,* Volume 3: Issue 1, January 2003.

Abbreviations

ACCORD	African Centre for the Cooperative Resolution of Disputes
AERC	African Economic Research Consortium
AFSSRN	Asian Fisheries Social Science Research Network
AIDA	Accessible Information on Development Activities
AIDS	Acquired Immune Deficiency Syndrome
APQC	American Productivity and Quality Centre
ASARECA	Association for Strengthening Agricultural Research in Eastern and Central Africa
ASEAN	Association of Southeast Asian Nations
ASEAN-ISIS	ASEAN Institutes of Strategic and International Affairs
ASK	Ain o Salish Kendra
BMZ	Bundesministerium für wirtschaftliche Zusammenarbeit und Entwicklung (Federal Ministry for Economic Cooperation and Development, Germany)
CACM	Central American Common Market
CAD	Canadian Dollar
CAHW	community animal health worker
CANDID	Creation, Adoption, Negation and Distortion of Ideas in Development
CCR	Centre for Conflict Resolution
CDF	Comprehensive Development Framework
CEE	Central and Eastern Europe
CERGE-EI	Centre for Economic Research and Graduate Education – Economics Institute
CFPS	Centre for Foreign Policy Studies
CGIAR	Consultative Group on International Agricultural Research
CIDA	Canadian International Development Agency
CSCAP	Council for Security Cooperation in the Asia Pacific
CWDS	Centre for Women's Development Studies
DAC	Development Assistance Committee (of the OECD)
DAH	Decentralised Animal Health
DAHC	Decentralised Community-Based Animal Health Care
DFAIT	Department of Foreign Affairs and International Trade (Canada)

DFID	Department for International Development
DG	Development Gateway (formerly Global Development Gateway)
DRC	Development Resource Centre (World Bank)
EADI	European Association of Development Research and Training Institutes
EC	European Commission
ED	Executive Director
EEPNET	Environmental Economics and Policy Network
EERC	Economic Education and Research Consortium
EGDI	Expert Group on Development Issues
ERF	Economic Research Forum
ERRC	European Roma Rights Centre
ESB	Education Sub-Board (Open Society Institute)
ESRC	Economic and Social Research Council
EU	European Union
EUMAP	EU Accession Monitoring Program
Eurodad	European Network on Debt and Development
FWLD	Forum for Women, Law and Development
G-24	Group of 24
GDG	Global Development Gateway (now Development Gateway)
GDN	Global Development Network
GDNet	the on-line Network associated with the GDN
GLR	Great Lakes Region
GNP	Gross National Product
GPPN	Global Public Policy Network
GRP	Global and Regional Research Program
GTZ	Deutsche Gesellschaft für Technische Zusammenarbeit (German Agency for Development Cooperation)
HIPC	heavily indebted poor countries
HIV	Human Immunodeficiency Virus
HO	Home Office
ICEG	International Centre for Economic Growth
ICRIER	Indian Centre for Research on International Economic Relations
ICT	Information and Communication Technology
IDA	International Development Association
IDB	InterAmerican Development Bank
IDRC	International Development Research Centre
IDS	Institute of Development Studies
IDT	International Development Target
IEA	International Economics Association
IFI	International Financial Institution
IFPRI	International Food Policy Research Institute
IGD	Institute for Global Dialogue
ILO	International Labour Organisation
IMF	International Monetary Fund

IMPACT	International Model for Policy Analysis and Agricultural Commodity Trade
INGOs	international non-governmental organisation(s)
IPF	International Policy Fellowship (Centre for Policy Studies, Central European University)
IQHEI	Institut québécois des hautes études internationals
ISO	International Organisation for Standardisation
ISS	Institute for Strategic Studies
ITDG	Intermediate Technology Development Group
JBIC	Japanese Bank for International Cooperation
JEEAR	Joint Evaluation of Emergency Assistance to Rwanda
JICA	Japan International Cooperation Agency
KM	Knowledge Management
KNETs	Knowledge Network(s)
KS	Knowledge Sharing
KVB	Kenya Veterinary Board
LACEA	Latin American and Caribbean Economic Association
LATN	Latin American Trade Network
LGI	Local Government and Public Service Reform Initiative (Open Society Institute)
MDG	Millennium Development Goal
MMCP	Managing Multiethnic Communities Project (LGI)
MNC	multinational corporation
MSF	Médecins sans Frontières
NAFTA	North American Free Trade Agreement
NEPAD	New Partnership for Africa's Development
NGO	non-governmental organisation
NORAD	Norwegian Agency for Development Cooperation
NORRAG	Network for Policy Review Research and Advice on Education and Training
ODI	Overseas Development Institute
OECD	Organisation for Economic Cooperation and Development
OSI	Open Society Institute
Oxfam	Oxford Committee for Famine Relief
PAC	Partnership Africa Canada
PEAP	Poverty Eradication Action Plan
PHARE	Poland and Hungary Action for Restructuring of the Economy
PRGF	Poverty Reduction and Growth Facility
PRISM	Performance Reporting and Information System for Management
PRSP	Poverty Reduction Strategy Paper
RAPID	Research and Policy in Development
RAPnet	Research and Policy Network
RAWOO	Raad voor het Wetenschappelijk Onderzoek in het kader van Ontwikkelingssamenwerking (Netherlands Development Assistance Research Council)

RBEC	Regional Bureau for Europe and the Commonwealth of Independent States (World Bank)
RDFN	Rural Development Forestry Network
RPP	Roma Participation Program
SADC	Southern African Development Community
SAIIA	South African Institute for International Affairs
SANEI	South Asia Network of Economic Institutes
SARC	South Asian Regional Cooperation
SAREC	Swedish Agency for Research Cooperation with Developing Countries
SARN	South Asian Research Network
SCF	Save the Children Fund
SDC	Swiss Development Cooperation
SIDA	Swedish International Development Cooperation Agency
SLA	Sustainable Livelihoods Approach
SPIA	Standing Panel on Impact Assessment
TAC	Technical Advisory Committee
TAN	Transnational Advocacy Network(s)
TWN	Third World Network
UCT	University of Cape Town
UDN	Uganda Debt Network
UK	United Kingdom
UN	United Nations
UNCTAD	United Nations Conference on Trade and Development
UNDP	United Nations Development Programme
UNICEF	United Nations Children's Fund
UNU	United Nations University
US	United States
USAID	United States Agency for International Development
USD	United States Dollar
VASEM	Vietnam Agricultural Spatial Equilibrium Model
WB	World Bank
WBI	World Bank Institute
WCED	World Commission on Environment and Development
WDR	World Development Report
WTO	World Trade Organisation

1 Global knowledge networks and international development

Bridges across boundaries

Simon Maxwell and Diane Stone

Introduction: bridging research and policy

This book is a contribution to the burgeoning literature on bridging research and policy in international development. The wider literature is concerned with how research can best influence policy, and conversely with how policy can make better use of research. Our particular concern is with policy that applies across national borders, and with the potential contribution of global knowledge networks.

The case for global policy surely needs no making: global warming, trade, financial stability, security – these are all examples of global problems that need global solutions. The role of research in helping to find solutions is, however, more difficult. What kinds of ideas count in current debates, and whose? What links exist between research and policy at global level? And what are the accountabilities? Will global development 'narratives' be the exclusive property of rich and well-connected northern institutions? Or will there be substantive contributions from all players? That is where networks come in.

Networks can play an important part in helping to create a policy process that is research rich, inclusive and accountable – at least in theory. Even so, the virtues of networks are not straightforward. We find that access can be unequal, transaction costs high, and sustainability problematic. This is true even of well-funded and well-meaning initiatives like those taken by the World Bank. There is a way forward, but it requires development agencies and actors to think in new ways about knowledge management.

We will come to that question. However, we need to begin with the more general topic of bridging research and policy. This is not straightforward, either. A linear model, in which careful research leads inexorably to better policy, is widely derided. As Clay and Schaffer (1984) remark, 'the whole life of policy is a chaos of purposes and accidents' (see also Grindle and Thomas 1991). Alternative policy models include disjointed incrementalism (Lindblom 1980), the interactive model (Grindle and Thomas 1991), mixed scanning (Walt 1994), policy as argument (Juma and Clark 1995) and ideas about the 'tipping point' (Gladwell 2000).

Several of the papers here venture into this territory. Clarke and Squire set the issue in the general context of institutional development and path dependency, drawing on the ideas of Douglass North. More particularly, Court and Young from the Overseas Development Institute (ODI), Ryan and Garrett from the International Food Policy Research Institute (IFPRI) and Carden and Neilson from the International Development Research Centre (IDRC) help us to understand the link between research and policy. These organisations all have an interest, not only in their research being policy-relevant, but also in being seen and used by decision-makers.

The terms 'research', 'ideas' and 'policy' need elaboration. McNeill talks about *ideas* and describes them as 'collective images' which 'powerfully influence ... policy'. These ideas become wrapped up in research. Court and Young are both less poetic and less instrumental: they draw on work of the OECD (1981) to define *research* as 'any systematic effort to increase the stock of knowledge'. Their definition of *policy* is equally pragmatic: any 'course of action', including actions on the ground as well as declarations or plans. Policy, they remind us, is what policy does. However, policy is also what does *not* happen.

Another important issue concerns *where* policy is enacted. As will become evident as the reader progresses through this volume, we do not limit our understanding of policy-making and implementation to the national context. Instead, the policies of international organisations and development agencies apply across national boundaries. Indeed, the chapters addressing the Open Society Network and the South Asian Research Network draw attention to the regional impact of both policy and research. Moreover, the chapters by Stone and by Carden and Neilson heighten our understanding not only of how policy is informed and shaped through transnational research networks but also how policy can be crafted in fora beyond the state.

Why is the link between research and policy difficult to make?

Drawing on the papers here, as well as on earlier reviews (see Sutton 1999; Stone *et al.* 2001; Crewe and Young 2002; de Vibe *et al.* 2002), we can identify three streams of explanation of why the link between research and policy is difficult. These are:

1   supply-side accounts;
2   demand-led explanations; and
3   socio-political thinking on knowledge utilisation.

Inadequacies in either the supply or demand for policy-relevant research are well accounted (see Lepgold and Nincic 2001). A less coherent, but more diverse set of explanations draws parallels between knowledge and power.

The first set of explanations identifies problems in the character of research supply. In many developing and transition countries, there is an inadequate supply of policy-relevant research. This is a public goods problem, in that there is insufficient public funding to educate and employ policy researchers, while it is too costly for private investors to fund research that is freely available to other users

(Squire 2000). Where countries enjoy a pool of talented researchers, this community may lack the tools – communications technology, data sets and other resources – that allow them to produce research suitable for policy use. Yet, even in ideal research circumstances, the supply of policy-relevant research may be very weak, because researchers are poorly informed about the policy process and how research might be relevant. Researchers can also often be ineffective communicators (Commission on the Social Sciences 2003). The popular perception is perhaps not surprising, that academics and researchers live in an 'ivory tower'.

The second set of explanations for poor research use has to do with the flawed demand for research. At a basic level, demand may be undeveloped because politicians are ignorant about the existence of policy-relevant research. Even if policy-makers are aware of useful policy research being undertaken, they may be incapable of absorbing and using research. John Maynard Keynes once remarked: 'there is nothing a Government hates more than to be well-informed, for it makes the process of arriving at decisions much more complicated and difficult' (quoted in Minogue 1993: 17). Research is a lengthy process, whereas politicians are driven by daily political concerns in a 'pressure cooker' environment. Researchers are often insensitive to the pressure for immediate action which decision-makers face (Oh 1997: 4). Alternatively, there may be a tendency for anti-intellectualism in government, that mitigates against the use of research in policy-making. This problem can be exacerbated in developing countries. As noted by a researcher in Ghana:

> In developing countries, policy makers are just suspicious of the political affiliations and intentions of academic researchers. Where democracy has weak roots and political survival is the order of the ruler, there is a tendency among the ruling body to ignore and maintain the impression that researchers are out of tune with reality.[1]

Consequently, another consideration affecting the demand for research is its politicisation. Research findings are easy to abuse, either through selective use, de-contextualisation or misquotation. Decision-makers might do this in order to reinforce existing policy preferences or prejudices. Alternatively, they gather and utilise information to support their policy positions as well as to legitimise decision outcomes.

A third set of explanations deals with the politics of research, or what Neilson (2001) at IDRC refers to as 'political models' of knowledge use (*inter alia*, Fischer 2003; Keeley and Scoones 2003; the essays in Stone 2000). Here, the concept of research 'user' becomes more blurred and at the same time, understanding where and how research might have influence becomes more diffuse and atmospheric. For instance, an organisation or group of researchers may have huge impact on the media or among NGO communities but little or no input into policy development. Conversely, even where there is a constructive dialogue between decision-makers and experts, there may be joint technocratic distance from the general public and those communities for whom research is intended to help.

Another important consideration in poor research impact is the contested validity of knowledge(s). Dominant ideologies, prevailing institutional arrangements, the nature of regime in power, the culture of public debate (or lack of it) and the prevailing idea of truth represent strong tendencies that structure what is considered 'relevant' or 'useful' knowledge (Flyvbjerg 2001). Finally, there are deeper questions about what is knowable. Our attention is then drawn to different epistemologies and 'ways of knowing'. The most common distinction drawn is between indigenous understandings of the world, and Western rationalist (scientific) approaches. Similarly, different professional perspectives and expert orthodoxies develop in communities of practice and knowledge networks.

The model developed at ODI by Court and Young presents a useful way of summarising the main elements of these arguments, in the diagram reproduced as Figure 1.1. This stresses the quality of the evidence, the context, and the links between the two. Where there are significant problems on the supply side then the 'Evidence' circle becomes an island in isolation from the 'Political Context' circle, where the 'Links' circle may be much smaller or might not even exist. Where problems of knowledge utilisation are found on the demand side then the 'Political Context' is de-linked from the 'Evidence' and whatever 'Links' that might have been developed by researchers with actors based in civil society. The third set of political explanations coincides with the Court and Young diagram, except that the three circles may overlap much more substantially than represented.

How can the links be improved?

A set of prescriptions can be seen to follow from these ideas, addressed in the papers here which report on evaluations, either from a piece of research forward to policy, or from a piece of policy back to the research which helped inspire it. The cases range from Roma policies in Eastern Europe to blood diamonds in Africa, through policies for debt relief and the concept of sustainable development.

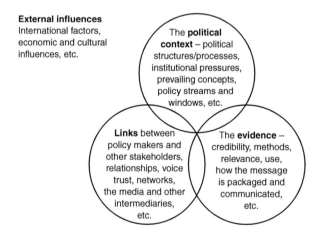

Figure 1.1 The RAPID framework: context, evidence and links
Source: Court and Young (this volume)

If the problem of knowledge utilisation is located on the supply side, then approaches to improve research communication and dissemination are needed. This could involve initiatives such as the establishment of research reporting services (on web-sites and traditional media); encouraging training activities for researchers, such as media workshops, exercises in public speaking, or training in how to write policy briefs. For instance, the UK Department for International Development has funded id21 – a fast-track research reporting service to bring UK-based development research findings and policy recommendations to policy-makers and development practitioners worldwide.[2] Similarly, in a heavy tome, Save the Children has produced a 'practical guide' for research on development (Laws 2003).

Another alternative is to cultivate intermediaries – a 'research broker' or 'policy entrepreneur' – with a flair for interpreting and communicating the technical or theoretical work. This is usually an individual, but sometimes a think tank or network plays a similar role in marketing knowledge and popularising research.

If the problem of research use is located on the demand side, then strategies might focus on improved awareness and absorption of research inside government, expanding research management expertise, and developing a culture of 'policy learning'. Government agencies and international organisations do face pressures to become 'intelligent consumers' of research and effective 'knowledge managers'. Administrative reforms might include establishing in-house policy evaluation units, sabbaticals for civil servants in a university or research institute, the creation of civil service colleges, or in-house bureaucratic training on research management and 'evidence-based policy'.

Such measures often assume that knowledge utilisation in government is a technical problem that can be resolved with technical 'fixes' and improved knowledge management. However, a larger part of the problem lies in understanding flaws and imperfections in the policy process. The gap in the execution of policy is the difference between the policy-makers' objectives and what actually happens at the point of policy delivery. Policy-makers – either in national governments or international organisations – have a 'control deficit' that results from not implementing the policies themselves but being reliant upon local government officials, NGOs or other partners in policy. A simple top-down hierarchical view of policy implementation from executive down through ministries or departmental agencies cannot be assumed. Policy is thrown off course by factors such as bureaucratic incompetence or resistance. Modification of policy is inevitable in the implementation phase where 'street level' bureaucrats play an important role, mediating policy between the centre and the local environment, and between decision-making elites and the public (Lipsky 1980).

Political explanations of the research utilisation process stress the need for the kind of long term engagement of researchers with policy-makers that creates common understandings and identities. This implies developing practices that take researchers beyond supplying or brokering research in a one-way direction and allow a more productive exchange between decision-makers and implementers on what does and does not work in the transition from theory to practice.

Practices could include mechanisms that bring researchers into government, for example through internships, or co-option onto advisory committees. The emphasis is on shared problem definition within policy networks of researchers, policy-makers and other key stakeholders as the dynamic for effective change.

What do all these ideas mean for researchers?

There are more researchers working on international development now than at any time. The number includes many in developing countries – as Mbabazi *et al.* remind us in their paper (Chapter 10), which discusses think tanks and research networks in sub-Saharan Africa.

For these researchers in particular, we have three main sets of advice from current work. None of the following is to be taken as a fail-safe recipe for policy influence. Yet, all underscore the need for researchers and research institutions to understand and operate within the policy process.

First, Ryan and Garrett provide a summary of the main lessons derived from their work at IFPRI. Their case studies include agricultural and food policy research projects in Bangladesh, Malawi, Pakistan and Vietnam, among others. They find that policy impact is highest when research is:

i   both of high quality and seen to be independent;
ii   timely and responsive to the needs of policy-makers;
iii carried out through long term collaboration in-country, and with an in-country presence by the international research institute;
iv   delivered to a receptive policy environment;
v   based on good empirical data and simple analysis;
vi   presented in such a way as to balance more immediate impacts and sustainable ones;
vii carried out with the right partners and collaborators;
viii used to build a consensus for change among stake-holders; and
ix   carefully located in cross-country experience.

A good example of IFPRI's work is its research on ration shops in Pakistan, part of a global programme of work on how to reduce the cost of food subsidies and target expenditures more effectively. IFPRI brought a reputation for independence and rigour to the work in Pakistan, based on its international status, but also on a decade-long involvement in the country, including via resident staff. Its research was carried out in close collaboration with local research institutes and with the Ministry of Food and Agriculture. The research generated new data that helped to structure and clarify a highly charged debate about the potential impact on poor consumers of phasing out the ration scheme. And the research was presented in such a way that it could be taken up and used by senior political figures in the office of the Prime Minister.

Second, and covering similar territory, Court and Young provide a useful synthesis, drawing lessons for researchers from their own field studies. These include both local policy processes, like the introduction of para-professional vets in Kenya, and also international ones, like the adoption of Poverty Reduction Strategy Papers as the main vehicle for delivering enhanced debt relief. In their chapter, they construct a table based on the diagram portrayed above, identifying what researchers need to know, what they need to do, and how to do it. Moreover, their framework and set of recommendations form the basis for capacity building workshops recently initiated at ODI and, at the time of printing, delivered in London, New Delhi and Marrakesh.

Finally, one of us (Maxwell) has engaged with the question of how researchers can become better policy entrepreneurs, and has identified four styles – outlined in Figure 1.2 – each image backed up by theory in the literature on policy.

The researcher as 'story-teller'. Building on the literature about the importance of policy narratives in shaping policy (Roe 1991), this style draws attention to the need for researchers to present research findings in such a way that they are useful to policy-makers, helping them to frame problems and identify practical solutions. As Roe observes for rural development, it 'is a genuinely uncertain activity, and one of the principal ways practitioners, bureaucrats and policy-makers articulate and make sense of this uncertainty is to tell stories or scenarios that simplify the ambiguity' (1991). This is not to say that policy narratives are not sometimes contested and do occasionally oversimplify (see Leach and Mearns 1996). Our role model of a most proficient story-teller is Scheherezade.

The researcher as 'networker'. There is a large literature which demonstrates that policy-making usually takes place within communities (policy or epistemic communities) of people who know each other and interact to create or contest shared wisdom on policy. The resulting conclusions therefore emphasise that researchers need to invest in networks that include policy-makers (Haas 1992; Hasenclever *et al.* 1997). The role model here is Paul Revere, who famously raised the American militia against the British in 1775, drawing, according to Gladwell (2000), on his networking skills.

The researcher as 'engineer'. The third model comes from the literature on 'street-level bureaucracy' (Lipsky 1980) and is informed by the phrase: 'policy is what policy does'. As already noted, there can be a significant implementation gap between what politicians and policy-makers think they are doing and what actually happens on the ground. Researchers therefore need to work not just with the senior level policy-makers, but also with those who implement. Who better to represent that way of working than an engineer noted for his bridge building skill – Isambard Kingdom Brunel?

The researcher as 'fixer'. The fourth and final model of the policy entrepreneur in our field is the 'fixer'. The examples could include Rasputin and Machiavelli; cult figures who had the ear of political leaders. This model is about understanding the political dynamics and personalities within the policy process, knowing when to try and market research findings and to whom. Outside the corridors of power, these types of skills are also often well understood by lobbyists and political campaigners (Chapman and Fisher 1999).

© Alain Thomas

a) The Storyteller

© 'Sunshine', Clinton Avenue Elementary School

b) The Networker

© National Portrait Gallery

c) The Engineer

© Bob Atchison

d) The Fixer

Figure 1.2 Four styles of policy entrepreneurship

'Le Sultan, Schéhérazade et Dinarzade' © Alain Thomas www.alain-thomas.com. Reprinted with permission. 'Paul Revere' Source: http://comsewogue.k12.ny.us/showcase2000/amrev/home.htm Reprinted with permission. Portrait of Isambard Kingdom Brunel by Robert Howlett. © National Portrait Gallery. Reprinted with permission. 'Rasputin' Source: http://www.alexanderpalace.org/alexandra/XV.html © Bob Atchison. Reprinted with permission.

ODI work on this topic emphasises that successful research entrepreneurship probably needs a combination of all these styles. Most researchers are better at some than others.[3] Researchers either need to develop new skills or work in teams that bring different skills together (see Maxwell 2003b).

Bridges across boundaries: what are the issues?

Development questions are increasingly questions of global concern that are met with responses on a multilateral basis. One of the binding agents, or glue, for collective action is the sharing of knowledge. However, making the link between research and policy, difficult enough within national boundaries, becomes much more difficult when dealing with global problems. This is not only because the context is more complex, but also because Gramscian ideas about power and hegemony apply with special force in an unequal and competitive world: power both frames and shapes discourse (Gramsci 1971). As McNeill observes:

> in the international system, it is important to achieve consensus across institutions ..., and between member states; and shared ideas play an important part in such consensus. But inter-institutional rivalry is common within the multilateral system, and institutions gain international prestige partly by having good ideas. Ideas are thus an important source of power.

Three separate problems can be identified: the question of whose ideas are heard; the issue of linking ideas to action; and accountability.

Whose ideas are heard?

The issue of 'whose knowledge counts?' is a familiar one in development, from a long tradition of work on the neglect of indigenous technical knowledge (Chambers 1993; 1997). In some of the papers here, the emphasis is on the active exclusion from debate of certain ideas, certain types of people, certain institutions and certain disciplines. Put crudely, the argument is that those who count are Northern economists, usually male, and usually working in the World Bank or one of the major bilateral agencies.

Rai develops a general framework within which the trans-boundary argument can be located. She builds on a tradition of 'standpoint theory', which examines issues from a feminist perspective, and 'subaltern theory', which takes the perspective of the marginalised rather than that of the dominant elites. There are some serious critiques here, for example in the assertion that 'traditional epistemologies worked to systematically exclude the possibility that women could be the agents of knowledge' or that 'the stories of the marginalised ... were not accounted for in the histories of the dominant elites'.

Who are the agents of knowledge in the Annual Meetings of the World Bank and the IMF or in the WTO? The papers here are clear that the agents are a select group, and that their voices do carry weight. McNeill, for example, reviewing the way in which ideas are taken up, synthesised and used in policy-making, uncovers the power of ideas, but also that institutions like the World Bank 'acquire both the power of ideas and the power over ideas'. The title of his research project, the 'Creation, Adoption, Negation and Distortion of Ideas in Development' (CANDID) tells an immediate story about power. His three case studies are the informal sector, sustainable development, and social capital, but the conclusions from these studies surely carry more widely in research on development.

The power of institutions is closely related to the power of the economics discipline. McNeill, again, makes much of this, discussing the influence of the 'economic/technocratic nexus'. For example, he analyses the stance of the World Bank inspired Global Development Network, finding evidence that economics occupies a privileged position and also claims a special status for itself. He concludes that

> there are strong structural factors within the discipline of economics that make it difficult for economists to adopt other perspectives; and this becomes apparent even in something as concrete as a conference timetable and choice of presentations.

The exclusion problem is not limited to the World Bank and the other multilateral agencies. King has carried out a careful study of knowledge management in a series of other development agencies, both bilateral and multilateral. He finds great enthusiasm for knowledge management as a technique, drawing on private sector experience to try and turn development agencies into learning organisations. At the same time, however, he finds that the emphasis is internal rather than external, more concerned with capitalising on tacit knowledge within agencies than with increasing access or voice from the ultimate clients in developing countries. He calls this 'agency-centricity'. The one exception is Swedish Sida, which has explicitly set out to make learning a two way process involving developing countries. Similarities with the latter approach can be found in Carden and Neilson's study of IDRC, an agency that has also found great value in developing long term research relationships with research communities in developing countries.

What links to action?

It might not matter that certain voices were excluded if ideas did not count internationally, but the evidence is that they do. McNeill is again eloquent on this, demonstrating the way in which his three case study ideas were taken up and used. Social capital is perhaps the best example, making the transition in only a few years from an academic volume (Putnam's well-known book of 1993, 'Making Democracy Work') to being the 'new buzzword of the Western development community'. The World Bank, inevitably, particularly its economists, had a lot to do with importing the social captial idea into this organisation. There are other cases. For example, Mbabazi *et al.* describe the power of ideas produced in 'track two' diplomacy linking governmental and non-governmental policy networks (see also Simon 2000). Their examples are the agreement on blood diamonds and the debt reduction programme in Uganda.

What accountability?

When ideas are influential, then those who supply them need to be accountable. This is especially so because the trend towards multi-level governance challenges the sovereignty of national decision-makers (Peters and Pierre 2000). Stone analyses the new policy-making environment as an 'agora', a public space in which 'market and politics meet and mingle' (Nowotny *et al.* 2001). It may be the case that this meeting and mingling provides new opportunities for civil society to participate in a new and more democratic 'global polity'. Equally, however,

> the agora may be an unequal environment. Rather than organisational density and diversity disrupting hierarchies and dispersing power, they can also represent new constellations of privatised power. Instead of being civil society manifestations of bottom-up, non-statist globalisation, networks and other formations may be viewed as mutually implicated in the affairs of states and international organisations.

When it comes to knowledge and ideas, there is a particular responsibility on the 'gatekeepers', those who help to manage the flow of information. King illustrates the dilemma in his analysis of the Development Gateway, another World Bank initiative in the field of knowledge management. This is a project of 'breathtaking comprehensiveness', in which a crucial role is played by 'Topic Guides', who assemble material, guide discussion, synthesise lessons and provide overall quality control. King runs through the super-human qualities required of topic guides, as knowledge managers, networkers, reviewers, disseminators, synthesisers, policy analysts and scholars. His key point, however, is about the difficult and conflictual role of gatekeeper and about the complexity of accountability to the project, to the funders, and to members of the various communities of practice that make up the Gateway community.

Global knowledge networks: what have we learned?

If we are to move forward, we need to begin by distinguishing different kinds of international network. Stone provides a three-way taxonomy. The first is transnational advocacy coalitions, often found alongside social movements. The second is the global public policy network, usually a quasi-corporatist alliance of governments, agencies and civil society working together to deliver health care or a similar public good – an example might be the Global Fund to Fight AIDS, Tuberculosis and Malaria. And the third is the global knowledge network, or KNET, defined as follows:

> Knowledge networks incorporate professional bodies, academic research groups and scientific communities that organise around a special subject matter or issue. Individual or institutional inclusion in such networks is based upon professional and/or official recognition of expertise, as well as more subtle and informal processes of validating scholarly and scientific credibility. The primary motivation of such networks is to create and advance knowledge as well as to share, spread, and, in some cases, use that knowledge to inform policy and apply to practice.

The number of KNETS is rising rapidly; Stone provides many illustrations. There are many different ways of classifying KNETs, which Stone explores: by issue, in terms of ideology, by organisational style, by commitment to policy. And what do they actually do? Stone identifies two broad functions: first the transnational communication and dissemination of knowledge; and, second, acting as interlocutors with external audiences. In short, they are often engineering the 'Links' highlighted in the Court and Young model.

So far, so good – but are KNETs subject to the kinds of pitfalls identified earlier, or can they be genuine vehicles for democratic and accountable policy-making? In Rai's term, is there potential for a new kind of 'cosmopolitics'?

Certainly, there are risks and grounds for scepticism. In discussing the World Bank inspired Global Development Network (GDN), for example, both McNeill and King are worried about the hegemony of economics and the framing of the agenda by dominant institutions and individuals. Many others raise concerns, about whether networks legitimise or challenge power (Rai as well as Krizsan and Zentai), or about governance and accountability (Stone). For example, Stone analyses a number of KNETS as epistemic communities, discourse coalitions and embedded knowledge networks. She finds some which are powerfully linked to interests, for example the Evian Group, which conducts trade-related research and convenes high-level dialogues on the future role of the WTO. It is, says Stone, 'informally connected to powerful social forces within the WTO, the EU and leading corporations' and 'supportive of the neo-liberal order'.

Yet, proximity and affinity to power do not, by necessity, translate into policy influence. We must caution ourselves against assumptions about both political impact, on the one hand, and exclusivity, on the other. There are also grounds for optimism – in four different ways.

First, as Clarke and Squire emphasise, networks evolve. The Global Development Network, for example, has broadened its subject matter and governance, drawing in different disciplines, establishing itself as an independent foundation, and considering a move to a developing country. Path dependency, as Clarke and Squire point out, can be constraining – but there is always scope for positive change. Their contribution here traces the history of the GDN and concludes that

> GDN has drawn on the new institutionalism of Professor North regarding the importance of building flexible institutions, and the need to incorporate ongoing learning from one location to the next and over time.

Second, it is possible to build networks that involve 'dissidents' or 'subaltern' players and that are sustainable. In their chapter, Krizsan and Zentai discuss how the vision behind the Open Society Institutes formed throughout Central and Eastern Europe, and beyond, meant sustaining an environment favourable to alternative ways of thinking. In another contribution, Mbabazi *et al.* analyse the success of partnerships between governments, researchers and NGOs. In Uganda, for example, the 'consensual knowledge' of this mixed community, about the impact of high debt repayments, led eventually both to debt forgiveness and to better poverty reduction programmes. In her chapter on the South Asian Research Network

(SARN) on gender, law and governance, Rai identifies four conditions for success: interpersonal networks that facilitate recruitment and participation; strong links between individuals and organisations, based upon multiple allegiances; inter-organisational links that foster trust; and trust between participants and funders.

Third, it is possible for Southern-based organisations to influence policy. Carden and Neilson provide three examples: the Latin American Trade Network, the Asian Fisheries Social Science Research Network, and the Technical Support Service to the Group of 24. These operated in different ways, but all exhibited the potential for networks as 'platforms for action'. For example, the Latin American Trade Network worked closely with middle-ranking officials and was able to make constructive inputs to trade policy in Argentina, Paraguay, Peru and several countries in Central America. A central feature of all the networks was that ownership was strongly held within the networks rather than by donor organisations.

Fourth, there are important lessons for donors, and again these come strongly out of the IDRC study by Carden and Neilson. They stress that donors need to be persistent and take a longer term framework, that funding for capacity building be built into grants alongside research funding, and that an adequate investment in communication and dissemination be given real rather than token consideration.

Putting these ideas together, one of us (Maxwell 2003a) has written about ways to organise transnational knowledge networks focused on policy. This time there are three possible models.

The first might be thought of as the Microsoft option: a hegemonic research organisation, imposing common standards and selling a homogeneous product throughout the world. It only takes a moment's thought to dismiss this. Quite apart from the heterogeneity of national situations and the need to service development communities in many and highly diverse countries (a problem which has not stopped Microsoft, it might be said), the variety of institutional relationships and funding arrangements make this approach unfeasible. Even if it were feasible, the model implies a lack of diversity that is not appropriate to a research industry.

A second approach is more like McDonald's; a large franchise operation, inde-pendently owned, but with all 'outlets' (= research centres) working with common products and styles, to the point where the product is entirely homogeneous. The local context might be a little easier to manage in this model, but again, the lack of diversity would be problematic.

The third option can be derived from the idea of 'competitive collaboration' found, for example, in the furniture industry in the Third Italy. Here, firms collab-orate on design and marketing, but compete on production. Quality control may be assured centrally. A high degree of trust between members is necessary. Another similar model is to be found in airline alliances: each airline retains its distinctive identity and brand name, but there is collaboration in marketing and a certain amount of operational integration, for example by code-sharing. Again, quality control is critical and trust is essential.

In practical terms, and at a minimum, there is obviously a role for better knowledge management, in order to foster relationships and assist research units to operate better in the marketplace. A more ambitious exercise is for coordinating bodies (like GDN?) to be more active in brokering partnerships, taking the first steps towards an alliance model. To take this idea further, the next step would be a more concerted effort to work together, perhaps identifying research or policy problems of common interest, and then setting up linked programmes under an alliance 'brand'. Here, the alliance would facilitate a kind of 'policy code-sharing', and offer benefits to all parties.

This model of policy code-sharing is currently being put into practice by the European Association of Development Research and Training Institutes (EADI) on the subject of European Development Cooperation.[4] There are linked activities in different countries and a central web-site to report findings. Managed by a multi-national steering committee, the project is intended to provide a vehicle for research, dissemination and debate, a forum in which the perspectives of different actors can be shared and developed. Many benefits are likely to arise – coherence in debates on development, integrated research projects, improved networking and exchange – that will contribute to a distinctive 'European development identity' in the international development arena. As two other chapters in our volume detail, the development of 'codes' have become important devices for research communication and network sustainability.

Conclusion

> knowledge itself does not make any difference; rather the application of knowledge 'on the ground' is what matters.
>
> (Sawamura 2001: 6)

This remark was made by a Japanese official reflecting on the role of Japan International Cooperation Agency in its development funding. We agree, but we also caution that there are no simple answers, problem-solving tactics or techno-cratic solutions that can be rationally devised to overcome the research–policy disjunction. Policy is a chaotic and sometimes irrational process: different policy environments, institutional structures and political arrangements produce different sets of opportunities and constraints for dialogue, call forth varying strategies for policy researchers, and have dramatically diverse implications from one political system or policy sector to the next.

We should emphasise also that research is not a panacea for policy. Social and economic problems will persist. As noted by another researcher in a GDN electronic discussion, it is a 'romantic notion that if research and policy work together from the onset one can see better results.'[5] Politics, values and ideology are an inevitable part of policy-making and are reflected in the funding and commissioning of research, and the political selection and application of research results.

Nevertheless, the papers in this volume do tell us that knowledge can make a difference, and that knowledge-workers, in other words researchers, can influence policy. This is true nationally, but also internationally. Global knowledge networks provide a model of the kind of vehicle that can help researchers influence policy, and help policy-makers use research effectively. They need to be the right kind of network, however: democratic, inclusive, mutually respectful, and open to change. Not many current networks meet these demanding criteria for genuine policy code-sharing. But many could build these bridges.

Notes

1 Many anecdotes and detailed information about the problems of decision-makers not using policy-relevant information can be found in the electronic discussions 'GDN Priorities' and 'Bridging Research and Policy' convened by the Global Development Network in 1999 and 2001. This quote was taken from Kwabia Boateng, GDN Priorities, e-discussion 3 November 1999.
2 See http://www.id21.org.
3 For a questionnaire that enables researchers to test their own capacities, see http://www.odi.org.uk/RAPID/Lessons/Entrepreneurship.html. Additionally, a more detailed presentation of the models and issues can be found at http://www.odi.org.uk/RAPID/Meetings/Presentation_14/Maxwell.html.
4 See http://www.eadi.org/edc2010.
5 Quoted from Gul Najam Jamy, 6 November 2001. Available online at http://www2.worldbank.org/hm/hmgdn/html.

References

Chambers, R. (1993) *Challenging the Professions. Frontiers for Rural Development.* London: Intermediate Technology Publications.

Chambers, R. (1997) *Whose Reality Counts? Putting the First Last.* London: Intermediate Technology Publications.

Chapman, J. and Fisher, T. (1999) *Effective Campaigning*. London: New Economics Foundation.

Clay, E. J. and Schaffer, B. B. (eds) (1984) *Room for Manoeuvre: An Exploration of Public Policy in Agriculture and Rural Development.* London: Heinemann.

Commission on the Social Sciences (2003) *Great Expectations: The Social Sciences in Britain.* London: Academy of Learned Societies for the Social Sciences. Available online at http://www.the-academy.org.uk.

Crewe, E. and Young, J. (2002) *Bridging Research and Policy: Context, Evidence and Links.* ODI Working Paper No. 173. London: Overseas Development Institute. Available online at http://www.odi.org.

de Vibe, M., Hovland, I. and Young, J. (2002) *Bridging Research and Policy: An Annotated Bibliography.* ODI Working Paper No. 174. London: Overseas Development Institute. Available online at http://www.odi.org.

Fischer, F. (2003) *Reframing Public Policy: Discursive Politics and Deliberative Practices.* Oxford: Oxford University Press.

Flyvbjerg, B. (2001) *Making Social Science Matter: Why Social Science Inquiry Fails and How It Can Succeed Again.* Cambridge: Cambridge University Press.

Gladwell, M. (2000) *The Tipping Point: How Little Things Can Make a Big Difference.* London: Little, Brown and Co.

Gramsci, A. (1971) *Selections from the Prison Notebooks.* New York: International Publishers.

Grindle, M. and Thomas. J. (1991) *Public Choices and Policy Change: The Political Economy of Reform in Developing Countries.* Baltimore: John Hopkins University Press.

Haas, P. (1992) 'Introduction: Epistemic Communities and International Policy Coordination' *International Organisation* 46 (1): 1–35.

Hasenclever, A., Mayer, P. and Rittberger, V. (1997) *Theories of International Relations. Cambridge Studies in International Relations.* Cambridge: Cambridge University Press.

Juma, C. and Clark, N. (1995) 'Policy Research in Sub-Saharan Africa: An Exploration' *Public Administration and Development* 15: 121–37.

Keeley, J. and Scoones, I. (2003) *Understanding Environmental Policy Processes: Cases from Africa.* London: Earthscan Publications.

Laws, Sophie with Harper, Caroline and Marcus, Rachel (2003) *Research for Development: A Practical Guide.* London: Sage.

Leach, M. and Mearns, R. (eds) (1996) *The Lie of the Land: Challenging Received Wisdom on the African Environment.* Oxford: James Currey.

Lepgold, Joseph and Nincic, Miroslav (2001) *Beyond the Ivory Tower: International Relations Theory and Issues of Policy Relevance.* New York: Columbia University Press.

Lindblom, C. E. (1980) *The Policy-Making Process.* Englewood Cliffs, NJ: Prentice Hall.

Lipsky, M. (1980) *Street-level Bureaucracy: Dilemmas of the Individual in Public Services.* New York: Russell Sage Foundation.

Maxwell, S. (2003a) 'Development Research in Europe: Towards an (All)-Star Alliance?' *The European Journal of Development Research* 15 (1, June): 194–8.

Maxwell, S. (2003b) *Policy Entrepreneurship.* Transcript of a talk at ODI, 11th June 2003. Available online at http://www.odi.org.uk/RAPID/Meetings/Presentation_14/Maxwell.html.

Minogue, M. (1993) 'Theory and Practice in Public Policy and Public Administration', in M. Hill (ed.) *The Policy Process: A Reader.* Hemel Hempstead: Harvester Wheatsheaf.

Neilson, Stephanie (2001) IDRC-Supported Research and Its Influence on Public Policy. Ottawa: Evaluation Unit, IDRC. Available online at http://www.idrc.ca/evaluation/litre view_e.html.

Nowotny, Helga, Scott, Peter and Gibbons, Michael (2001) *Re-Thinking Science: Knowledge and the Public in an Age of Uncertainty.* Oxford: Polity Press.

OECD (1981) *The Measurement of Scientific and Technical Activities: Proposed Standard Practice for Surveys of Research and Experimental Development* (Frascati Manual). Paris: OECD.

Oh, Cheol H. (1997) 'Issues for New Thinking of Knowledge Utilization: Introductory Remarks' *Knowledge and Policy: The International Journal of Knowledge Transfer and Utilization* 10 (3): 3–10.

Peters, B. Guy and Pierre, Jon (2000) 'Developments in intergovernmental relations: towards multi-level governance' *Policy and Politics* 29 (2): 131–5.

Putnam, D. (1993) *Making Democracy Work: Civic Traditions in Modern Italy.* Princeton University Press.

Roe, Emery (1991) 'Development Narratives, Or Making the Best of Blueprint Development' *World Development* 19 (4): 287–300.

Sawamura, Nobuhide (2001) 'Local Spirit, Global Knowledge: a Japanese Approach to Knowledge Development in International Co-operation' *NORRAG News* (29): 6–8.

Simon, Sheldon (2002) 'Evaluating Track Two Approaches to Security Diplomacy in the Asia-Pacific: the CSCAP Experience' *Pacific Review* 15 (2): 167–200.

Squire, Lyn (2000) 'Why the World Bank Should Be Involved in Development Research', in G. L. Gilbert and D. Vines (eds) *The World Bank: Structure and Policies.* Cambridge: Cambridge University Press.

Stone, D., Maxwell, S. and Keating, M. (2001) Bridging Research and Policy: An International Workshop. Warwick, UK, July 2001. Working Paper available online at http://www.csgr.org.

Stone, Diane (ed.) (2000) *Banking on Knowledge: The Genesis of the Global Development Network.* London: Routledge.

Sutton, Rebecca. (1999) *The Policy Process: An Overview.* ODI Working Paper No. 118. London: Overseas Development Institute.

Walt, G. (1994) *Health Policy: An Introduction to Process and Power.* London: Zed Books.

2 Bridging research and policy in international development

Context, evidence and links

Julius Court and John Young

Introduction

Reducing poverty and meeting the Millennium Development Goals (MDGs) will require improved policies around the world (UNDP 2003). However, policymakers and other stakeholders often don't know which policies are most suitable and how they can best be implemented in different contexts. Research is one way for policymakers and other stakeholders to enhance the processes of policy formulation and implementation.

Although research clearly matters, there remains no systematic understanding of what, when, why and how research feeds into development policies. While there is an extensive literature on the research–policy links in OECD countries, from disciplines as varied as economics, political science, sociology, anthropology, international relations and management, there has been much less emphasis on research–policy links in developing countries. The massive diversity of cultural, economic and political contexts makes it especially difficult to draw valid generalisations and lessons from existing experience and theory. In addition, international actors have an exaggerated impact on research and policy processes in developing contexts. A better understanding of how research can contribute to pro-poor policies, and systems to put it into practice, could help improve development outcomes.

There has been increasing interest in these questions in the international development sector. Work for the International Institute for Environment and Development identified a six-point programme for improving impact (Garrett and Islam 1998). The Overseas Development Institute (ODI) has been researching research–policy linkages since 1999, with an early report providing a 21-point checklist of what makes policies happen (Sutton 1999). ODI set up the cross-cutting Research and Policy in Development (RAPID) programme focusing specifically on the uptake of research into policy.[1] The link between research and policy has been a key issue for the Global Development Network (GDN) since its inception in 1999. The UK Department for International Development (DFID) has recently completed a major review of work as part of its effort to develop a new research policy (Surr *et al.* 2002).

This is the context for the ODI Bridging Research and Policy project. To guide the research, the project completed a literature review (de Vibe, Hovland and

Young 2002) and developed a framework for understanding research–policy links (Crewe and Young 2002). The framework clusters the issues around three broad areas:

- Context: politics and institutions;
- Evidence: approach and credibility; and
- Links: influence and legitimacy.

The project then completed detailed episode studies on research–policy linkages with the objectives to test the integrated framework; increase understanding of the linkages between development research, policy and practice; promote evidence-based international development policy; and guide further research.

The research project includes four case studies of specific policy changes which assess the relative influence of research on the policy change. The four case studies are:

- The adoption of the Poverty Reduction Strategy Paper (PRSP) initiative by the IMF and World Bank in September 1999 (Christiansen and Hovland 2003).
- The launch of the Sphere project in 1996 to strengthen the accountability of international humanitarian agencies in the wake of the much-criticised response to the Rwanda crisis (Buchanan-Smith 2003).
- The reluctance to legalise private para-professional livestock services in Kenya, despite their spread on the ground and good evidence that paravets can provide an effective, cost-efficient, and safe service (Young *et al.* 2003).
- The emergence and adoption of the Sustainable Livelihoods Approach (SLA) in DFID's 1997 White Paper as a guiding principle of UK development policy less than a decade after it originated (Solesbury 2003).

The approach taken focused on a clear change in policy and then worked back to assess the key issues that led to the policy change and the relative impact that research played. This was done by constructing an historical narrative of key policy decisions and practices, along with important documents and events, and identifying key actors. This approach is different from the common approach of evaluating the impact of individual research projects, which tend to focus specifically on the research rather than other issues that may matter in influencing policy.

This chapter provides a synthesis of the findings from the ODI episode studies. It is structured as follows. The second section outlines the framework used for investigating the links between research and policy and discusses the methodology. The third section provides an outline of the four case studies assessed in this work. The fourth section provides a discussion of the emerging themes and highlights interesting findings that relate to the main streams of theoretical thinking on research and policy. The fifth section discusses issues around how the framework can be applied and makes some recommendations for researchers. The final section highlights a few conclusions regarding the framework, method and emerging lessons.

The framework and method

Definitions

In preparing the episode studies, the project decided to use relatively open definitions of research and policy. This was important given the preliminary nature of the work, the diversity and complexity of the study topics and the relative lack of existing case studies.

Like others, we thought it was difficult, and often unhelpful, to provide an overly specific definition of research since the exact meaning will depend on the context. For the case studies in the ODI Bridging Research and Policy project we considered research as 'any systematic effort to increase the stock of knowledge'.[2] This included therefore any systematic process of critical investigation and evaluation, theory building, data collection, analysis and codification related to development policy and practice. It includes *action research*, that is self-reflection by practitioners oriented toward the enhancement of direct practice.

Policy also has a wide range of definitions. In collecting case studies, we considered policy to be the 'course of action' including declarations or plans as well as actions on the ground. We also adopted a broader view in assessing the impact of research on policy change – one that went beyond impact on formal documents or visible practices. The cases were thus intended to explore how research can influence policymaker's horizons, policy development, declared public policy regimes and policy implementation or practice (Lindquist 2003). Following Carol Weiss (1977), it is widely recognised that although research may not have direct influence on specific policies, the production of research may still exert a powerful indirect influence through introducing new terms and shaping the policy discourse. The case studies included the impact of research on public policies, changes in practice on the ground and examples of including new issues into policy discussions.

The RAPID framework

Traditionally, the link between research and policy has been viewed as a linear process, whereby a set of research findings is shifted from the 'research sphere' over to the 'policy sphere', and then has some impact on policymakers' decisions. At least three of the assumptions underpinning this traditional view are now being questioned. First, the assumption that research influences policy in a one-way process (the linear model); second, the assumption that there is a clear divide between researchers and policymakers (the two communities model); and third, the assumption that the production of knowledge is confined to a set of specific findings (the positivistic model).

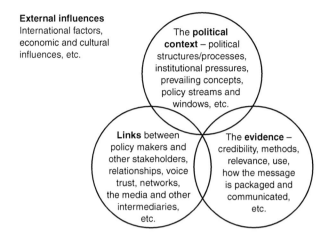

Figure 2.1 The RAPID framework: context, evidence and links

Literature on the research–policy link is now shifting away from these assumptions, towards a more dynamic and complex view that emphasises a two-way process between research and policy, shaped by multiple relations and reservoirs of knowledge (see for example Garrett and Islam 1998; RAWOO 2001). This shift reflects the fact that this subject area has generated greater interest in the past few years, and already a number of overviews of the research–policy linkage exist (e.g. Keeley and Scoones 2003; Lindquist 2003; Neilson 2001; Stone, Maxwell and Keating 2001; Sutton 1999). However, there are still a limited number of case studies (Puchner 2001).

The case studies were addressed through the lens of the RAPID framework (Court and Young 2003), as shown in Figure 2.1. This framework should be seen as a generic, perhaps ideal, model. In many cases there will not be much overlap between the different spheres or the overlap may vary considerably.

The political context

The research–policy link is shaped by the political context. The policy process and the production of research are in themselves political processes, from the initial agenda-setting exercise through to the final negotiation involved in implementation. Political contestation, institutional pressures and vested interests matter greatly. So too, the attitudes and incentives among officials, their room for manoeuvre, local history, and power relations greatly influence policy implementation (Kingdon 1984; Clay and Schaffer 1984). In some cases the political strategies and power relations are obvious, and are tied to specific institutional pressures. Ideas circulating may be discarded by the majority of staff in an organisation if those ideas elicit disapproval from the leadership.

The evidence and communication

Experience suggests that the quality of the research is clearly important for policy uptake. Policy influence is affected by topical relevance and, as importantly, the operational usefulness of an idea; it helps if a new approach has been piloted and the document can clearly demonstrate the value of a new option (Court and Young 2003). A critical issue affecting uptake is whether research has provided a solution to a problem. The other key set of issues here concern communication. The sources and conveyors of information, the way new messages are packaged (especially if they are couched in familiar terms) and targeted can all make a big difference in how the policy document is perceived and utilised. For example, marketing is based on the insight that people's reaction to a new product/idea is often determined by the packaging rather than the content in and of itself (Williamson 1996). The key message is that communication is a very demanding process and it is best to take an interactive approach (Mattelart and Mattelart 1998). Continuous interaction leads to greater chances of successful communication than a simple or linear approach.

Links

Third, the framework emphasises the importance of links; of communities, networks and intermediaries (e.g. the media and campaigning groups) in affecting policy change. Some of the current literature focuses explicitly on various types of networks, such as policy communities (Pross 1986), epistemic communities (Haas 1991), and advocacy coalitions (Sabatier and Jenkins-Smith 1999). Issues of trust, legitimacy, openness and formalisation of networks have emerged as important issues in GDN work. Existing theory stresses the role of translators and communicators (Gladwell 2000). It seems that there is often an under-appreciation of the extent and ways that intermediary organisations and networks impact on formal policy guidance documents, which in turn influence officials.

Method

ODI applied the framework to three case studies of policy change, within areas where the institute already has substantial research and policy experience (PRSPs; Humanitarian Accountability; and Animal Health in Kenya). ODI also worked with the Evidence Network to prepare another case study (Sustainable Livelihoods). The case studies were developed separately by their authors, but the same basic process was followed in each case and there were regular meetings to report and discuss the findings.

Each case constructed an historical narrative leading up to the observed policy change in each case study. This involved creating a timeline of key policy decisions and practices, along with important documents and events, and identifying key actors. The next step was to explore why those policy decisions and practices took place and assess, using the framework, the relative role of research in that process. This was done through interviews with key actors, reviewing the litera-ture and cross-checking conflicting narratives.

The approach is distinct in current debates since it starts from the clear policy change and then works backwards to assess the key issues that made a difference. It is argued that this gives a more realistic view than the normal approach of the broad range of factors other than research that influence policy, which tend to start with an individual research project and then track how the research outputs have been used (see Ryan and Garrett chapter in this volume). Tracking forward probably over-emphasises the importance of research vis-à-vis other factors.

However, the approach also has drawbacks and limitations. Since policy processes are complex, multi-layered and change over time, it is difficult to iden-tify the key factors that caused policy to change (or not) and isolate the impact of research. The standard challenges of unconscious selection of informants and memory are ones that are common to case studies; we believe they have been ameliorated by seeking the views of a wide range of informed stakeholders. Moreover, inputs were drawn from a range of other sources including literature reviews, workshops and authors' own experiences. The process was iterative in preparing each episode study; key facts and/or inconsistencies were cross-checked with key informants. The study authors report that the approach allowed them to capture, in depth, the range of issues that mattered in the four cases. In sum, we do feel that the cases allow us to draw meaningful conclusions about research–policy linkages.

The case studies

Poverty Reduction Strategy Papers[3]

In September 1999, the World Bank and IMF adopted a new approach to aid: Poverty Reduction Strategy Papers (PRSPs). PRSPs are official documents that define the national strategy for poverty reduction. They are important because preparation of a PRSP is an eligibility criteria for low income countries for con-cessional lending from the World Bank (IDA) and IMF (PRGF programme), as well as being one of the criteria for access to debt relief under the Enhanced Heavily Indebted Poor Countries (HIPC) programme. How did the idea of the Poverty Reduction Strategy Paper (PRSP) come to be adopted? What was the role of research in this process – both 'academic research' in general and the 'applied policy research' within the World Bank and IMF? The case study traces the vari-ous factors, including the role and relative influence of research, that contributed to this far-reaching policy shift.

Accountability of humanitarian aid[4]

After the varied and sometimes poor performance of NGOs in response to the Rwanda refugee crisis in 1994, it was not a surprise that there were efforts to strengthen the accountability of humanitarian agencies and find ways of improving performance in humanitarian response. But even after the immediate crisis had passed and media attention had moved on, what led to the policy shift represented by the publication of the 'Humanitarian Charter and Minimum Standards for Disaster Response' in 2000 ('Sphere 2000')? This case study assesses the range of issues that led to the decision to launch the Sphere project in 1996 and the nature of the policy shift as well as implementation during the first year of Sphere's existence. Specifically, how important was the research – particularly Study 3 of the Joint Evaluation of Emergency Assistance to Rwanda (JEEAR), which was critical of some NGO performance in the Rwanda crisis?

Livestock services in Kenya[5]

Livestock services were among the first sectors targeted for privatisation under structural adjustment programmes, particularly in sub-Saharan Africa. The veterinary profession however was very slow to respond, and the increasing financial constraints effectively paralysed government services in the late 1980s and early 1990s. Given the problems, non-governmental organisations introduced a new model of community-based livestock services (similar to barefoot doctors, but for vets). Intermediate Technology Development Group (ITDG) was one of the early pioneers in the mid 1980s, and adopted an action-research approach with a clear objective to use the results, if positive, to influence the policy environment to allow the approaches to be widely replicated. Despite the outstanding success of the new decentralised community-based animal health care (DAHC) approaches and their proliferation throughout the arid and semi-arid parts of Kenya, there remains no legislation relating to the approach. It has been over 15 years and community-based livestock services remain illegal. The case study explores why key policy decisions and practices took place and assesses the role of research in that process.

Sustainable livelihoods[6]

In 1997, the White Paper on international development made the 'sustainable livelihoods approach' (or SLA) a core principle of the strategy for poverty reduction of the UK's Department for International Development (DFID). This case study offers an explanation of how the SLA concept, which had first appeared in research literature in the 1980s, became such a core development issue in UK development assistance policy. How did the idea of the sustainable livelihoods approach come to be adopted? The study focuses on the interactions between research, policy and practice, highlighting the different types of individuals and institutions that enabled the uptake of the approach.

Cross-cutting issues

The key question is: why are some of the ideas that circulate in the research–policy arenas picked up and acted on, while others are ignored and disappear?' We structure our discussion around the three arenas in the RAPID framework. Our analysis illuminates some of the key theoretical strands of theory in the literature pertinent to the four ODI case studies.

Context: politics and institutions

The ODI cases certainly support the literature and the findings of other studies (Court and Young 2003) that the political institutional context is the most important arena affecting the uptake of research into policy. Political contestation, institutional pressures and vested interests matter greatly. In certain political contexts, research may be completely ignored. So too the attitudes and incentives among officials, history, and power relations greatly influence policy processes.

Kingdon (1984) argues that 'political streams' – the wider political environment including issues of government changes and public opinion – are a key influence on the agenda-setting process. This is clearly reflected in the sustainable livelihoods case. SLA was in tune with wider international shifts towards sustainable human development rather than economic growth. There was also an imperative at the institutional level as DFID strove to redefine its role and mark the change of government in 1997.

Lindquist (1988) describes routine, incremental, fundamental and emergent policy processes – each of which has different implications for the uptake of research. Most policy decisions are routine policy processes (merely modifying previous decisions) and there is little scope for research uptake. Incremental processes deal with selective issues as they arise, may make use of whatever analysis is close at hand, but are unlikely to involve a comprehensive review of all the associated issues. However, many of the ODI cases describe situations where more fundamental or emergent policies are being made[7] or what Kingdon (1984) calls policy windows where more radical solutions are needed. Policy windows provide opportunities where research can have a substantial impact, but they tend to occur suddenly by chance or due to an external crisis.

All the ODI cases tended, to different degrees, to have a general context where it was increasingly apparent that change was needed and then where specific issues spurred the policy change (or not). Thus, in addition to literature above, the cases also seem to reflect the argument by Gladwell (2000) that social change is brought about by tipping points, a relatively minor occurrence which galvanises trends that have been building up 'beneath the surface'. In the Sphere case it was the general concerns about accountability, highlighted dramatically by the response of humanitarian agencies to the Rwanda crisis. In the Kenya case, evidence about the spread of para-professional veterinarians or paravets contributed to the alarm of the Kenya Veterinary Board (KVB), resulting in their letter in the national press threatening to punish livestock owners and veterinarians involved in paravet programmes. This was clearly the 'tipping point'. Beforehand there was a long period where community animal health workers (CAHWs) schemes gradually proliferated, generating powerful evidence of their value, and providing an issue around which different groups of stakeholders, supporters and antagonists could form formal and informal networks. The letter brought the work of all the different actors, including the KVB itself, into focus and resulted in a process where all stakeholders came together to develop a new policy framework with emphasis in favour of the approach.

The degree of policymaker demand is one of the main issues that distinguishes cases of research uptake from those which have little impact. Demand, in various ways, was critical to the emergence of Sphere. By the first half of the 1990s, there was no longer an unquestioning acceptance of the activities of humanitarian agencies in emergency situations. However, it was the scale and intensity of the humanitarian crisis in Rwanda in 1994 – and the spotlight on the response by the agencies – which created the demand for major changes. The same is true in the PRSP case. The 1997 Asia Crisis and the continued weak economic performance in sub-Saharan Africa led to a widespread sense of there being 'a problem' with international development policy and spurred questions about the roles of the IMF and World Bank. There was a backdrop of substantial external pressure building up around the debt issue, particularly from the NGO movement such as Jubilee 2000 and from the US administration to ensure that resources freed up by debt relief would be 'well spent'.

It is not just demand, however, but also consensus. This was most notable perhaps in the Sphere case study, where the high profile failures in Rwanda and the pressures for reform – plus the credible solution proposed – made building a consensus much easier. Similarly the PRSP case study concludes that the most important contextual factor was the major convergence of debates and controversies in the field of international development. Poverty reduction had become a central concern for the UK Department for International Development (DFID). There was also the need to operationalise the new conceptual framework for aid put forward by World Bank President James Wolfensohn – the Comprehensive Development Framework (CDF) – in early 1999. The case study notes that:

> The simultaneous recognition of similar sets of problems and similar ideas for solutions by various actors in the international development field in the late 1990s is probably the reason why the PRSP idea, which was a substantial challenge to current practice, took hold relatively easily and rapidly.

By contrast, the lack of consensus on legislation for the Animal Health sector in Kenya was glaring. The need for reform – and the widespread use of an approach that provided a solution – was not enough to spur legal reform due to the troubled political context. The animal health policy process had become the sort of complex, highly politicised process described by Sutton (1999) and Keeley and Scoones (2003), with increasingly polarised views developing in the different camps, and no mechanism for dialogue and resolution. Personalities and personal relationships were at least as important as any formal relationships and structures.

However, policy is not just about statements and laws; it is also about implementation. The work of Lipsky (1980) on how 'street level bureaucrats' have an enormous influence on how policies are implemented is also very relevant. Street level bureaucrats are the employees of an organisation who are responsible for implementation and, Lipsky argues, ultimately decide how policy is to be translated into practice. All the cases indicate that paying attention to how the policies will be put into practice is an important element of policy change. The Kenya case provides a powerful demonstration, where effective community-based approaches to animal health care were adopted by practitioners across the arid Northern region despite the fact they were illegal. Vets in the field, finding themselves with virtually no operational budgets, adopted the new approaches as the only way they could continue to provide any services at all. The SLA case also particularly highlights how the role of 'developers' was crucial to the eventual adoption of the approach.

It is interesting that all four cases give an indication that new actors – in this case NGOs – are playing an unexpectedly significant role in developing policy-making. In the Sphere case this was obvious since it was all about NGOs. In the Kenya case, however, ITDG, church groups and local Kenyan actors played a key role. In the PRSP case there was increasingly sophisticated analysis by development charities and the advocacy coalition around the debt campaign. The SLA approach highlighted a range of think tanks, NGOs and foundations. Many would argue that this is a positive step in its own right, facilitated by the fact that policy-making regimes are becoming more open. The cases suggest that the increase in actors tends to translate into greater use of evidence in development policymaking. But more work is needed to better assess where, how and to what degree these new actors actually make a difference.

Evidence: credibility and communication

In terms of the evidence domain, there are a set of issues which seem to come out most clearly and which make a big difference to whether research is taken up – the relevance of the findings to current policymaker concerns, the credibility of the evidence and, perhaps most importantly, whether the research provides the solution to a problem. A first issue that emerges from the case studies is that research appears to have a much greater impact when it is topically relevant. For an impact in the near term, research needs to relate to the policy issue of the day. In the Sphere case, a key reason Study 3 of the Joint Evaluation had an immediate impact on policymakers was because it was directly related to a crisis that had dominated news reports.

But there are often time delays. The PRSP case emphasises how 'academic' research through the 1970s, 1980s and 1990s had an indirect influence by shifting the international development discourse towards poverty reduction, participation, and aid effectiveness. This research highlighted problems with development practices and set the stage for the policy reviews of the 1990s. In this sense, the case can be seen as an example of the 'percolation' model described by Weiss (1977), where certain research gradually percolates into policy networks and influences the general policy framework. As highlighted above, the SLA case is also one where research 'filtered' into the policy arena – and then was substantially assisted to influence a specific policy orientation.

The quality of the research is very important for policy uptake. All the cases emphasise the issue of credibility. In the SLA case, the credibility of some of the key researchers, their clarity in expressing complex processes and often personal means of communication combined with the diverse sources of the evidence that helped foster uptake within DFID. In the Sphere case, the independence of the evaluation ensured that the sometimes unpopular findings were protected from censure. But credibility depends on the user. As the PRSP case put it:

> It (research) was considered most credible when it was commissioned by the IFIs themselves or other donors, demonstrated analytical rigour, and was communicated in a language that was accessible and relevant to World Bank and IMF staff and other donor agencies.

In the Kenya case, it was action research that was convincing; formal, academic research had little impact.

At another level, it is extremely clear that operational usefulness is critical. Research that had an operational orientation or action research seemed to have a great impact in the cases. The fact that researchers in the Rwanda evaluation had practical experience was emphasised. The Kenya and SLA cases highlight that it was important that a new approach has been piloted and researchers and communicators could clearly demonstrate the value of the new option. In the PRSP case, 'applied policy research' in the late 1990s, the HIPC review for example, focused more on providing policy recommendations and operational solutions. In addition, the positive experience of the Poverty Eradication Action Plan (PEAP) had a strong influence in convincing policymakers in the IFIs of the value and feasibility of PRSP-type strategies.

A critical issue affecting uptake is whether research provided a solution to a problem. The CAHW approach in Kenya was the solution for how to provide services in arid areas in a climate of minimal funding. The PRSP was the solution to a variety of problems faced by the IFIs and donor governments. As the case study notes: 'In summary, the PRSP was an operational solution that solved several internal problems and provided an answer to external pressures, particularly for the IFIs but also within different bilateral organisations.' The Sphere process was the solution to the conundrum of the accountability of humanitarian agencies. The SLA provided the answer to DFID's search for an innovative approach to development assistance. This reflects the marketing literature (e.g. Lambin 1996), which suggests that people buy products that provide a solution to a problem.

But it is not just the evidence that matters – how findings are communicated is crucial, since policymakers cannot be influenced by research unless they are actually aware of its existence. Interestingly the issue of credibility does not just concern the quality of the research but also the way that research is packaged to make it palatable to policymakers. The evidence from the case studies does support much of the existing literature that the format of the research outputs also matters for policy impact. The Sphere cases specifically emphasised that the evaluation 'findings and recommendations were clearly presented, and were often targeted at particular groups of actors'. The SLA case emphasised similar points, but also the power of visual images. This very much supports the literature which emphasises that, frequently, 'seeing is believing' (Philo 1996). In the Kenya case, evidence generated by working CAHW schemes, communicated directly to visitors by livestock owners and the animal health staff directly involved in them, seems to have been much more important than research reports. Early on, this evidence contributed to the rising popularity of such programmes with donors and field veterinarians.

The cases also provide evidence to support the literature (Mattelart and Mattelart 1998) that it is best to take an interactive approach to communication. It seems that continuous interaction leads to greater chances of successful communication than a simple or linear approach. This seems to be most evident in the SLA case, where key individuals had extensive discussions over periods of time. Evidence of the conceptual and practical use of the SLA approach accumulated over the decade preceding the 1997 White Paper. Solesbury notes that in the SLA case, 'the conventional view of research informing policy which frames practice: Research ⟶ Policy ⟶ Practice could be better represented as a triangle where all components inform each other'.

Links: influence and legitimacy

Much of the literature on bridging research and policy emphasises that the links between researchers and policymakers are critical. Key issues include feedback, dialogue and collaboration between researchers and policymakers; the role of networks and policy communities; and issues of trust, legitimacy and participation. However, it is also apparent that there are many issues that remain unanswered in this arena. This section focuses on relevant issues in this area that emerge from the four ODI case studies.

Kickert *et al.* (1997) and Robinson *et al.* (1999) describe how networks play a vital role in policy change. They regard policymaking as a series of negotiations about competition, coordination and cooperation which can be completed efficiently through formal and informal networks. The Sphere case is probably the best example here. It highlights how the links between researchers and policymakers were

> institutionalised in the structure put in place for the Joint Rwanda Evaluation ... Thus, a critical and cooperative link was established right at the beginning between those who commissioned the 'research', and the policymakers at whom the findings were directed.

This maximised the sense of ownership and buy-in in conducting the evaluation and implementing the findings.

However, all the other three cases also demonstrate the importance of networks. The PRSP case study describes the 'high level of contact' and 'multitude of links' among policymakers, researchers and NGOs. As one informant noted, 'none of the players is more than two handshakes away from any of the others'. The Kenya case highlights that the first ITDG Vets Workshop in 1988, which brought together decentralised animal health (DAH) practitioners from several projects around the country, marked a significant increase in interactions between researchers/practitioners and policymakers in Kenya, and ITDG's international DAH workshop strengthened the emerging international network of practitioners and links between policymakers and practitioners.

The cases also reflect much of the literature regarding the ways networks can facilitate knowledge sharing, coordination and cooperation. But a key question that remains is: what are the characteristics of networks that best enable them to act as a bridge between research and policy? Hass (1991) describes how 'epistemic communities' – colleagues who share a similar approach or a similar position on an issue and maintain contact with each other across their various locations and fields – create new channels for information and discussing new perspectives. Such communities are believed to be particularly effective if they include a few prominent and respected individuals. Epistemic communities did seem to be important in the SLA, PRSP and Sphere cases.

In 'The Tipping Point', Gladwell (2000) describes why some individuals are trusted more than others, and are effective 'salesmen' of ideas, and how salesmen, networkers and 'mavens' (people who collect information) all contribute to the spread of ideas through 'social epidemics'. Individual contacts between researchers and policymakers also emerge from the ODI case studies as an important aspect of bridging research and policy. For example, the Sphere case describes two key policy entrepreneurs as salespeople and networkers; two other people played critical connector roles.

Also important to prove the legitimacy of policy advice based on research are the 'downward' links to the populations and communities that will be affected by the policies (Fine *et al.* 2000). Recent work for the Rockefeller Foundation (Figueroa *et al.* 2002) emphasises that social change will be more sustainable if the affected community owns not just the physical inputs and outputs, but also the process and content of the communication involved. The issue of legitimacy is most emphasised in the Sphere case. In the Rwanda evaluation and Sphere process, great effort was given to inclusion and the legitimacy this conferred seems to have contributed enormously to the project's impact. The Kenya case demonstrates that, although it often takes a great deal of time, working with local communities to develop effective and sustainable examples of new approaches is essential to acquire the legitimacy to be able to advocate for widespread changes.

Two of the cases particularly emphasise the importance of three-way feedback processes between researchers, policymakers and practice. The SLA case does this most emphatically, highlighting the role of a number of individuals and institutions who worked as 'testers, developers, champions, communicators, interpreters and advocates' of SLA to facilitate its adoption within DFID. So too the PRSP case highlights the interactions between academic researchers, policy researchers, donors, the Boards of the IFIs and street-level bureaucrats within the Bank and IMF.

Finally, it is worth noting that all the cases involve an element of the transnational interactions of researchers, policymakers and donors and the utilisation of research by international policy communities. This is most noticeable in the PRSP case, which focused on an international policy process but also emphasised the role of the Jubilee Debt Relief campaign, very much a trans-national advocacy network as described by Keck and Sikkink (1998). The humanitarian sector portrayed in the Sphere case represents a global public policy network (Reinicke and Deng 2000). In the Kenya case, it was an international NGO, ITDG, which facilitated the transfer of an idea across sectors and continents. While these were not cases of pure knowledge networks, the set of associations in each case clearly were crucial to the transfer of knowledge internationally.

Applying the framework and recommendations for researchers

It is worth commenting on the validity of the RAPID framework. All the cases conclude that the framework provides a useful guide for organising analysis of policy change in a systematic way. There seem to be two particular strengths that emerge. The first is comprehensiveness. Much existing theory on bridging research and policy provides a narrow insight on a single aspect of research and policy processes, rather than an overarching way to approach the problem as a whole. As important, perhaps, the framework was useful as a tool which facilitated comparisons between different instances of policy change. This allows the framework to be used to suggest recommendations in a middle ground between very specific issues (that may only be applicable in a certain time and place) and very general (and thus banal) suggestions. This leads us to believe that the framework is worth commending to others – with the provisos below.

The project suggests that the configuration of the three spheres in the framework seemed to vary according to the case. In the PRSP case, for example, there was a great overlap between the '*links*' sphere, where policymakers, researchers and NGOs were in frequent contact with each other, and a '*political context*' where similar sets of problems and ideas for solutions were emerging from various actors simultaneously. This was in contrast to the case of Livestock Services in Kenya, where the '*links*' between livestock owners and veterinarians were advancing successful DAHC practice on the ground, but were far removed from the underlying '*political context*' of policymaking and legislation, which was largely unaware of its existence. The analytic framework then, should be viewed as a trio of floating spheres of variable size and degree of overlap, rather than a solid mesh with 'context', 'evidence' and 'links' held as equally important, and equally overlapping, in every case.

The SLA case in particular highlighted two elements which fall outside the framework: time and chance. In terms of time, the adoption of the SLA in the 1997 White Paper occurred over a decade after the conceptualisation of the SLA approach. Time is also a particular issue in two of the other cases – in terms of the filtering of academic research in the PRSP case and the extensive time lag in Kenya between the initiation of a new approach and its formal policy adoption (still pending). The SLA case also notes, akin to the findings of Clay and Schaffer (1984), that chance plays a role through a number of 'lucky encounters, overlapping diaries, and external decisions'. This idea also reflects the ideas of Stacey (1995), who draws on chaos theory to describe the 'nonlinearity' of networks and

Table 2.1 Impact on policy: what can researchers do?

What researchers need to know	What researchers need to do	How to do it
Political context		
• Who are the policymakers?	• Get to know the policy-makers, their agendas and the constraints they operate under.	• Work with the policymakers.
• Is there policymaker demand for new ideas?	• Identify potential supporters and opponents.	• Seek commissions.
• What are the sources/ strengths of resistance?	• Keep an eye on the horizon and prepare for opport-unities in regular formal processes.	• Line up research with high-profile policy events.
• What is the policymaking process?	• Look out for – and react to – unexpected policy windows.	• Reserve resources to be able to move quickly to respond to policy windows.
• What are the opportunities and timing for input into policy processes?		• Allow sufficient time and resources.
Evidence		
• What is the current theory?	• Establish credibility over the long term.	• Build up respected programmes of high-quality work.
• What are the prevailing narratives?	• Provide practical solutions to problems.	• Action-research and pilot projects to demonstrate benefits of new approaches.
• How divergent is the new evidence?	• Establish legitimacy.	• Use participatory approaches to help with legitimacy and imple-mentation.
• What sort of evidence will convince policymakers?	• Build a convincing case and present clear policy options.	• Clear strategy and resources for communication from start.
	• Package new ideas in familiar theory or narratives.	• 'Seeing is believing'.
	• Communicate effectively.	
Links		
• Who are the key stakeholders in the policy discourse?	• Get to know the other stakeholders.	• Partnerships between researchers, policymakers and communities.
• What links and networks exist between them?	• Establish a presence in existing networks.	• Identify key networkers and salespeople.
• Who are the intermediaries and what influence have they?	• Build coalitions with like-minded stakeholders.	• Use informal contacts.
• Whose side are they on?	• Build new policy networks.	

their impact on the policy process. Clearly people using the framework must guard against determinism. The framework is a useful tool to cluster and simplify identification of the key issues that matter at a particular time. Applying the framework at different points during a policy process will highlight different issues. Within many policy processes there will be particular times when chance creates a particular constellation of factors which facilitate change.

So what should researchers do if they want to achieve policy impact? Evidence from ODI's work so far suggests preliminary recommendations in three areas. First, there are some things researchers need to know about the political context, issue area (evidence) and key actors and networks (links). Second, there are some things researchers need to do in each of these areas. Third, evidence is emerging about the most effective way to go about things. Some of these are summarised in Table 2.1. We emphasise that this is not a blueprint but a menu of options for review and consideration based on specific contexts.

Conclusions

Although too early to make extensive recommendations, the analysis of the theory and preliminary case studies undertaken so far already provide some useful insights for policymakers, researchers and donors to promote more evidence-based policy. We wish to highlight six conclusions below.

First, we believe the RAPID framework provides a useful tool to analyse research–policy issues. The four case studies demonstrate how the three spheres – political context, evidence and links – functioned as a useful structure onto which specific instances of influence on policy could be mapped. Applying the framework to these case studies has provided a more holistic understanding of research–policy processes, and indications how they may be refined as a tool for promoting evidence-based policy.

Second, the method employed is worth consideration by others in this field. Rather than tracking the impact of research, the approach was to focus on a clear change in policy and then assess the key issues that led to the policy change and the relative impact of that research. While it suffers limitations of case study work, we believe these can be minimised to provide researchers in this area with an additional approach that can help generate a comprehensive and accurate understanding of research–policy processes.

Third, our work suggests that 'context is key'. Political Context – especially the level of demand for change, the nature of contestation and openness to new ideas – has emerged as critical in terms of policy change and has a degree of impact over and above other factors. Importantly, however, it is very clear that whilst 'political context' at the moment of policy shift is a critical factor, we are not suggesting that this context is immovable, unstoppable or deterministic of policy outcomes. Chance may create policy windows, otherwise contexts change slowly. In either case though, it is possible to maximise the impact of research through a proper understanding of how the 'context' can be influenced by 'evidence' and 'links'.

Fourth, we believe that we have the clearest understanding of the 'evidence' arena. The influence of evidence depends on credibility (including analytic rigour and/or person doing research), relevance, and whether research provides the solution to a problem. The way evidence is communicated is also vital (with the importance of packaging and an interactive approach to communication).

Fifth, our understanding of the 'links' arena remains the most limited. Although it is relatively simple to draw a 'family tree' of the key individuals and partnerships involved in a particular policy episode, it is harder to understand how more diffuse networks influence the research–policy process. The current theoretical literature provides myriad typologies of 'formal and informal networks', 'epistemic communities', and 'downward links', all of which seem to be evident and important in the case studies. They do not, however, add up to a comprehensive analytic tool for understanding what makes links work. Further research needs to be done to address serious outstanding issues: what are the characteristics of networks which enable them to act as a bridge between research and policy? and 'where, how and to what degree do networks actually make a difference to policymaking?'.

Sixth, all the cases involve fascinating elements of the trans-national interactions of researchers, policymakers and donors. While focused around specific events in Washington DC., the PRSP case included a global cast of researchers and policymakers in a process of policy change that spanned the globe. The Kenya case involved the translation of a Chinese idea (barefoot doctors) into a different sector (animal health) in a completely different part of the world (arid Kenya). There was also an international dimension to the transfer of knowledge in both the SLA and Sphere cases. In a globalising world, trans-national knowledge sharing is increasingly important, but our knowledge remains limited. More effort to understand more systematically the formal and informal processes at work makes a great deal of sense.

Notes

1   See http://www.odi.org.uk/rapid.
2   This was based on and remains similar to the OECD definition: 'creative work undertaken on a systematic basis in order to increase the stock of knowledge, including knowledge of man, culture and society, and the use of this stock of knowledge to devise new applications' (OECD 1981).
3   See Christiansen and Hovland (2003).
4   See Buchanan-Smith (2003).
5   See Young *et al.* (2003).
6   See Solesbury (2003).
7   It is important to note that the process of collecting cases probably underemphasises the importance of routine and incremental decisions and overemphasises the importance of fundamental or emergent ones.

References

Buchanan-Smith (2003) *How the Sphere Project Came into Being: A Case Study of Policy-making in the Humanitarian Aid Sector and the Relative Influence of Research.* ODI Working Paper No. 215. London: Overseas Development Institute.

Christiansen and Hovland (2003) *The PRSP Initiative: Multilateral Policy Change and the Relative Role of Research.* ODI Working Paper No. 216. London: Overseas Development Institute.

Clay, E. J. and Schaffer, B. B. (1984) *Room for Manoeuvre: An Exploration of Public Policy in Agricultural and Rural Development.* London: Heinemann Educational Books.

Court and Young (2003) *Bridging Research and Policy: Insights from 50 Case Studies.* ODI Working Paper No. 213. London: Overseas Development Institute.

Crewe, Emma and Young, John (2002) *Bridging Research and Policy: Context, Evidence and Links*. ODI Working Paper No. 173. London: Overseas Development Institute. Available online at http://www.odi.org.

de Vibe, Maja, Hovland, Ingeborg and Young, John (2002) *Bridging Research and Policy: An Annotated Bibliography.* ODI Working Paper No. 174. London: Overseas Development Institute. Available online at http://www.odi.org.

Figueroa, M. E. *et al.* (2002) *Communication for Social Change: An Integrated Model for Measuring the Process and Its Outcomes.* The Communication for Social Change Working Paper Series No. 1. New York: Rockefeller Foundation. Available online at http://www.comminit.com/stcfscindicators/sld-5997.html.

Fine, M. *et al.* (2000) 'For Whom? Qualitative Research, Representations, and Social Responsibilities', in N. Denzin and Y. Lincoln (eds) *Handbook of Qualitative Research.* Thousand Oaks: Sage.

Garrett, J. L. and Islam, Y. (1998) *Policy Research and the Policy Process: Do the Twain Ever Meet?* Gatekeeper Series No. 74. International Institute for Environment and Development.

Gladwell, M. (2000) *The Tipping Point: How Little Things Can Make a Big Difference.* London: Little, Brown & Co.

Haas, E. B. (1991) *When Knowledge is Power: Three Models of Change in International Organisations.* Berkeley: University of California Press.

Keck, M. and Sikkink, K. (1998) A*ctivists Beyond Borders: Advocacy Networks in International Politics.* Ithaca NY: Cornell University Press.

Keeley, J. and Scoones, I. (2003) *Understanding Environmental Policy Processes in Africa: Cases from Ethiopia, Mali and Zimbabwe.* London: Earthscan Publications.

Kickert, W. *et al.* (1997) 'A Management Perspective on Policy Networks' in W. Kickert, E. H. Klijn and J. F. M. Koppenjan (eds) *Managing Complex Networks.* London: Sage.

Kingdon, J. W. (1984) *Agendas, Alternatives, and Public Policies.* New York: Harpers Collins.

Lambin, J. (1996) *Strategic Marketing Management.* London and New York: McGraw-Hill.

Lindquist, Evert A. (1988) 'What do Decision-Models Tell Us about Information Use?' *Knowledge in Society* 1 (2): 86–111.

Lindquist, Evert A. (2003) 'Discerning Policy Influence: Framework for a Strategic Evaluation of IDRC-Supported Research'. Ottawa: International Development Research Centre.

Lipsky, M. (1980) *Street-level Bureaucracy: Dilemmas of the Individual in Public Services.* New York: Russell Sage Foundation.

Mattelart, A. and Mattelart, M. (1998) *Theories of Communication: A Short Introduction.* London: Sage.

Neilson, S. (2001) *Knowledge Utilisation and Public Policy Processes: A Literature Review.* Ottawa: Evaluation Unit, IDRC.

OECD (1981) *The Measurement of Scientific and Technical Activities: Proposed Standard Practice for Surveys of Research and Experimental Development* (Frascati Manual). Paris: OECD.

Philo, G. (1996) 'Seeing and Believing,' in P. Marris and S. Thornham (eds) *Media Studies: A Reader.* Edinburgh: Edinburgh University Press.

Pross, P. (1986) *Group Politics and Public Policy.* Toronto: Oxford University Press.

Puchner, L. (2001) 'Researching Women's Literacy in Mali: A Case Study of Dialogue among Researchers, Practitioners, and Policy Makers', *Comparative Education Review* 45 (2): 242–56.

RAWOO (2001) *Utilization of Research for Development Cooperation: Linking Knowledge Production to Development Policy and Practice*, Publication no. 21. The Hague: Netherlands Development Assistance Research Council.

Reinicke, W., Deng, F. *et al.* (2000) *Critical Choices: The United Nations, Networks and the Future of Global Governance.* Ottowa: International Development Research Center.

Robinson, D., Hewitt, T. and Harriss, J. (1999) 'Why Inter-Organisational Relationships Matter', in their (eds) *Managing Development: Understanding Inter-Organisational Relationships.* London: Sage.

Sabatier, P. and Jenkins-Smith, H.C. (1999) 'The Advocacy Coalition Framework: An Assessment', in P. Sabatier (ed.) *Theories of the Policy Process.* Boulder: Westview Press.

Solesbury, W. (2003) *Sustainable Livelihoods: A Case Study of the Evolution of DFID Policy.* ODI Working Paper No. 217. London: Overseas Development Institute.

Stacey, R. (1995) 'The Role of Chaos and Self-Organisation in the Development of Creative Organisations', in A. Albert (ed.) *Chaos and Society.* Amsterdam: IOS Press.

Stone, D., Maxwell, S. and Keating, M. (2001) *Bridging Research and Policy. An International Workshop.* Warwick, UK, July 2001.

Surr, Martin, Barnett, A., Duncan, A. and Speight, M. (2002) 'Research for Poverty Reduction: DFID Research Policy Paper'. DIFD Development Committee Meeting, 24 October.

Sutton, R. (1999) *The Policy Process: An Overview.* ODI Working Paper No. 118. London: Overseas Development Institute.

UNDP (2003) *Human Development Report 2003 Millennium Development Goals: A Compact among Nations to End Human Poverty.* New York: Oxford University Press.

Weiss, Carol (1977) 'Research for Policy's Sake: The Enlightenment Function of Social Research' *Policy Analysis* 3 (4): 531–45.

Williamson, J. (1996) 'Decoding Advertisements' in P. Marris and S. Thornham (eds) *Media Studies: A Reader.* Edinburgh: Edinburgh University Press.

Young, J., Kajume, J. and Wanyama, J. (2003) *Animal Health Care in Kenya: The Road to Community-Based Animal Health Service Delivery.* ODI Working Paper No. 214. London: Overseas Development Institute.

3 The impact of economic policy research

Lessons on attribution and evaluation from IFPRI

James G. Ryan and James L. Garrett

Introduction

Donors and governments institute complex monitoring and evaluation mechanisms to demonstrate the value of their investments in programmes and projects, yet demonstrated value is not necessarily enough to justify funding. For example, economists and scientists have extensively documented the rates of return to investment in agricultural research and development at around 80 per cent per year (Alston *et al.* 2000). Yet funding for the centres of the Consultative Group on International Agricultural Research (CGIAR), of which the International Food Policy Research Institute (IFPRI) is a part, has fallen by 8 per cent in real terms in the last ten years. At the same time, evidence of the impact of research on policy is scarce. Yet between 1997 and 2001 the proportion of overall spending dedicated to economic policy research in the CGIAR rose more than 30 per cent, going from 11 to 14 per cent, to USD 49 million (CGIAR 2002).

In recent years, IFPRI, the lead economic policy research institute of the CGIAR, has faced growing demands for clearer demonstration of impact. This has been challenging, however, as methodologies for impact assessment of social science research are not well developed. Cause-and-effect relations in the biological and physical sciences are much clearer than in the policy arena, which depends to a greater extent on human behaviour. The costs and benefits of a particular technology are thus more straightforward to calculate than that of a policy finding or recommendation, where numerous political factors and actors complicate the connections between research results, actions and outcomes. Few researchers have turned their attention to methodological issues of evaluating the impact of social science research, and so there are virtually no 'best practices' available (Maredia, Byerlee and Anderson 2001).

In response, a symposium held at IFPRI in 1997 focused on the development of quantitative economic approaches for impact assessment (Smith and Pardey 1997). Participants presented ideas on how to assess social science research quantitatively, but concluded that at this stage case studies, instead of general quantitative analyses, were more appropriate for drawing conclusions about impact and the means to achieve it. Consequently, IFPRI commissioned a number of case studies. The studies, (many of them summarized in Garrett 1999) covered a range of activities in which IFPRI was involved – from direct policy advice, to the building of general knowledge, to training – and provided a foundation for IFPRI's current approach to impact evaluation.

This chapter reviews methods and approaches of impact evaluation in economic policy research. A discussion of the main lessons from case studies on ways to heighten, and also analyse, the impact of economic policy research on policy decisions and welfare outcomes follows. The paper then outlines a framework for evaluation that IFPRI is using to guide its next steps in this area.

Documenting and measuring impact

A research institution has at least four rationales for documenting and measuring impact. They are basically to improve:

- accountability and credibility;
- quality and relevance;
- programme and project design and implementation;
- future planning and prioritizing.

To a significant extent, the primary purpose of impact studies determines the appropriate approach. If accountability is the major reason for evaluation, the evaluator may choose programmes or projects purposively, rather than randomly. Choosing the more 'successful' candidates may more convincingly justify the investments in the institution to the public, clients and donors. However, such 'cherry picking' may not be as informative to an institution that is interested mainly in improving its quality, relevance and effectiveness. In such instances, sampling 'failures' as well as 'successes' may offer more insights.

Approaches. Impact evaluations can employ quantitative or qualitative approaches, or a mixture of both. Quantitative approaches attempt to assess and attribute the welfare impacts of economic policy research, but a virtual void has existed in the economics literature with respect to the quantitative calculation of benefits and returns to social science research (Smith and Pardey 1997). The IFPRI 1997 symposium presented new thoughts on conceptual and methodological issues in quantitative assessments (Gardner 1997b; Norton and Alwang 1997; Timmer 1997; Zilberman and Heiman 1997). Suggested frameworks generally followed models used by economists to measure rates of return to agricultural research and development. These approaches rely on market models or regression analysis to estimate costs of investment and the value of resulting benefits (Alston *et al.* 2000). They use standard financial analysis procedures to account for timing and variations in the streams of costs and benefits. Empirical applications of these approaches remain scarce (but see Norton and Schimmelpfennig 2001; Ryan 2002).

These quantitative methods are particularly useful to assess historical trends in rates of return, compare returns across different geographical, environmental and political conditions, and to assign investment priorities. However, these methods cannot provide insight into the policy process and how policymakers use research information. Just as assessments of investment in agricultural research and development do not describe how technologies enhance production or which of the seed's genes need to be tweaked, quantitative approaches do not illuminate how economic research influences policy choices or which policy actors should be targeted with research information. Policymaking remains a black box, giving little idea of how the research had an impact, if any, or how it could be improved or communicated more effectively.

Qualitative evaluations describe the processes by which research outputs influence policy formulation. They take the form of retrospective narratives (Adams 1983; Babu 2000; Islam and Garrett 1997; Richardson 2001; Ryan 1999b). They involve interviews with professional peers, policymakers and their advisers and analysts. These sorts of evaluations elicit familiarity with the research, how the research compares with alternative sources of information, and what influences it had on the timing and design of policy.

One of the most impressive retrospective narratives is that of Campbell and Squires (1998). They describe the evolution of policies on the management of dolphin kills and tuna fishing in the seas around Australia and the role that biological and economic policy research played in policy development. Biological research on the synergy between dolphins and tuna and population dynamics began 20 years prior to the emergence of the problems of overexploitation of the tuna fisheries and the related problem of dolphin kills. This research was critical to later bio-economic modelling, which was used to establish policies regulating tuna catches. Biological and economic research were complementary in influencing policy in this instance. This is a good example of anticipatory research producing public goods.

Evaluators can also blend quantitative and qualitative approaches. Ryan (1999a) describes how research interacted with the institutional and political environment to lead Vietnam to relax rice export quotas and liberalize internal restrictions on rice trading. He then employs a quantitative model to estimate the value of policy changes to rice farmers, the government and consumers over time.

Counterfactual analyses are a variant of the mixed approach. These ask what might have occurred without a policy change. Burfisher, Robinson and Thierfelder (2001) examine what would have occurred to jobs and trade balances in the US without the North American Free Trade Agreement (NAFTA). The authors then compare these results to scenarios with NAFTA in place. While the study does not allow attribution to individual institutions or research, it does allow ex post verification of the accuracy of *ex ante* economic policy research.

Regardless of which approach is used, analysts still confront at least eight key issues in the design and conduct of the studies (Ryan 2001).

1. Scale and scope. Although evaluators can conduct impact evaluation at different levels of analysis (institution, programme, thematic body of work, project), most case studies are at the project level. Project-level studies are easier methodologically because the generation of research information and its dissemination often occurs within limited time and space. However, an international organization such as IFPRI produces knowledge as an international public good. For example, country policy analysts can employ methodologies or policy findings developed in one context in their own, or findings can change common ways of looking at problems, leading to multiple changes in policy decisions across countries, institutions, and individuals (Farrar 2002).

These sorts of impacts are difficult to trace and capture. As one moves beyond the project level, more and more actors become involved, with exponentially greater sources of information and motivations. This limits the evaluator's ability to attribute policy responses to individual actors or specific pieces of research. The need for greater accountability encourages a focus on the project level, where impacts are easier to trace. However, this short-term drive for accountability has inherent moral hazards. It encourages an institution to focus on projects where impact is more easily attributable and avoid longer-term and arguably more risky international public-good policy research. It may slant the perception of the nature of the institute (and ultimately slant the research portfolio through incentives for project work), in that projects are only a part of total research programme activity and an even smaller part of institute activity. In addition, it rewards those donors who provide country-level support tied to projects, while those donors whose funding allows flexibility across topics or across countries do not receive indications of the 'impact' of their investment, creating negative incentives for donors as well (Farrar 2002).

2. Timing. The policy process is not linear, or continuous. Gaps, jumps and lags in this process are present from the time an issue first arises in public discussion to when policymakers place it on the policy agenda and then make, announce and implement policy choices (Garrett and Islam 1998). Due to long lead and lag times between the completion of research and the accrual of any welfare impacts as a result of policy change, evaluations conducted soon after research is completed may not reveal any impacts as it is premature to look for them. This raises another issue, termed the 'Cassandra problem' by Smith and Pardey (1997): what is the value of 'good research advice' not taken? Or of delays in taking the advice? Perhaps advice continually not taken has value in that an analyst can then articulate the opportunity costs of a 'wrong' decision (that is, estimate the cost of the alternative to not taking the advice). In such instances, decision makers presumably are not giving due weight to concerns with economic efficiency, the presumed objective of the 'good research'. Alternatively, the so-called 'good advice' might indeed arise from flawed research, with the policymakers then having 'good reasons' not to accept it.

Time lags in the production, use and ultimate impact of research information can make the value of anticipatory research on future policy concerns especially high. Research findings that are readily available when policymakers need them reduce time lags in 'production' and 'adoption'. Alternatively, research not available when policymakers need it will, obviously, have limited impact. Anticipatory research not done can have a high opportunity cost in terms of reductions in welfare if decision makers make a wrong policy choice as a result of not having appropriate information. But it can be difficult to marshal resources for anticipatory research, to work on issues that do not seem 'current'.

3. Supply- versus demand-side approaches. Ideally, impact assessment would start on the demand-side from the point at which a major policy initiative occurs (the point of initial 'demand' for the information). It would then work backwards from the outcome towards the research itself, assessing what institutions and researchers have played a significant role in informing or influencing the policy change. Instead, most impact case studies have started at the level of the research project and tracked how the research outputs (the 'supply side') were used. The need for attribution has dictated this approach, but it may lead to loss of information about the importance of other projects, institutions and sources of information.

4. Importance of surprise. Surprise – the addition of new information to a policymaker's understanding – is the essence of quantitative Bayesian approaches to measuring impact. However, research has also shown the value of confirmatory research that reinforces current understanding and policies (Weiss 1980). So surprise is not necessarily a sine qua non of impact. Likewise, anticipatory research that alerts policymakers to possible future scenarios and surprises can reduce the time lag between appearance of an issue and action.

5. Attribution. Many actors participate in the policymaking process, and they rely on various sources of information when making or influencing policy decisions. It is difficult then to attribute 'impact' to any one source, as the multitude of actors, themselves with differential influence on the decision, rely on a multitude of sources. Attribution becomes even more difficult when we recognize that even this 'one' information source can represent a collaborative effort. In public research, partnerships and collaboration among non-profits, universities and governments are key and becoming the norm. Determining contributions to decisions in such an environment may not only be difficult but politically unwise and deceptive. Donors need to focus on the impacts produced jointly and synergistically by partnerships.

6. Choice of indicators. Choice of the indicators of impact also involves judgement. First, what is really the impact of research? At what level and what kind of impact should the evaluator look for? Should evaluators look at what the research organization produces, including the format and quality of information? Or how the organization provides information to policymakers and whether it enters into the policy process and influences policy choices? Or does research have impact only when policymakers choose and then effectively implement policies that affect final outcomes of interest, such as reductions in malnutrition or poverty?

Garrett and Islam (1998) argue for a traditional principle of monitoring and evaluation: that evaluators can directly hold an organization responsible only for those outcomes over which it has significant control. In this case, given the nature of the policy process and of how policymakers use research information, is it sensible to hold a research organization responsible for a government's particular policy choices and for the effectiveness of those choices in improving social welfare or economic growth? Garrett and Islam (1998) argue that it is not. Rather, evaluation should look more at the quality of the research outputs, the effectiveness of communicating those outputs and contributing to policy debates, and the potential (rather than necessarily actual) outcomes of the policy recommendations, or choices, based on research findings.

Ryan (1999a, 2002) maintains that this focus on quality of research output, processes and potential outcomes is necessary but not sufficient for impact assessment. One must also look at post-decision impacts if an institution is going to be able to differentiate its product from others and sustain funding support. Socioeconomic welfare is an obvious impact indicator of this nature. Distributional outcomes are another. Generally, portrayal of distributional outcomes has proved more influential than showing the economic losses due to current policies (that is, quantifying efficiency gains from policy change). Also, articulation of local impacts is often more influential in changing policies than global estimates.

Bibliometric indices that survey how often others cite the research offer another measure of higher-level impacts on overall scientific knowledge. The improvement of data quality as a result of policy research can also be a legitimate indicator, as is evidence of increasing demand for research by policymakers matched by additional investment in research and development. Calculating the economic value of the time saved in effecting policy changes is a valid measure of impact as well, as is qualitative information of the influences and impact of the research drawn from retrospective narratives. Historical narrative is especially valuable when the assessment starts with a demand-side approach.

Indicators are difficult to identify when the research reinforces the status quo, rather than resulting in distinct policy changes. It is equally difficult to assess situations where the research results in inappropriate policies or 'poisoned wells'. Bayesian approaches, for example, cannot handle such outcomes.

7. Sampling. A number of organizations use case studies to assess impact, posing several important methodological questions. Should case study choice be random or purposive? Each approach has pros and cons, and no clear consensus has emerged. Interviewing and elicitation techniques remain a concern when evaluating policy research, especially when the selection of interviewees depends to a significant extent on the researchers themselves. These concerns are valid for quantitative approaches as well, and statistical sampling methodologies can go a long way toward addressing such concerns. Qualitative researchers have developed other methods to deal with sampling problems. For example, to identify bias and triangulate results evaluators differentiate among audience types and employ different data-gathering techniques. Use of independent peers offers objectivity and lends credibility to the impact evaluation. However, limited budgets may reduce the study to a selection of only a small sample of projects and programmes, leading to 'cherry picking'.

8. Ex ante and ex post assessments. Both *ex ante* and *ex post* approaches are important to impact assessment. A part of standard monitoring and evaluation, a logical framework can employ an *ex ante* assessment to gauge the success of policy research in achieving its objectives. Even though all projects in a portfolio may not undergo formal independent *ex post* assessment, there is still considerable value in researcher teams documenting outputs, outcomes/influences and policy responses. This promotes internal learning and enhances institutional effectiveness. However, independent peer impact evaluation is still needed to ensure credibility and accountability. All assessments require databases of outputs, outcomes/influences and policy responses to enable the evaluator to verify them, track their influence and measure their impact.

Lessons from case studies

Case studies commissioned by IFPRI to assess the centre's impact provide some lessons for both enhancing IFPRI's future impact and designing and conducting future impact studies. The five studies were as follows (see also Garrett 1999):

- IFPRI and the abolition of the wheat flour ration shops in Pakistan (Islam and Garrett 1997);
- rice policy changes in Vietnam and the contribution of policy research (Ryan 1999a);
- IFPRI's 2020 Vision initiative for food, agriculture and the environment (Paarlberg 1999);
- food security and resource allocation impacts of IFPRI research in Bangladesh (Babu 2000);
- policy research and capacity building by IFPRI in Malawi (Ryan 1999b).

In our view, nine factors emerged from the above studies as important to the success of economic policy research, and the subsequent generation of meaningful impact.

1. High quality, independent research. All case studies noted that decision makers looked to IFPRI to produce quality research free of any apparent political bias. Being a CGIAR Centre seemed to confer this attribute in the minds of partners and stakeholders. The availability of peer-reviewed methodologies, such as the International Model for Policy Analysis and Agricultural Commodity Trade (IMPACT) for the 2020 Vision project and the Vietnam Agricultural Spatial Equilibrium Model (VASEM) in the case of work with the Vietnamese Ministry of Agriculture, lent credibility to the advice that emerged. The 2020 study noted a major source of 'impact' was that, in spite of its advocacy role, IFPRI never sensationalized the hunger and poverty issues or compromised professional judgements. 'These high professional standards maintained by the 2020 initiative are one reason it came to be trusted by both donors and developing-country policy leaders' (Paarlberg 1999).

Objectivity, independence and peer-reviewed outputs seem prerequisites for the acceptability of policy advice, but these attributes take time to cultivate. In many cases, however, policymakers need information in short order. Time is of the essence. Yet the need to present results quickly to have impact poses a risk to quality, and inappropriate advice can offset any gains from timeliness. In Vietnam, for example, researchers provided early results to policymakers as they continued to refine the model and have their work peer-reviewed for publication. Fortunately later results differed only in degree rather than kind and did not vitiate the earlier conclusions or policy advice. In Malawi, however, early results concluded improved credit access by smallholders increased incomes and food security. Later research came to the contrary conclusion using the same databases. The policy conclusions for the two cases would obviously be quite different.

IFPRI's role as an 'honest broker' also enhanced its credibility. Although some contend that competitive tendering for projects with donors and banks, as was the case in Pakistan, Vietnam and Bangladesh, can compromise independence, no evidence exists that stakeholders in those countries held that opinion. Commissioned research may actually improve the level of impact because stakeholders clearly want the information and plan to use it. In addition, independence was a primary reason that governments and donors commissioned the research from IFPRI in the first place. Governments and donors generally respected IFPRI's professionalism and integrity. The 2020 study by Paarlberg (1999) also acknowledged that IFPRI's position as a neutral institution vis-à-vis the 'pro-World Bank' and 'anti-World Bank' views allowed it to emerge as a respected voice.

Quality research and reputation are not sufficient conditions to influence the policy process and generate impact. For example, although the food security and nutrition monitoring data and analysis in the Malawi study were regarded as among the best in Africa, their availability and use in policy analysis have not led to a significant improvement in food security and nutrition among the vulnerable groups in that country.

2. Timeliness, responsiveness and communications. Whilst IFPRI cannot take credit for the policy changes per se, IFPRI research can give policymakers confidence that a change will have beneficial effects. Information then is useful in speeding up policy decisions, increasing cumulative benefits over the long term. In Pakistan, research on leakages in ration shops corroborated existing but limited research on the subject. IFPRI then provided specific and reputable data on which to formulate policies. Similarly the work on tobacco quotas in Malawi revalidated the decisions to relax them and allow smallholders to grow the crop.

Communication of key results prior to publication of project reports and refereed publications helped researchers gain time, and enhanced the usefulness and impact of the results. Through seminars, workshops, training programmes, policy briefs, and working papers, researchers proffered timely data, information and advice. IFPRI used this information to play both information and advocacy roles.

Involving the key ministries of government from the outset in design and feedback enhanced timely response on the part of IFPRI and encouraged timely use by Ministries. In Bangladesh, researchers shared sensitive results with the concerned Ministries prior to their public release. The final reports took account of the comments received but did not alter the results. This advance sharing built trust, according to Babu (2000). IFPRI was also responsive to emergent needs of policymakers. Once models such as IMPACT and VASEM were calibrated and validated, researchers and analysts could use them to respond quickly to policymakers' questions, ensuring they saw IFPRI as an institute able to offer advice in real time on emergent issues.

Training research staff in communications (presentation skills, interaction with the mass media, and public awareness) can have high payoffs. These skills allow staff to work comfortably to broaden the audience for research findings beyond the original clients or partners and hasten the policymaking process (with information as input), as all five studies showed. For example, the Southern African Development Community food security programmes grew out of the Malawi project as a result of active networking and communication of results. However, the project may have over-emphasized the written word at the expense of the spoken word, and policy process benefits rather than impact. Moreover, as the 2020 study indicated, policy researchers – IFPRI's intellectual peers – have traditionally been the primary audience. If policy impact is to be a higher priority, then IFPRI should recognize the diversity of policy audiences and tailor research communication for them.

3. Long-term collaboration and in-country presence. The studies indicated that having experienced staff living and working in countries and regions over extended periods is advantageous. This helps to build mutual confidence and understanding. Resident researchers enabled IFPRI to identify 'windows of opportunity', where the contemporary research could build on past research to constructively contribute to policy formulation and capacity building.

The Bangladesh study showed that a continuous presence allowed researchers to set and revise priorities through regular consultations with government officials. This increased the relevance and impact of the research. Government officials in Bangladesh brought IFPRI into planning for a follow-up to the rural rationing programme, abolished partially in response to IFPRI research. The successful food-for-education programme was the result. Similarly, IFPRI quickly responded to the need for work on procurement pricing and open tendering, giving effect to the policy change it had helped engineer to privatize and liberalize markets. The Pakistan impact study cites the nine-year association of IFPRI with the country along with out-posted staff as increasing the likelihood of use of the information and research. That is, '[the research fellow's] presence on the ground ensured continuity of dialogue and flow of information, and was punctuated by the visits of larger IFPRI teams from Washington' (Islam and Garrett 1997). On the other hand, the working paper series on food security and nutrition policy in Malawi's Bunda College stopped after the departure of the IFPRI staff.

In these examples, a residential presence allowed IFPRI to participate in planning and discussion sessions that might not otherwise have seemed to merit a separate visit from Washington. The advent of video conferences may make maintaining such a 'presence' easier and feasible, even if researchers do not reside in the country. Yet, technology seems unlikely to replace the personalized knowledge and contacts in a country that ease incorporation into these important initial discussions.

For sustained impact, more than a few years of a residential presence in a country appear necessary. Eicher (1999) contends that 25 to 50 years of sustained effort is needed in Africa to strengthen the 'agriculture knowledge triangle' involving research, extension and agricultural higher education. He advocates long-term scientific technical assistance by posting scientists from industrial nations in universities, national agricultural research institutes and ministries of science and technology. Timmer (1997) supports long-term country involvement with the same policymakers so that advisers are able to observe whether the policies they advocate in fact work. Perhaps the time is ripe for one or two IFPRI regional programmes in sub-Saharan Africa involving the posting of a critical mass of IFPRI scientists for the longer haul, along with libraries, databases and training programmes (see Ryan 1999b).

Another rationale for a physical presence of IFPRI staff over extended periods is the acknowledged long lead and lag times between the generation of process benefits and the realization of socioeconomic impacts from resulting policy changes. Reducing these lags will require constant advocacy and responsiveness. The continuous presence of staff allows a better understanding of the challenges involved in implementing policy, which can help in articulating the ultimate impacts of policy research. As well as bridging research and policy, there is a need to bridge policy and action. Closing both gaps are neglected areas of research at IFPRI and more generally. As the Malawi study attests, despite almost ten years of IFPRI involvement, four of them in a residential mode, and the quality data, research and publications that resulted, there has not been any discernible impact on the food security and well-being of the poor and vulnerable in that country. Should not IFPRI 'stay the course' to help ensure such ultimate impact? Should it do more 'embracing and sitting' and less 'hitting and running'?

Residential staff can orchestrate spillovers to other countries, regional institutions and IFPRI projects, by virtue of their presence and the contacts and reputations they develop. For example, in Malawi former students in the Masters programme at Bunda College were involved in later IFPRI projects on market reforms and regional integration. The resident IFPRI staff member also encouraged the use of the project's food and nutrition security information by the World Bank agricultural services project. As a quid pro quo he was able to convince the Bank to include an agricultural policy training and research component. Such spillovers are only possible with a residential presence. Unfortunately, despite their influence on impact, long-term residencies of the type envisaged here are not easy to sustain using current funding levels and shorter-term project modalities. More long-term core funding is inescapably required, as this sort of presence is key.

4. A conducive and receptive policy environment. A policy environment where the decision makers are eager for quality data, information and advice and where there is a momentum for change is the most favourable for achieving both process benefits and real socioeconomic impact. This was clearly the case in Vietnam, Bangladesh, Malawi and Pakistan. The currency of the topic, timeliness of the research and a sense of ownership by the collaborators and, importantly, the key policymaking audiences are critical ingredients for success. A topic that is demand-driven is imperative. A feature of the policy environments in all the case-study countries was a particular concern that any policy changes have an economic efficiency rationale and not come at the expense of the poor and their food security. IFPRI's ability to address this specific set of trade-off questions in a convincing way was instrumental in effecting significant policy changes.

In Pakistan the focus on the impact on poor consumers of de-rationing helped diffuse criticisms that the closure of ration shops would lead to consumer unrest. The IFPRI study showed that corruption in the ration shops was rampant and few poor consumers in fact used them. In Vietnam one of the most influential aspects of the IFPRI research was satisfying policymakers that relaxing rice export controls would not harm household food security and the poor. The design of the food-for-education programme in Bangladesh responded to concern that the earlier decision to abolish rural ration shops might harm the rural poor if some new initiative did not replace it.

A major comparative advantage of IFPRI is an ability to examine poverty, distribution and food security questions in a way that facilitates policy changes. Pointing out the economic efficiency gains of changes did not seem as instrumental in the policy decisions as were the data, analysis, information and advice on the distributional and food security outcomes. In other words it was IFPRI's influence on the political economy of the decision making processes that led to impact.

This is consistent with Gardner's (1997a) research that estimates of deadweight losses from US farm programmes by economists were not as influential as advocacy by them to newspaper editorialists, government experts and commodity grant representatives, to the effect that commodity programmes were costing billions to taxpayers, but accomplishing much less for farmers. The Pakistan study also found that the government was more concerned about the impact of the subsidies for ration shops on the budget than with the impact on Gross National Product. Maredia, Byerlee, and Anderson (2001) point out from their review of best practices that much more attention needs to be given to the distributional consequences of research than has been the case. Rodrik (1996) contends that policy changes with larger redistributive consequences per dollar of efficiency gains will be more difficult to achieve. He calls this the political cost–benefit ratio. The more dollars that have to be reshuffled per dollar of efficiency gain the less the chances of reform.

The Bangladesh and Vietnam impact studies estimated cost–benefit ratios of IFPRI's policy research and related activities in those countries. However, they could not translate these into meaningful measures of the impact of these efficiency gains on food security and poverty. These examples highlight the need for improved methods and higher priority for identifying and measuring the distributional impacts of cost-effective interventions targeted at the poor and food insecure.

5. *Importance of empirical data and simple analysis.* The country impact studies made the strategic importance of quality data and simple analysis evident. Results helped illuminate the policy debates, with household survey data perhaps most significant in influencing policy decisions. In Malawi, sample household survey findings helped convince the government that even though the macro-arithmetic of national food production per capita showed that food security was not an issue, the majority of households did not have an adequate diet and almost one-half of children were severely malnourished. The availability of household sample survey data within a few weeks of its collection across the whole country was also critical in designing an effective drought relief response, thereby averting a potential national disaster. In Vietnam presentation of preliminary results from household surveys on the extent and location of food insecurity was instrumental in alerting policymakers to the importance of increased rice exports and prices to the food security of smallholders, who were

the majority of the poor. This sensitized them to later policy advice. In both Pakistan and Bangladesh the information IFPRI assembled about the extent of leakages in the rationing programmes was arguably the most powerful influence on policymakers. Again, the availability of primary data on distributional issues by a credible international player with no stake in the outcome was key. It provided the ammunition for governments to respond to the various vested interests that may have opposed change.

6. Trade-offs between more immediate impacts and sustainable ones. Reliance on project funding and competitive contracting is not necessarily conducive to the long-term residencies frequently so important to achieving sustained impact. A long-term continuous and close involvement allows training and capacity-strengthening activities to be factored into the programme in ways that both complement the short-term objectives and enhance the ability of partners and collaborators to sustain the momentum in the longer term.

Experience in Malawi and Vietnam suggests that involving ministries as collaborators in the research helps to reduce lags in achieving influence and impact from policy research. However, staff of ministries may have limited ability to refine and use the economic models and other analytical tools and so maintain the momentum of the research beyond the end of the project. Pressures of new issues and frequent staff changes are also not conducive to sustainability. Linking with universities and other research institutes can build capacity or allow governments to understand how to access research beyond the immediate project task.

A concern for IFPRI is to ensure sustainability when it leaves a country, to avoid a vacuum that may vitiate previous and potential impact. IFPRI's 2020 Network in Eastern and Southern Africa is one such example of extending impact. This network now connects to existing ones on economics and policy under the auspices of the Association for Strengthening Agricultural Research in Eastern and Central Africa (ASARECA). Whilst Malawi would have preferred IFPRI staff to continue to contribute directly to the Masters programme at Bunda College, IFPRI made the conscious decision that after several years Malawians should assume the responsibilities.

7. Choosing partners and collaborators. Collaborators should have an interest in and capability for carrying out the work, as well as acknowledged independence and authority. In Pakistan IFPRI involved both the Ministry of Food and Agriculture and the Pakistan Institute of Development Economics in its programme on ration shops. This had peers and policymakers involved jointly in the planning and conduct of the policy studies, which seems an optimal mix. However, staff in Malawi and Bangladesh have limited capacity for food policy analysis, even after years of training and collaboration with IFPRI. This suggests that IFPRI needs to encourage ministries to rely more on independent think tanks like the Agricultural Policy Research Unit in Malawi and the Bangladesh Institute of Development Studies for data, research and analysis, with a combination of core and project funding from the ministries. IFPRI could then work with both types of institutions in a synergistic tripartite arrangement.

'Policy champions' at high levels of government are crucial to playing the necessary advocacy roles in the executive and legislative arms of government. In Pakistan, Sartaj Aziz, the adviser to the Prime Minister, played this role. In Vietnam, Cao Duc Phat, then Director of the Department of Agricultural and Rural Development Policy in the Ministry of Agriculture and Rural Development, was critical. In Bangladesh, the IFPRI project leader, Akhter Ahmed, a Bangladeshi, played the role of champion. Although on a priori grounds one may question the wisdom of having a national as leader of an international team because of the political pressures that might be brought to bear on him or her, it seems that this did not prevent the achievement of significant process benefits and impact.

8. Building consensus for change among stakeholders. The international public goods nature of IFPRI's outputs implies both an opportunity and an obligation to proffer them widely. Free availability is paramount to all interest groups likely to be affected by policy changes. At the same time, IFPRI must ensure partners and collaborators respect its freedom to publish and provide data and information, even when they may make the government uncomfortable.

In the case of the Pakistan, Vietnam and Bangladesh projects, partners had no reluctance to publicize the information and recommendations, to a large extent because governments were already wishing to head in that particular policy direction. Indeed in Bangladesh a press leak occurred from some in-house seminars in November 1991, which were discussing the results of the research on the ineffectiveness of the rural rationing. When the Minister of Finance read the newspaper story he called the Secretary of Food for an explanation. He then also raised it in the Cabinet, which asked the Minister of Food to develop a proposal to abolish the rural rationing programme. IFPRI shared its information on the savings to the government from its abolition. The Ministry of Food then used this information in subsequent Cabinet submissions, and ultimately abolished the scheme in May 1992.

The message here is that whilst perhaps unintended, media publicity helped build a consensus and in the process saved valuable time. Without compromising integrity or skewing results, a research organization can utilize the media strategically. Certainly on some occasions, partners will prefer that the results of studies are kept in-house. But research organizations must ensure that they have the freedom to publish in professional outlets and in the media.

In Vietnam, consensus-building did not involve the media in the same manner. IFPRI engaged in an extensive series of seminars and workshops among disparate partners and stakeholders with a similar message about the benefits of liberalization of domestic and export markets for rice. In Vietnam the policymaking environment is diffuse and consensus-building is an essential prerequisite to effecting change. An international market-oriented research institute with integrity, independence and quality research was seen as a neutral agent for change.

The 2020 Vision programme had significant success in catalysing consensus among international policy leaders, and noticeable success among developing country policy leaders. Fora such as IFPRI Research Updates were useful for airing vastly different perspectives on topical policy issues. Paarlberg (1999) sees high value in bringing individuals and institutions with differing views together, not only through the written word but in settings where they can talk and listen to one another.

9. The value of IFPRI's cross-country experience. The cumulative experience of IFPRI in undertaking policy research and capacity strengthening in many countries serves to underpin its efforts in individual countries. Such experience is one of the main comparative advantages IFPRI has to offer. This experience and its research structure can increase the probability of success, save time and reduce the likelihood of wrong policy advice. The food-for-education programme, for example, derived from IFPRI's extensive research on the design of targeted food and nutrition programmes. Work by Kherallah and Govindan (1999) guided other countries on the appropriate sequencing of market reforms, using the Malawi experience. IFPRI also drew on 12 country studies of food subsidies to design a study of the same issue in Pakistan. Previous work in Egypt was especially relevant. IFPRI has also sometimes arranged study tours by senior policy advisers and analysts to help them understand the issues and to examine 'best practice'.

In summary, the case studies instituted by IFPRI in the past five years have proved to be effective in articulating impact, thus satisfying the accountability imperative, the primary rationale. IFPRI management has noted that donors have not been harping as much on the need for documented *ex post* evidence of impact, as was the case earlier. They seem content with an Impact Assessment Discussion Paper series. In addition, the case studies in this series have highlighted lessons that the institute is using in the ex ante planning and conduct of its future research and related activities. This was the second of the four rationales for conducting impact evaluation.

IFPRI's current strategy and approach

The early imperative for impact evaluation in the mid-1990s was to enhance accountability to IFPRI's donors in order to justify the wisdom of their investments. The 1997 Symposium concluded that case studies were the appropriate way to articulate, measure and document the impact of economic policy research. The accountability imperative arose because of increasing competition for declining agricultural research and development funding from donors, and policy research had to compete with alternative investments. The hope was that by providing quantitative estimates of the economic benefits, especially to the poor, one would be able to demonstrate that policy research had comparable impacts to other research themes, as documented by Alston *et al.* (2000). Ultimately, IFPRI did not pursue the more 'global' quantitative approach. Rather, IFPRI undertook a series of case studies, beginning in 1998, and came to adopt a mixture of quantitative and qualitative approaches to assess impact primarily at the project level.

The Board of Trustees approved an operational strategy to institutionalize impact evaluation at IFPRI in 2000. The process was discussed in detail with all staff at the IFPRI Internal Program Reviews in both 2001 and 2002. In 2001, IFPRI's management initiated a number of pilot exercises involving ex ante impact evaluation on new projects as a component of the new strategy. IFPRI also began to go beyond the project level to conduct evaluations of some of its thematic research programmes. The first such study was Alwang and Puhazhendhi's (2002) examination of the impact of IFPRI's multi-year multi-country research programme on microfinance. The second was by Ryan (2003) on agricultural projection modelling at IFPRI.

The case studies provided ex post evaluations somewhat distant from the daily operations of staff. IFPRI seeks now to incorporate some aspects of impact evaluation in all its research activities and to improve IFPRI's ability to operate as a learning organization. In 2002–3, all research staff were requested to narrate instances where their research outputs had influenced policy and had subsequent social or economic impacts. These were conducted in focus groups of 4–6 staff from the different research divisions in order to stimulate cross-fertilization and validation.

IFPRI's current approach to impact evaluation is to categorize the products from economic policy research and related activities as outputs, outcomes/ influences, policy responses and welfare impacts (Table 3.1). Outputs are activities or efforts that can be expressed quantitatively or qualitatively. Outcomes or influences are measures of the use that clients or partners make of the outputs. They reflect the value placed on them as intermediate products, which in turn are inputs into the policymaking process. Outcomes and influences can be usefully separated into initial, intermediate and longer-term. Policy responses imply a degree of attribution of the effects of the intermediate outputs and outcomes/influences on the formulation of new, or reinforcement of existing, policy. Impacts are measurable effects of the attributed policy responses on the well-being of the ultimate beneficiaries of the research, namely the poor, the food and nutrition insecure and the environment. It could also include perceptions of peers and policymakers about such impacts.

These products are generally sequential. Evidence becomes more difficult to assemble as one moves from outputs to impacts. Generally, the responsibility of staff and management for documentation and evaluation decreases on the same continuum. The role of independent peer evaluators increases (Figure 3.1).[1]

For this framework to function, staff must record output and outcome/ influence indicators as a matter of course. Increasingly, this is happening at IFPRI. These indicators will relate directly to milestones and achievements in work plans at the beginning of the year. IFPRI staff will also record policy responses, subject to subsequent verification by independent peer impact evaluators that can be captured effectively in narratives. This is not meant to be a top-down compliance approach, but instead a performance management approach. Eventually it could become a regular part of staff evaluation.

Investors in public research and development are no longer satisfied with activity-based progress reports. They expect outcome/influence and impact evaluation: that is, objective assessments of the actual effects of the funded programme on the target population (Easterling 2000). For research institutions to deliver on this requires responsibility and accountability at the staff level. Suitable databases of indicators of outputs, outcomes/influences and policy responses need to be

Table 3.1 Some indicators of the products of policy research

Outputs	Outcomes/Influences	Policy responses	Impacts
Publications • number and type • refereed/non-refereed	*Publications* • citations, use in curricula, circulation numbers, sales, requests, web hits	Changes in policies attributable to policy research	Reduced poverty
Methodologies • description • value-added	*Methodologies* • use of new methodologies	Reinforcement of existing policies	Improved food and nutrition security
Training • number of trainees • extent of training • duration of training • number and type of manuals	*Training* • trainee promotions • number of others trained by IFPRI trainees	Implementation of policy changes	Sustained livelihoods of the poor
Seminars/Symposia/Conferences • number • type • number of participants	*Seminars/Symposia/Conferences* • number of policy-makers present and influence on policy • invitations to IFPRI staff to present key-note and other papers at other meetings – number, organizations and whether expenses are paid	Changes in institutions	Enhanced natural environment
Press releases • number • type	*Press releases* • number of press releases published and in what fora; letters to editors spawned as a result		
Press conferences • number • type	*Press conferences* • number of press articles that resulted and in what fora		
Capacity-strengthening of partner institutions	*Capacity strengthening* • invitations to IFPRI staff and management to be on committees adjudicating policy changes in partner organizations and countries • refereeing assignments of IFPRI staff, requests for additional research in response to earlier outputs • degree of success in acquiring additional resources for policy research to partner institutions		

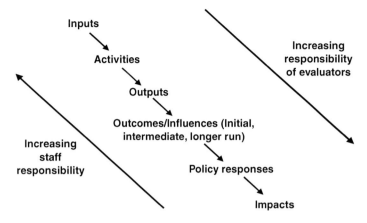

Figure 3.1 Framework for impact evaluation

developed and maintained so they become a sustainable part of the corporate memory that is not lost when individual staff leave. Given the often-long period between the conduct of economic policy research and the generation of real impact, such databases are imperative.

Indicators at staff level are then aggregated to the appropriate project-, programme- or institute-levels. Benchmarks are important for all of these. These can be before-and-after comparisons that document the gap between goals or milestones and actual achievements. A framework that ties outputs to processes and assumptions can provide a useful way of linking such ex ante with ex post impact assessments. This is now a feature in the CGIAR (Balzer and Nagel 2001). For a more comprehensive impact assessment a comparison with best practices of others (i.e. with-and-without IFPRI) is desirable.

Conclusions

Progress has been made in the last five years in the conduct of various case studies of the impact of economic policy research and in drawing lessons for the future. Some progress has also been made in the development of methodologies for quantifying impact in economic terms. However, a number of issues remain. These include attribution, measurement and the enhancement of impact.

'Demand-side' approaches seem preferable to 'supply-side' ones. The former uses major policy events as the starting point and works retrospectively to establish the separate influences of the many research suppliers and other factors on policy responses. It may be easiest, and most logical, to measure joint impacts of various players rather than separating out the contributions of individual institutions. Impact assessment will also most likely use a mixture of both qualitative and quantitative methods. Retrospective narratives are an essential component of the former and indeed provide the basis for quantitative estimates and can help address the elusive issue of attribution. Most importantly, if impact evaluation itself is to be effective in enhancing the impact of research and researchers, the process must be institutionalized. Staff and management should take responsibility for recording outputs, outcomes/influences and policy responses related to their research. Independent evaluators can verify these and endeavour to translate them into meaningful measures of their impact on economic welfare and assess what share might be attributed to policy research institutions and their partners. Researchers must see such a system as integral to learning and improving their own actions.

Researchers also have a responsibility to ensure the public dissemination of their findings. To the extent that the independence and credibility of the researcher and the institution are not compromised, a degree of advocacy is also appropriate. With the increased availability of information technology and impetus for participatory democracy and good governance in developing countries, there is increased scope for credible policy research to be accessed by disparate groups and thereby generate public debate and so better inform the policy process. In this context, credible research on the distributional consequences of alternative policies will arguably have more influence and impact than will measures of the implications for economic efficiency.

Finally, we need to continue to undertake more case studies in order to further refine approaches and methodologies for impact evaluation and help to define 'best practices'. There is also scope for more multidisciplinary research into policy processes in order to better position policy research to have strategic influence, as is being proposed in the Food Consumption and Nutrition Division of IFPRI (Haddad and Pelletier 2003). But we should go beyond into bridging the gap between policymaking and implementation. In other words, 'bridging policy and action' should complement 'bridging research and policy'.

Note

1   The graphic is not meant to imply the policy process is linear but only to portray the responsibilities of staff and evaluators in assessing impact.

References

Adams, R. H., Jr. (1983) 'The Role of Research in Policy Development: The Creation of the IMF Cereal Import Facility' *World Development* 11 (7): 549–63.

Alston, J. M., Chang-Kang, C., Marra, M. C., Pardey, P. G. and Wyatt, T. J. (2000) 'A Meta-analysis of Rates of Return to Agricultural R & D. Ex Pede Herculem?' *Research Report* No. 113. Washington, DC: International Food Policy Research Institute.

Alwang, J. and Puhazhendhi, V. (2002) *The Impact of the International Food Policy Research Institute's Research Programme on Rural Finance Policies for Food Security for the Poor.* Impact Assessment Discussion Paper No. 16. Washington, DC: International Food Policy Research Institute.

Babu, S. (2000) *Impact of IFPRI's Policy Research on Resource Allocation and Food Security in Bangladesh.* Impact Assessment Discussion Paper No. 13. Washington, DC: International Food Policy Research Institute.

Balzer, G. and Nagel, U. (2001) 'Logframe Based Impact Monitoring within the CGIAR System. Annex 4 Background Papers', in TAC Secretariat *The Future of Impact Assessment in the CGIAR: Needs, Constraints and Options.* Proceedings of a Workshop Organized by the Standing Panel on Impact Assessment (SPIA) of the Technical Advisory Committee (TAC), 3–5 May, 2000. Rome: Food and Agriculture Organization of the United Nations, pp. 54–78.

Burfisher, M. E., Robinson, S. and Thierfelder. K. (2001) 'The Impact of NAFTA on the United States' *Journal of Economic Perspectives* 15 (1, Winter): 125–44.

Campbell, H. and Squires, D. (1998) 'The Role of Research in Fisheries Management: Conserving Dolphins in the Eastern Tropical Pacific and Exploiting Southern Bluefin Tuna in the Southern Ocean', Chapter 6, in S. R. Tabor and D. C. Faber (eds) *Closing the Loop: From Research on Natural Resources to Policy Change*. Policy Management Report No. 8. European Centre for Development Policy Management and the International Service for National Agricultural Research, pp. 52–87.

CGIAR – Consultative Group on International Agricultural Research (2002) *Annual Report 2001*. Washington, DC: CGIAR Secretariat, World Bank.

Easterling, D. (2000) 'Using Outcome Evaluation to Guide Grant Making: Theory, Reality, and Possibilities' *Non-profit and Voluntary Sector Quarterly* 29 (3): 482–6.

Eicher, C. K. (1999) *Institutions and the African Farmer*. Issues in Agriculture No. 14. Washington, DC: Consultative Group on International Agricultural Research.

Farrar, C. (2002) Personal communication to J. G. Ryan.

Gardner, B. L. (1997a) 'Returns to Policy-related Social Science Research in Agriculture.' Paper prepared for the IFPRI workshop The Benefits of Policy-oriented Social Science Research. Washington, DC: International Food Policy Research Institute.

Gardner, B. L. (1997b) 'Measuring the Benefits of Agricultural Economics Research: Discussion' *American Journal of Agricultural Economics* 79 (5): 1551–3.

Garrett, J. L. (1999) *Research That Matters: The Impact of IFPRI's Policy Research*. Washington, DC: International Food Policy Research Institute.

Garrett, J. L. and Islam, Y. (1998) *Policy Research and the Policy Process: Do the Twain Ever Meet?* Gatekeepers Series No. 74. London: International Institute for Environment and Development.

Haddad, L., and Pelletier, D. (2003) 'The Nutrition Policy Process: A Proposal for a Global and Regional Research Programme (GRP)' Draft consultation document for discussion and comment. Washington, DC: International Food Policy Research Institute.

Islam, Y. and Garrett, J. L. (1997) *IFPRI and the Abolition of the Wheat Flour Ration Shops in Pakistan: A Case Study on Policymaking and the Use and Impact of Research*. Impact Assessment Discussion Paper No. 1. Washington, DC: International Food Policy Research Institute.

Kherallah, M., and Govindan, K. (1999) 'The Sequencing of Agricultural Market Reforms in Malawi' *Journal of African Economies* 8 (2): 125–51.

Maredia, M., Byerlee, D. and Anderson, J. R. (2001) 'Ex Post Evaluation of the Economic Impacts of Agricultural Research Programmes: A Tour of Good Practice'. Annex 3 Overview Papers, in TAC Secretariat *The Future of Impact Assessment in the CGIAR: Needs, Constraints and Options*. Proceedings of a Workshop Organized by the Standing Panel on Impact Assessment (SPIA) of the Technical Advisory Committee

(TAC) 3–5 May, 2000. Rome: Food and Agriculture Organization of the United Nations, pp. 3–43.

Norton, G. W. and Alwang, J. (1997) 'Measuring the Benefits of Policy Research' *American Journal of Agricultural Economics* 79 (5): 1534–8.

Norton, G. W. and Schimmelpfennig, D. E. (2001) 'Using Bayesian Approaches to Value Policy Research.' Paper presented at the Ministry of Foreign Affairs, Netherlands–IFPRI Workshop on Assessing the Impacts of Policy-Oriented Social Science Research. The Hague, Netherlands, November 12–13.

Paarlberg, R. L. (1999) *External Impact Assessment of IFPRI's 2020 Vision for Food, Agriculture, and the Environment initiative.* Impact Assessment Discussion Paper No. 10. Washington, DC: International Food Policy Research Institute.

Richardson, B. (2001) 'The Politics and Economics of Wool Marketing, 1950–2000' *Australian Journal of Agricultural and Resource Economics* 45 (1) March: 95–115.

Rodrik, D. (1996) 'Understanding Economic Policy Reform' *Journal of Economic Literature* 34 (1, March): 9–41.

Ryan, J. G. (1999a) *Assessing the Impact of Rice Policy Changes in Vietnam and the Contribution of Policy Research.* Impact Assessment Discussion Paper No. 8. Washington, DC: International Food Policy Research Institute.

Ryan, J. G. (1999b) *Assessing the Impact of Policy Research and Capacity Building by IFPRI in Malawi.* Impact Assessment Discussion Paper No. 11. Washington, DC: International Food Policy Research Institute.

Ryan, J. G. (2001) *Synthesis Report of Workshop on Assessing the Impact of Policy-oriented Social Science Research in Scheveningen, the Netherlands November 12–13, 2001.* Impact Assessment Discussion Paper No. 15. Washington, DC: International Food Policy Research Institute.

Ryan, J. G. (2002) 'Assessing the Impact of Food Policy Research: Rice Trade Policies in Viet Nam' *Food Policy* 27 (1): 1–29.

Ryan, J. G. (2003) *Evaluating the Impact of Agricultural Projection Modelling Using the 'IMPACT' Framework.* Impact Assessment Discussion Paper No. 17. Washington, DC: International Food Policy Research Institute.

Smith, V. H. and Pardey, P. G. (1997) 'Sizing up Social Science Research'. *American Journal of Agricultural Economics* 79 (5): 1530–3.

Timmer, C. P. (1997) 'Valuing Social Science Research and Policy Analysis' *American Journal of Agricultural Economics* 79 (5): 1545–50.

Weiss, C. H. with Bucavalas, M. J. (1980) *Social Science Research and Decision-making.* New York: Columbia University Press.

Zilberman, D. and Heiman, A. (1997) 'The Value of Economic Research' *American Journal of Agricultural Economics* 79 (5): 1539–44.

4 Power and ideas

Economics and global development policy

Desmond McNeill

Introduction

In the international system, it is important to achieve *consensus* across institutions (bilateral and multilateral), and between member states. Shared ideas play an important part in such consensus. But inter-institutional *rivalry* is common within the multilateral system, and institutions gain international prestige partly by having good ideas. Ideas are thus an important source of power.

A second claim of this paper is that economic ideas play a particularly important role. This discipline enjoys great power within the multilateral institutions. But it is not well equipped to take account of social and historical context, and indeed social phenomena generally. Economics seeks to be value-free, and derives much of its strength from its claim to analytical rigour. But many economists either ignore power or deal with it in a way that, arguably, distorts comprehension.

To illustrate the interplay between these two arguments, the dynamics of the annual conference in 2000 of the Global Development Network will be considered. This was a large international meeting of development researchers from different disciplines, who convened under the overall banner of 'Beyond Economics'. Notwithstanding the title and theme of the conference, the research questions, methods and models of economics appeared to prevail. How can we explain the kind of institutional and disciplinary hegemony seen in Tokyo? As developed in the next two sections, I address how 'ideas' are taken up, synthesised and instituted in policy using three brief case studies – the informal sector, sustainable development and social capital – to reveal the extent to which the economics discipline combined with multilateral institutions such as the World Bank acquire both the power of ideas and the power over ideas.

Towards an interpretive framework

The role of ideas in multilateral development institutions is the subject of study under a research programme entitled the CANDID project (Creation, Adoption, Negation and Distortion of Ideas in Development).[1] In this study, we focus on case studies of a few selected 'ideas' and the major multilateral institutions. In each case, the aim is to trace:

- how an 'idea' is taken up by the development assistance community;
- how it is interpreted and translated into policy;
- how it is modified, in response both to debate and to feedback from implementation experience.

An 'idea,' in the context of this research, is defined as a concept that powerfully influences development policy. It is more than simply a slogan or 'buzzword', but may nevertheless be vulnerable on analytical or empirical grounds. It arises and is developed in the interplay between the academic and policy domains, but it derives its credibility for policy largely from its basis in academia.

We analyse how ideas are processed within the multilateral system, and also thereby seek to assess the varying importance of these different fora. A further aspect of interest is how the interface between academia and multilateral institutions operates, and on whose terms. More specifically, what is the role of economics? To what extent does this discipline determine the language and the criteria of rigour that are applied?

In our study we found inspiration in the perspectives of Gramsci (1971) and Cox (1992); the former for his theories of hegemony, and the latter for the application of such theory specifically to the field of international political economy. Also, we seek to establish a middle ground between the realist and constructivist positions within international relations theory. In broad terms, the constructivist perspective implies that the identities and interests of the actors within the multilateral system are constructed by social interaction around competing interpretations of different ideas. But any framework for understanding the relationship between power and ideas in the multilateral system must also take seriously the basic logic of political realism: outcomes cannot be properly analysed without regard for the distribution of power.

Since we here are talking about ideas as collective images we need to establish a clear connection between ideas and institutionalisation. Whereas traditional international relations/international political economy scholars such as Kindleberger (1973) and Keohane (1984) use the term hegemony in a narrow sense, meaning dominance by one state over a group of other states, another interpretation can be derived from Gramsci: hegemony as a structure of dominance. In this interpretation, whatever group or entity holds the hegemonic position it is sustained not merely by force, but by broadly based consent through the acceptance of an ideology and of institutions consistent with this structure. In other words, a hegemonic structure of world order is one in which power primarily takes a consensual form. Here we find Cox's concept of 'framing' most useful (see below). As he puts it: 'Hegemony frames thought and thereby circumscribes action' (1992: 179). An effective frame is one that makes favoured ideas seem like common sense, while unfavoured ideas are unthinkable.

To be practical, multilateral institutions therefore take up and seek to establish global consensus around certain 'ideas' that they see as important for their policy purposes and international image. Legitimacy in the making of development policy is sought by grounding the proposals in a theoretical base and in supporting empirical analysis. In multilateral institutions, whose constituency is relatively ill defined, this is perhaps especially important. In such a context, economic ideas experience relative ease in disciplinary institutionalisation.

Economics seeks to be neutral, allowing values to be introduced into decision-making processes only explicitly – at the stage of prescription. In practice, of course, values enter in at every stage – including explanation and even description. And who is to define economics, and how? To define its boundaries is also, to a large extent, to determine how it is studied. In economics, as Schumpeter observed, ideology enters on the very ground floor: 'Analytical effort is of necessity preceded by a preanalytic cognitive act that supplies the raw material for the analytical effort' (1954: 41). As such, economics differs from other disciplines in being operative at all levels: from the very theoretical through to the practical; from description and analysis to policy. This is a major reason for its special power.

It is sometimes assumed that the 'values' with which economics is concerned are economic growth and efficiency alone, and there is therefore seen to be a conflict between, for example, economic efficiency and equity, or economic growth and the environment. This is too simplistic. But there is a more subtle sense in which economic perspectives frame the discourse of development, and exert enormous influence over both research and policy. It is this phenomenon with which I am concerned here.

The extent to which the economic 'paradigm' has prevailed in the enactment of policy ideas varies. In some cases there is evidence of fruitful combination, in others major issues are still unresolved, and there is either interdisciplinary strife or analytical confusion. It is important to remember that development economics stands in an uneasy relation both to development studies and to economics (Meier 1994). Within development studies, economics has always been a powerful, perhaps even dominant discipline. Within economics, however, development economics has generally had a low status. The development economist has thus been torn between two 'social and epistemological communities': mainstream economists on the one hand and other social scientists of development on the other. Both no doubt claim to be rigorous, but their perspectives and approaches may differ radically.

Three case studies

The ideas we have chosen to study in CANDID span about 25 years. I will here refer briefly to three of these: the informal sector (from the 1970s), sustainable development (1980s), and social capital (1990s).[2] In this period there have been major social and political background changes, both local and global. Ideas have been shaped by – and to some extent have themselves shaped – the political/ideological context of development thinking. In this respect, all three represent compromise positions.

Informal sector

The idea was coined by an anthropologist, Keith Hart, on the basis of his experience in Ghana (Hart 1973). It refers to economic activities that largely escape recognition, enumeration, regulation and protection by the government. The idea was taken up and developed in a long and fruitful collaboration between staff (most of them economists) from an applied research institution (Institute of Development Studies, Sussex – IDS) and the International Labour Organisation (ILO) who undertook joint work on the World Employment Programme through a series of country studies and city studies. The concept was taken up in the very influential book *Redistribution with Growth* (Chenery *et al.* 1974), which was the outcome of collaboration between IDS and the World Bank. Today, despite substantial criticism, there is no doubt that the idea of the informal sector has had enormous influence on both theory and practice. It has been criticised both theoretically and in relation to the policies that have been based on it; and it has been misused, misunderstood and redefined. Despite, or perhaps even partly because of this, it has for a very long time shaped the structure and content of debate about urban employment, and urban development more generally.

What part has economics played in the informal sector debate? First, the very recognition of the sector has been crucial. Existing categories, shaped by the nature of developed economies, and the discipline of economics (and national income accounting) had previously caused the 'working poor' to be overlooked. Once the 'sector' was recognised it then had to be rigorously defined and analysed. There was considerable, but not full, consensus that the analytical categories and tools of economics needed to be reviewed.

The informal sector 'idea' had important implications for policy. Broadly, it contributed to an argument for reconsidering the apparent conflict between equity and growth. The compromise – 'redistribution with growth' – was a reformist position (at least in the context of the radical 1970s). This applies both to the analysis and the policies proposed. As regards the latter, the emphasis was on raising productivity rather than asset redistribution; and the activities that resulted were often project level rather than systemic initiatives: provision of loans, training, etc.

In brief, the informal sector 'idea' brought together social scientists from different disciplines. It would be too much to claim, however, that the outcome was a wholly new and integrated analytical apparatus. For comparative purposes, what is important to note is the origins of the idea: precisely at the interface between academia and policy and between economics and other disciplines – arising out of a perceived conceptual vacuum. To quote *Redistribution with Growth*:

> This report has its origins in discussions between members of IDS and DRC/WB over the past several years. Our point of departure was the notable inconsistency between the general perception of income distribution and employment as major problems for developing countries on the one hand, and the analytical tools available to policy-makers on the other.
>
> (Chenery *et al.* 1974: v).

The power of the informal sector 'idea' was, I suggest, the extent to which it acted as a bridge, in several respects: a bridge between research and policy, between different disciplines, and – perhaps most important – between apparently conflicting positions. It held out the prospect of a consensus – something which is crucially important for policy-makers (though not necessarily for researchers). The danger is that agreement may be reached only by avoiding or concealing real differences of view. Prolonged discussions at international conferences end all too often with a compromise that is empty in analytical and policy terms. In the case of the informal sector, one reason that this concept was successful was that it helped to create what I call substantive consensus.

A consensus is, ideally, achieved both in analytical terms (what the informal sector is) and in policy terms (what needs to be done). Certainly this consensus became strained, in the case of the informal sector, and the concept distorted. The focus of much of this discord was, of course, the definition of the term itself. Here, the tension between researchers and policy-makers was very marked: the latter need not just simple definitions, but also ones that enable action to be taken.[3] I will not explore the details of the debates here, but simply make three comments. First, the question of definition was central in the discussion between radicals and reformists: whether the relation between formal and informal sectors is benign or malign – an issue which is necessarily very difficult to test empirically. Second, definitions varied between different disciplines: whether employment-focused or household/livelihood focused; whether generalisable or context-specific. Third, policy-makers tended to be far less concerned with the niceties of definition than researchers. The lack of a clear definition opens the way both for poor quality research, and also for a policy consensus which is more apparent than real. Like it or not, the idea of the informal sector had a significant impact on both development research and development policy – at least in the urban sector – over a ten- and perhaps even twenty-year period (Harris 1992).

Sustainable development

This 'idea' was even more policy-driven than the informal sector, in that it arose directly out of the unresolved – even perhaps unconsidered – conflict between two objectives: development (seen as economic growth) and environment. There is some debate as to who first coined the term, but no doubt that it was following the publication of *Our Common Future* (WCED 1987) that the idea took off. It represents a supremely successful example of agenda-setting. The idea of sustainable development has been tested both conceptually and empirically. It has been distorted, and often found wanting, but it still remains very important for policy debate.

Seen from the viewpoint of development studies, the 'idea' of sustainable development involved an expansion of the policy agenda. The environment was already a concern (albeit minor) in economics, and there existed a well-established sub-discipline known as environmental economics. This was sometimes criticised by non-economists as being too 'economistic' in its approach. Further, casting environmental issues in a global instead of a local perspective altered the agenda – raising the questions which often arise in development studies: whose values? whose analysis? whose priorities? The ensuing debate led to important discussions in the North, about the hegemony of economic ideas (as having little to do with development); and in the South about the hegemony of northern concerns (as emphasising environment 'at the expense of' development).

NGOs (non-governmental organisations) played a very significant role in putting sustainable development – and more generally the environment – on the multilateral agenda. Perhaps the most clear case is the World Bank where what might be described as an 'unholy alliance' between northern-based environmental NGOs and the US Treasury drew critical attention to Bank projects, notably in Brazil (Polonoroeste) and India (Narmada). The concept of 'sustainable development' not only entered the vocabulary of the World Bank, but led to the creation of a new Vice-Presidency for Environmentally Sustainable Development (Wade 1997).

There have occurred some significant developments in economic thinking with regard to the environment: for example, concerning the 'using up' of natural capital, and its implications for national income accounting; and around the distinction between 'strong sustainability' and 'weak sustainability'. Yet, some (from both natural sciences, and other social sciences) might claim that in analytical terms the concept of sustainable development has been distorted by becoming too technocratic. Economics is narrowly anthropocentric; so that in economics the environment is a resource, whose value is its market (or perhaps 'corrected market') value. Others would argue that in policy terms the idea of sustainable development has still failed to resolve the implicit conflict between economic growth and environmental conservation.

Social capital

The third 'idea', social capital, has a different history again, arising as it did from a book by a political scientist, Robert Putnam's *Making Democracy Work* (1993), which became extremely popular in an astonishingly short time; the new buzzword of the western development community. The term social capital can be traced to the social theories of Pierre Bourdieau and more recently James Coleman (1990) and from Putnam's own work, but it is in fact an old topic in social science. In Putnam's (1993) interpretation the concept refers to features of organisation, such as trust, norms and networks that can improve the efficiency of society by facilitating co-ordinated action. The main reason for its popularity among multilateral development institutions is that Putnam offers a hard-headed argument in favour of community, trust and shared values: they encourage economic growth.

It was actively taken up by the World Bank, which undertook two research programmes on the subject; organised a large conference in Washington in 1999; established a website; and published a number of papers, as well as an edited volume (Dasgupta and Serageldin 2000). Why did this happen?

There has, in recent years, been an increasing recognition, in the World Bank – and more generally among development assistance agencies – of the importance of community participation. There has also been a significant shift within the Bank towards the inclusion of political issues, notably through the Bank's work on 'governance'. These changes have given greater recognition to the need for insights from disciplines such as sociology and political science. The World Bank has always had an ambition – one which it has generally been rather successful at achieving – to be at the forefront of ideas; if not initiating them, then at least rapidly taking them over (Ranis 1997; Stern and Ferreira 1997). The discipline, and language, of economics has for many years been dominant within the World Bank, and especially its Research Department. New ideas must, therefore, in order to be accepted, survive criticism by this particular discipline. The reason why the concept of social capital is so attractive for the World Bank is that it allows for the dominant economic perspective to take into account sociological and political considerations that have increasingly been recognised as important. The concept fits well at the interface between economics and sociology (in the so-called 'new institutional economics'). Thanks to the work of Putnam, Coleman, and others, staff in the World Bank could thus adopt a new term which was at the forefront of both academic and popular debate; not only within the disciplines of sociology and political science but – most important (for the Bank) – perhaps also in economics. It is therefore understandable that research-minded Bank staff had an a priori interest in the idea.

But the rapid progress of the idea required its being actively taken up by those that count. The President of the Bank, James Wolfensohn himself, showed a special interest in participation and involvement of NGOs, which created a supportive context. The Chief Economist, Joseph Stiglitz, who had established a very high reputation for his work on the economics of information and institutions, played an important part. So too did one of the Vice-Presidents, Ismail Serageldin, who was adept at involving prestigious academics outside the Bank: such as Mancur Olson and Robert Putnam, but especially economists, such as Arrow and Solow (Dasgupta and Serageldin 2000). It was of crucial importance that senior economists both within and outside the World Bank took the concept seriously. In brief, a conjuncture of key individuals and structural factors may be said to have played their part in causing the concept of social capital to achieve such rapid prominence in the Bank. It is still too early to pass any final judgement on the fate of the 'idea' social capital. In the World Development Report 2000/2001 *Attacking Poverty* (World Bank 2001) the term is used, but it plays a far less prominent role in the final document than in the earlier draft that was posted on the web.

The UNDP, by contrast, has been much more cautious, or even reluctant, in its use of the term, which might be considered surprising in view of its traditionally greater emphasis on social as opposed to economic aspects (most notably, perhaps, reflected in the contrasts between the annual Human Development Reports of the UNDP and the World Development Reports of the World Bank). While the World Bank has been promoting the idea of social capital, the UNDP has been promoting the concept of 'global public goods'. Here a standard concept from economics ('public goods') has been extended into the global realm.

'Social capital' appeals to economists who see the opportunity to use their analytical tools and disciplinary perspectives on a new and interesting field. And also, perhaps, to other social scientists who see the possibility of exerting some influence on an economics-dominated discourse. This raises the question: whose category is it? It is new for economists (and, in a sense, for political scientists), but not for sociologists or anthropologists. Does it, then, successfully combine economic and sociological perspectives? And in whose terms – and hence *on* whose terms – is the debate? Is there room for a truly interdisciplinary position? These questions are relevant not only for the concept of social capital, but for the relationship between economics and other disciplines more generally.

A brief comparison of the three ideas

Each of these three ideas relates to an important policy issue, and is attractive because it appears to fulfil a bridging function: resolving a conflict, or filling a gap, and offering the promise of what I call 'substantive consensus'. What role does economics play in establishing such a consensus? And how has economics interacted with other disciplines in so doing? The answer will, of course, vary according to the discipline concerned. What is the relevant other? (Or perhaps more accurately, for which disciplines is economics the relevant other?) In the case of the informal sector the significant other discipline is anthropology or sociology. For sustainable development it is ecology, and perhaps the natural sciences more generally. For social capital it is political science and, perhaps, anthropology/sociology again. Consider, briefly, each 'idea' in turn.

In the case of the informal sector, it can be argued that an economic perspective led to the overlooking of an important phenomenon, but that this has now been corrected. And this had important consequences both for analysis and policy. It was thus the level of *description* which was crucial. Certainly the 'description' of the phenomenon (in this case employment) was substantially changed thanks to the introduction of the informal sector. This then had some impact on analysis and prescription. As regards the former, economics and other disciplines were to some extent complementary (for example combining qualitative and quantitative approaches, focusing on the household or social group as well as the 'firm' or production unit). Economic policies and instruments were, along with others, applied in response to the objectives identified. Certainly economics exerted a strong influence both on the discourse and on other disciplines. Nevertheless, I would suggest, there was mutual interaction, and economics as a discipline was even perhaps altered somewhat as a result.

In the case of sustainable development the initial impact was at the policy level. Here, so-called 'win-win' outcomes were soon identified, although it became clear that these by no means covered all conditions. But it also became clear that there were differences not only in prescription but also in analysis. The previous economic analysis of the issues was also significantly challenged, leading to some changes, which some would regard as merely an extension of the economic approach, and others as truly innovative and 'interdisciplinary'. These changes may in the long term have an effect also at the level of description: not simply by increasing the 'visibility' of the environment as an issue, but also altering the way in which it is categorised.

In the case of social capital it is with regard to analysis that the primary impact has so far been felt. Simply stated, it appears that economics earlier failed to take account of an important explanatory factor relating to economic performance. Whether one sees the developments that have followed since the adoption of the idea simply as economists catching up with other social scientists or as them enriching or even improving the already existing analysis of other disciplines depends on one's viewpoint (and future developments). The idea will, however, also have important implications at the policy level, though it remains to be seen precisely what these will be. Community participation has long been advocated – though not always so seriously acted upon. The 'idea' of social capital may give added weight to the arguments of those who favour a greater role for local communities; but it may also distort the way in which this is achieved.

'Beyond economics': the Global Development Network meeting in Tokyo

The power of economics, both within social sciences and in multilateral development institutions, is well established. This constitutes a very important type of framing. The disciplinary perspective of economics determines not only how issues are thought about, but to some extent, what issues are studied. It is therefore appropriate to address here the Global Development Network (GDN) as both a vehicle for the generation and dissemination of development ideas as well as more specifically for the conference it convened on the role of economics. I shall briefly review how economics fared – in relation to other disciplines – at this conference.

The annual conference in 2000 of the Global Development Network, held in Tokyo, met under the overall banner 'Beyond Economics: Multidisciplinary Approaches to Development'. Its title was a response to views expressed at the Inaugural Conference of the GDN, in Bonn in December 1999, where (as the background note announcing the conference put it) 'several participants ... pointed to the need to go beyond the narrow confines of standard economics in order to achieve a fuller understanding of development'. Although it is widely recognised that the study of development requires contributions from several disciplines, there is always a tension between economics and other social sciences, and it is often unclear what, in practice, a 'multidisciplinary' or an 'interdisciplinary' approach entails (see McNeill 1999b). What happens to 'ideas' in such a situation? Can they compete, with good ideas squeezing out bad, irrespective of institutional provenance? And how does economics compare (and compete) with other disciplines in such a situation?

There were very many parallel sessions, on such topics as 'infrastructure development', 'gender and the household', 'privatisation and beyond' and 'environmental and social sustainability'. Papers were delivered by researchers and practitioners from a number of different disciplines and a very wide range of countries. Consequently, my comments on the conference are based only on the plenary sessions.[4]

The first plenary was a panel session in which each of the four speakers had been asked to say something about what their own discipline has contributed to the study of development; highlight gaps in our knowledge; and suggest how disciplines can co-operate. Nicholas Stern, Senior Vice-President and Chief Economist, World Bank, spoke about 'making the world a better place through serious study ... not as an economic imperialist but to share ideas'. He listed five top ideas in economics and how they help to understand development:

> Choice, competition, capital accumulation and growth, information and risk, opportunity cost: put all these together and you see how powerful economics can be. But you need other social sciences also. We have to get markets working well, and the institutions supporting these markets ... . Empower poor people to participate in the growth process.

His views, and, I suggest, those of many other economists, are well summed up in the following statement from his presentation, to which I return below: 'Development economics is good economics applied to development ... . The angles of a triangle add up to 180 degrees whatever country you are in.'

Next to speak was a political scientist, Ashutosh Varshney, Professor, University of Notre Dame, USA, who discussed the political economy of development which he concisely summarised as being concerned with 'political explanations of economic outcomes, and economic explanations of political outcomes'. Third in line was Louk de la Rive Box, Professor, Universities of Maastricht and Utrecht, Netherlands, who related how he was once described as 'a cassava sociologist', indicating the low prestige attached by his peers to the career path he chose. He noted the 'lack of studies of cultural background in development projects' and the existence of 'a glass wall between the development community and the community that needs to be developed. The terms are not translatable.' He urged the audience to 'cherish the marginal ... acknowledge values ... take institutions seriously ...'. The last speaker was Lydia Makhubu, Vice-Chancellor, University of Swaziland, who gave a presentation on the importance of education. She spoke of inequality – 'the global village will be an unequal village' – and on the importance of the involvement of women.

These presentations were short – and my summaries of them certainly cannot do them justice. I will therefore not attempt to analyse them, but simply draw attention to the order in which the presentations were made, for this must have been the result of some discussion among the organisers. It is hard to avoid seeing an implicit hierarchy here: economist, political scientist, sociologist, educationalist – and tempting to go further and refer also to other hierarchical rankings: North/South, and male/female.

The second plenary was a working session, which included a lively debate about the dominance of economists in the GDN governance structure, both global and regional. Although beyond the scope of this paper, it is of some relevance to my central argument.

The third plenary was a paper titled 'Institutions and the Performance of Economies over Time' by the Nobel prizewinning economist Douglass North. He drew on the impressive body of work on the economics of institutions on which his reputation is based, and noted, *inter alia*, the limitations of an economic approach to development studies:

> Institutional change, [therefore], is a deliberate process shaped by the perceptions of the actors about the consequences of their actions … . Institutional change is typically incremental and path dependent. … While the rationality assumption has served economists well for a limited range of issues in micro-theory, it has devastating limitations in dealing with the process of economic change.
>
> (North 2001)

> I wish to emphasize the limits of our understanding because there is a certain amount of hubris evident in the annual surveys by the World Bank and in the writing of orthodox economists who think that now we have it right. But it is important that we understand that even if we have it right for one economy it would not necessarily be right for another economy and even if we have it right today it would not necessarily be right tomorrow … . The interface between economics and politics is still in a primitive state in our theories but its development is essential if we are to implement policies consistent with intentions.
>
> (North 2001)

The other keynote address was in the fifth plenary, by Amartya Sen, another Nobel prizewinning economist, with a formidable reputation both as an economist and as a philosopher. He intimated that the topic – Culture and Development – was not one that he felt quite comfortable with, but gave an eloquent and erudite presentation, making reference to writers from Ashoka, through Adam Smith, Montesquieu and Mill, to Tawney and Weber, Hirschmann, North and Morishima. He also cited the work of Ron Dore on Japanese ethos and economic development. Despite the broad sweep of the paper, he expressed some scepticism about grand theories, whose record has not been very gratifying: 'always one step behind the real world'. His comments most relevant for my purposes in this paper came in response to questions, where he rejected those who sought to draw simplistic generalisations, whether these were advocates of the market or of economic methodology. For example, in reply to a question from the Free Market Institute, Venezuela, Sen remarked that '(The theory of) the free market is also a grand theory'; and in response to a question from Ukraine that: 'A country is like a firm. The culture should be adequate to the market niche. How to tailor the culture to fit the market niche?' Sen commented that: 'Now the biggest planners are the free marketeers. The arrogance of planning may have been inherited by the other side, who think they can achieve radical change.'

What can we derive from a comparison of the three presentations by econo-mists: Stern (in the panel), North and Sen?

First, on economics, I return to Stern's point about the angles of a triangle always adding up to 180 degrees, which, in a way, exemplifies one of the central issues concerning social sciences and development policy: to what extent the social and historical context matters.[5] I do not claim that the angles of a triangle add up to some other number (although Einstein, famously, does). Rather, I sug-gest that the validity of economic theories is not of the same kind as a mathematical truth. The point was well made almost 40 years ago by Dudley Seers in his famous article 'The Limitations of the Special Case' (1963). It was made again at the conference, by Douglass North, in his replies to questions: 'According to formal economics there would be no Third World ... . Every soci-ety is different ... You have got to have an in-depth understanding.' But 'We have very simple-minded economics ... knowing what we know about the broad nature of development, (we need to) tailor it to the specific ... .'

Thus North and Sen (as is apparent from the quotations above) adopted a rela-tively moderate position with regard to what economics has to offer; casting doubt on its generalisability, the validity of grand theory, the merits of the market. And both argued for drawing on other disciplines. Sen, for example, referred to the importance of anthropologists, sociologists and historians. But many economists do not appreciate the need to involve other disciplines in the study of develop-ment. Even those that do, I suggest, often find it difficult to understand what this involves and how it can be achieved. The latter point was, I would claim, reflected in the way the conference presentations were organised. I am not suggesting that the organisers actively resisted a multidisciplinary approach. Rather, there are strong structural forces within the discipline of economics that make it difficult for economists to adopt other perspectives; and this becomes apparent even in something as concrete as a conference timetable and choice of presentations.

Second, on the role of institutions, I am rather doubtful to what extent the new institutional economics equips economists to analyse institutions in the broader sense of the term,[6] or in contexts very different from those of their own society. The approach of North, and of new institutional economics, is not so much 'beyond economics'. Instead, it takes economics beyond its existing boundaries – using economic concepts and methods to study institutions.[7] This may or may not prove to be a fruitful endeavour. But it is surely beyond doubt that it constitutes economic imperialism.

Some emerging issues

An important issue discussed at the Tokyo conference was the World Bank's ambition to create a global knowledge network based on the use of the Internet. It was T. S. Eliot, I believe, who emphasised the difference between information and knowledge, and between knowledge and wisdom. In this technological age, the sheer amount of information available has increased beyond our wildest dreams – or nightmares. But how can this information be useful for the purpose of making decisions? This was a matter for discussion at the meeting. The debate was not only on the practical and technical issues involved in supplying and gaining access to information though the Internet, but also on roles and responsibilities, including the aim of creating a 'global knowledge gateway'.

There is surely something paradoxical about the concept of a knowledge gateway in the age of the Internet. The great novelty of this new technology, as I understand it, is that everything is available to everybody. The situation is changing, however, as attempts are made to limit access; and to require payment for such information. On the other side, the sheer excess of information is creating a problem. That which is most effectively promoted, or most attractively packaged, may attract undue attention. This is generating a new and important function – of sifting out information: what is relevant and what is 'good quality'. But the issue then immediately arises: who is to judge?

There seem to be different tendencies at work: one is to establish a 'gate', implying gatekeepers, criteria for entry, etc. The other is to follow the practice of the Internet (so far) implying diversity and anarchy. Users themselves will – ideally – choose which they prefer. But what sort of knowledge (or information) will count? It may prove to be precisely the time- and space-specific that is most useful: not 'best practice' or 'global guidelines', but information about what is happening right now in a specific region of a country; what projects are planned; who has specialised knowledge which can be used, etc.

This issue is beyond the scope of this paper. I mention it, however, not only because it may prove to be one of the most important in future; but also because it may relate to the phenomenon of 'framing', and the dominance of an economic/technocratic approach with which I have been concerned. Will the development of Internet-based information exacerbate or mitigate this powerful tendency?

Concluding remarks

It is a coincidence that our study of the role of ideas in multilateral development institutions should have begun at the same time as the World Bank initiative to establish a Global Development Network. The GDN is not explicitly the subject of our research, but it is clearly of interest: both as an object of study in itself, and as further evidence of the power that ideas are thought to have in the arena of multilateral development institutions. Both here at this meeting of the GDN, and in the wider discourse on development policy, our contention in the CANDID project is that ideas tend to be 'framed'; that debate about them is structured (without anyone necessarily even being aware of it) in ways that powerfully modify the capacity of ideas to bring about substantive change. These processes are subtle and difficult to comprehend, but by the careful study of empirical experience – including events such as this meeting – it is possible to enhance understanding; and hence perhaps also the capacity for knowledge to bring about change.

My concern in this paper has largely been the power of economics and, to some extent, the related issue of the power of the World Bank: both the power of ideas and the power over ideas. The GDN raises numerous questions in this connection: of the relationship between research and policy, between different disciplines, between different multilateral institutions, between such institutions and 'civil society' – and many more. The network will be an important phenomenon worthy of study in its own right. On the basis of our research, and the evidence from the GDN meeting in Tokyo, a major question will, I suggest, concern the power of what I call the 'economic/technocratic nexus'. Will an economic perspective be dominant? Will this be challenged effectively by other disciplines, by NGOs, or simply by information/knowledge available through the network? Will the result be the dominance of one worldview, or two major competing alternatives, or perhaps 'a thousand flowers blooming'?

Notes

1 With Morten Bøås *et al.*, financed by the Norwegian Research Council.
2 For a more detailed account, see Bøås and McNeill (2004).
3 For further discussion on the criteria for a 'good' definition see McNeill (1999a).
4 I thus avoid the bias that would have been involved in basing comments on the particular parallel sessions that I chose to attend; but on the other hand I introduce another bias, by excluding the evidence from these diverse presentations. Quotations are verbatim from my notes taken at each session, except where they are based on the written text handed out and as cited. Further information and conference proceedings can be found at http://www.gdnet.org/activities/annual_conferences/second_annual_conference.
5 In fairness it should be noted that Stern's contribution was a brief and necessarily simple presentation of the economic perspective.
6 As opposed to, say, an urban water supply organisation – the topic of one of the papers in a parallel session, on which North was a commentator.
7 To put it succinctly: the old institutional economics – of Veblen and Polanyi, for example – treats markets as if they were institutions; while new institutional economics treats institutions as if they were markets.

References

Bøås, M. and McNeill, D. (eds) (2004) *Global Institutions and Development: Framing the World?* London: Routledge.
Chenery, H. *et al.* (1974) *Redistribution with Growth*. Oxford: Oxford University Press.
Coleman, J. (1990) *Foundations of Social Theory.* Cambridge, MA: Belknap Press.
Cox, R. (1992) *Approaches to World Order.* Cambridge: Cambridge University Press.
Dasgupta, P. and Serageldin, I. (eds) (2000) *Social Capital: A Multifaceted Perspective.* Washington, DC: The World Bank.
Gramsci, A. (1971) *Selections from the Prison Notebooks.* New York: International Publishers.
Harris, N. (ed.) (1992) *Cities in the 1990s: the Challenge for Developing Countries.* London: University College London Press.
Hart, K. (1973) 'Informal Income Opportunities and Urban Employment in Ghana' *Journal of Modern African Studies* 11: 61–89.
Keohane, R. (1984) *After Hegemony: Cooperation and Discord in the World Political Economy.* Princeton: Princeton University Press.

Kindleberger, C. (1973) *The World in Depression, 1929–39.* Berkeley: University of California Press.

McNeill, D (1999a) 'The Concept of Sustainable Development', in A. Holland, K. Lee and D. McNeill (eds) *Global Sustainable Development in the Twenty-First Century.* Edinburgh: Edinburgh University Press.

McNeill, D. (1999b) 'On Interdisciplinary Research: With Particular Reference to the Field of Environment and Development' *Higher Education Quarterly* 53 (4).

Meier, G. (1994) 'Review of Development Research in the U.K. Report to the Development Studies Association' *Journal of International Development* 6 (5): 465–512.

North, D. (2001) 'Mimeo', Paper presented at the GDN Conference, Tokyo, December. Available online at http://www.gdnet.org/pdf2/gdn_library/annual_conferences/second _annual_conference/north.pdf.

Putnam, R.D. (1993a) *Making Democracy Work: Civic Traditions in Modern Italy.* Princeton: Princeton University Press.

Ranis, G. (1997) 'The World Bank Near the Turn of the Century', in R. Culpeper, A. Berry and F. Stewart (eds) *Global Development Fifty Years after Bretton Woods.* New York: St. Martin's Press, pp. 72–7.

Schumpeter, J. (1954) *History of Economic Analysis.* London: Allen & Unwin.

Seers, D (1963) 'The Limitations of the Special Case' *Bulletin of the Oxford Institute of Economics and Statistics* 25 (2).

Stern, N. and Ferreira, F. (1997) 'The World Bank as an Intellectual Actor', in D. Kapur, J. P. Lewis and R. Webb (eds) *The World Bank: Its First Half Century.* Vol. 2, Washington DC: Brookings Institution Press, pp. 523–609.

Wade, R. (1997) in R. Culpeper, A. Berry and F. Stewart (eds) *Global Development Fifty Years after Bretton Woods,* New York: St. Martin's Press.

WCED – World Commission on Environment and Development (1987) *Our Common Future.* Oxford: Oxford University Press.

World Bank (2001) *Attacking Poverty.* Washington, DC: The World Bank.

5   Knowledge-based aid

A new way of networking or a new North–South divide?[1]

Kenneth King

Introduction

In the years since 1995, there has been a flurry of activity in many of the multilateral and bilateral development agencies concerning knowledge and information management (King and McGrath 2004). This should not perhaps be surprising; these agencies were in many cases set up in the 1960s to transfer 'know-how' and technology to the developing world.

This focus on knowledge and information management has coincided to a large extent with a parallel agency emphasis on new forms of more genuine and symmetrical partnership with the South, and with new modalities for delivering development assistance, such as sector wide approaches (NORRAG 1999). It becomes therefore natural to inquire whether the new knowledge preoccupations of the agencies are really complementary with these other developments.

We begin with a brief review of the sources and character of the new knowledge and information developments, focusing particularly on the World Bank and a number of bilateral development agencies. We then develop a critique, showing that the agencies have mostly been concerned with improving their own capacity rather than with improving the quality of engagement with the South. An alternative approach is possible, though current initiatives like the Global Development Network (GDN) the GDNet and the Development Gateway (DG) all fall some way short of the ideal.

Sources and character of the new knowledge and information developments

Undoubtedly, one of the most influential sources on these knowledge initiatives has been the private sector, and the business schools, think tanks, and consultancy firms associated with corporate America. North American business has in fact been the primary source, though there have been key figures and firms, such as British Petroleum from Europe (APQC 1998) and authors from Japan (e.g. Nonaka and Takeuchi 1995) who have also been influential in exploring the idea of the knowledge-based enterprise. It is important to reflect a little on this first influence since it is plain that the motivation in the corporate sector has been greater productivity, global competitiveness and ultimately profit. By contrast, though the international financial institutions and the regional banks are firmly in the market place, their role and mission are substantially different from transnational firms, and the regular bilateral development agencies are very different indeed from private firms, even if some of them have recently espoused public–private partnerships in support of development.

The World Bank was the first of the development organisations systematically to espouse becoming a knowledge agency or, in the words of its President, James Wolfensohn in 1996, the Knowledge Bank. Within a short time, the World Bank's mission to become the Knowledge Bank was drawing approving comment from business analysts, altruism notwithstanding:

> Though the mission tends towards altruism, the Bank is managed for commercial viability. Headed by a practical ex-Wall Street executive, this financial powerhouse generated approximately $1 billion in annual profits and maintains a pristine credit rating while lending between $15 and $20 billion a year to some eighty developing nations. The decision to embrace KM [knowledge management], therefore, is rooted in sound business principles – turning internal know-how into commercial success, achieving operational excellence, and forming more intimate ties with external customers.
>
> (O'Dell and Grayson 1998: 161).

Along with the best of the other knowledge firms, the World Bank would appear to have adopted some of the characteristic measures to make its 8000 staff feel more productive members of a large learning organisation. Thus, several of the key mechanisms that are the stock in trade of the new knowledge-rich firms, as they seek to become learning organisations, have been adopted, including the institutionalisation of informal knowledge sharing through 'thematic groups' and 'communities of practice'.

It is some of these same mechanisms that are under consideration in the knowledge initiatives and explorations of many other agencies such as DFID (Mathews and Thornton 2000), 'BMZ as a learning organisation' (BMZ 2000), or *Towards knowledge management: the vision of SDC* (Swiss Development Cooperation 1999). 'Community of Practice' is listed first in the IDB's possible components of a knowledge exchange programme (Beguin and Estrada 1999: 8). Canadian CIDA has very explicitly centred on communities of practice networks as the key to their strategy (Petillon and Chartrand 2000). JICA has also focused on the potential of networks in its exploratory project, and the European Commission, in its draft ideas about a 'Knowledge Exchange for Development', has pointed to the potential of 'communities of practice' (European Commission 2000).

We have suggested that, ultimately, the development agencies have taken their cue from best practice in the private sector, but in terms of direct borrowing the World Bank's earlier experience of knowledge management (KM) and knowledge sharing (KS) has been perhaps especially influential with other agencies. Thus a series of agency initiatives, such as JICA, DFID, CIDA, the IDB and the EC, all acknowledge the value of the World Bank's example. But it is interesting to note that development agencies continue to draw inspiration from best practice in the leading knowledge firms in the private sector. In the DFID paper on knowledge, for instance, the authors looked at the work of British Petroleum and Nokia, as well as development agencies and other government departments, and even in the June 2000 Workshop on Knowledge Management for Development, there were a series of inputs from private sector knowledge enterprises as well as from agency and NGO personnel (Bellanet 2000).

What is intriguing about these borrowings from the corporate sector is the importance that has been attached to making the most of the 'tacit knowledge' that resides in people but which has traditionally been difficult to access except amongst small groups of trusted colleagues. Through the 'communities of practice' notion popularised by management theorists such as Peter Senge, varieties of practitioner knowledge, tips, intuitions or best practice, which may well have been hidden in the heads of individual employees, are meant to be brought out into the open, and can then become part of the knowledge resource of the whole institution.

This knowledge currency of these communities of practice or thematic groups turns out to be rather a complex commodity. It is – to judge from the many illustrations of it in the literature – not only professional knowledge-in-practice, but also something much closer to topical tips, knack, stories, or sixth sense which makes up this knowledge embedded in people. This process is often referred to as companies making the most of the knowledge that is already there in their employees – or in the apposite words of O'Dell and Grayson's (1998) book *If only we knew what we know*.

What this might mean in terms of development organisations is worth exploring a little further. In the World Bank case, it suggests that the challenge is to make more accessible the best practice knowledge that is in the heads of the 8000 staff members scattered across the organisation, in headquarters and in the many country offices. For this to happen, it is admitted by those who directed the Bank's initial knowledge-sharing programme that there needs to be a shift in the culture – from competitive retention of knowledge to knowledge networking (World Bank 1998).

The 130-odd communities of practice or networks that have sprung up in the Bank since 1996 are meant to be the vehicles for this new readiness to share knowledge and information. What is also remarkable about the language in which communities of practice are discussed is that there is an ethical dimension that pervades it. There is an emphasis on unselfishness, on the importance of giving and sharing, on the need for commitment and solidarity. Some of the language is almost more reminiscent of communities of faith than of aid personnel. See, for example, this similar comment from the DFID report on Knowledge Management which picks out a series of essentially ethical ingredients in knowledge sharing:

> Management at all levels must be prepared to trust staff, listen to them, value their contribution and demonstrate this actively. Similarly, all groups need to

value the contribution of others. One of the key issues about developing a culture of knowledge exchange is the demonstration of humility by all, acknowledging the contribution that everyone can make, even if they are not considered expert.

(Mathews and Thornton 2000: 27–8).

How this requirement to share actually works out in reality is difficult to know with certainty though there is a good deal of anecdotal evidence about good practice being built up in different agencies. What does seem clear is that the first circle of sharing is certainly within the agency (e.g. the European Commission and its delegations), the second level is outside the agency, but probably still in the North (e.g. organisations in the European member states, such as the development research community), and only third would be Southern partner organisations (e.g. Southern centres of excellence).

In the agencies themselves, expectations of knowledge and information sharing are going to be treated very differently in different organisational and bureaucratic cultures. Thus in some situations where specialist knowledge is a very scarce commodity, there may well be strong temptations to retain rather than share. In other settings, where age is an important marker of status, hopes of knowledge networking across the boundaries of seniority may prove to be naïve (McGinn 1996). Equally in civil service structures, such as Japan's, where the generalist is regarded more highly than the specialist professional or technical personnel, it may also be problematic to install a culture of networking and knowledge sharing.

The recent moves towards decentralisation in the agencies have in some ways made knowledge sharing more challenging and essential. In some instances, such as the World Bank, Canadian CIDA and German GTZ, professional sector expertise which was centred in the headquarters has been dispersed to regional offices, or to geographical desks. But even where a strong central professional grouping is retained, along with pockets of decentralised expertise, as in DFID, there can develop a sense of isolation and remoteness from the immediacy of personal contact with a team. It is where communications technology may seem to provide the answer.

If a primary influence on knowledge management has come from the private sector, a second factor has been the information and communications technology (ICT) that has allowed corporate expertise to be accessed globally and shared almost instantly. This dramatically heightened productivity associated with the speed of global communications is frequently celebrated in the knowledge sharing literature. Thus a technical solution required within 48 hours by a Bank staff member in a particular country is met, just in time, because his or her world-wide community of practice is able to share the relevant experience from many other settings.

The quite extraordinary technical capacities for knowledge and information mapping, synthesising, sorting and disseminating help to explain the timing of the emergence of knowledge management during the 1990s. These ICT facilities have not only made possible the kind of global knowledge sharing associated with communities of practice in transnational firms and development agencies, but they also suddenly make possible previously unthinkable amounts of collection and synthesis. In development agencies, it is now feasible to integrate all the different databases that relate to different development sectors. The potential now exists, for example, for the digitising of all project and programme materials and also of all evaluation reports with the possibility for new levels of lesson learning across these. At the same time, agencies are aware that even where there is now the scope for the comprehensive collection of materials, the challenge of effective use will continue to be dependent on knowledgeable personnel, and a culture that rewards learning from experience and sharing.

In the matter of what information really needs to be collected and synthesised comprehensively, the fact that something massive can now be done relatively easily is no guide as to whether it is worth doing. Thus, if evaluation reports were little read in the old days of limited dissemination of paper reports, the fact that all evaluation reports ever completed in an agency are potentially available on line does not itself alter the audience for such reports. Unless the scope and reach of the new technology can be used to sift and critique what has been evaluated in new and much more powerful ways, the costs of digitising the evaluation reports may not be justified.

The same argument could be used of systems such as the comprehensive project database called the Performance Reporting and Information System for Management (PRISM) of DFID. Short of a system whereby really thoughtful project analysis is input for each project, there is no reason to believe that the lessons learned from across the whole database will be any more instructive than under the older systems. We shall return to the ambition to synthesise all development information when we look at the Development Gateway, but the DFID report has highlighted one of the key trade-offs between plenty and scarcity: that the more information is available, the more essential is it to have pathways through it via summaries, state of the art reviews and syntheses. There is a major cost to this kind of editing.

As with the potential participants in communities of practice, it turns out that much of the initial discussion in the KM/KS literature about data is about what could be called, in the analogy of the private firm, the company's own proprietary data. Thus it is DFID or JICA data that is under review for further joining up or integration, in the form of evaluation reports, project summaries or funded research reports. It is not the data generated by the partners or recipients.

Towards an alternative approach through North–South knowledge-networking

What is missing in all this discussion of informal networks, learning networks, and communities of practice are creative mechanisms whereby the hundreds of programme officers in the Northern agencies can engage in any very different way with their Southern partners, using some of the new knowledge possibilities.

This is not to say that the discussion of knowledge management in the agencies is carried on quite separately from the traditional partner organisations in the South. DFID, in its August 2000 paper, is probably not alone in suggesting that its own staff development in the knowledge sphere is ultimately going to be good for the South:

> We assume that, moving to become an organisation which manages knowledge, we will also be able to join better to our partners, and encourage more exchange with them. Since knowledge is one of DFID's products, creating a mechanism that makes us better knowledge managers will enable us both to influence, and to listen, more. It will also allow us to facilitate more knowledge exchange between our partners.
>
> (Mathews and Thornton 2000 para. 11.3.2)

If an agency were to begin from the perspective of being a unique organisation charged with the development of something other than itself, there would be a series of immediate insights as the new knowledge approaches were applied to current practice.

First, analysis might reveal that many of the regular networks associated with the agencies had little or no connection with the supposed Southern partners. Thus in many sectors, there are donor working groups that are almost exclusively made up of other donors.

Second, at the more fundamental level of knowledge sharing, it could be suggested that the new assumptions of 'genuine partnership' between North and South would have made it mandatory to start the explorations of knowledge sharing with the primary actors in the so-called recipient countries. This could have been salutary. For instance, a good deal of the initial knowledge management and knowledge sharing in the agencies has actually taken place behind the protection of an intranet, reinforcing the view that it is the agency's own staff development that is the primary objective. Whereas it would have been possible, presumably, for donors and their partners in developing countries jointly to say, 'Here is a new opportunity to apply additional knowledge to our partnership. Neither side has much expertise, but let us develop this together.'

The danger, otherwise, is that the North develops its communities of practice, rethinks its own evaluation and lesson-learning, constructs an appropriate website. And then, the developing world is invited to take advantage of the knowledge that has already been processed and prioritised.

There have been a few interesting illustrations of countries in the South dialoguing with the North about their knowledge needs (rather than their lending priorities). These would certainly include both Chile and South Africa. Apart from these, the agency which has possibly thought most radically and consistently about the multiple constituencies for knowledge would be Swedish Sida. Quite apart from the unit for organisational learning with its focus on Sida's own development as a learning firm, there has been a task force working on capacity development much more widely. It has had in view three audiences or constituencies – the Sida staff, the 1500-odd partners of Sida in Sweden, and the many partners in the developing world. These are the same three audiences that are central to all the agency's work. In the Sida mission statement's brief chapter 'Knowledge is the key to development', the emphasis on these three constituencies is clear: 'Sida will carry out a programme which systematically raises levels of knowledge and skills in partner countries, in Swedish partners, and at Sida' (Sida 1997: 30).

Unlike much of the knowledge management literature we have been referring to, the Sida task force addresses the challenge to capacity building in all three of these target constituencies (Sida 2000). In a brief document, Sida locates 'knowledge development' and sharing within a dynamic context of change in the developing world, as well as in the changes needed in the bilateral agency itself, and amongst its many Northern partners. Indeed, it deliberately uses the term 'knowledge development' to underline the fact that ideally knowledge is created in a two-way process. The document admits that a good deal of knowledge is still transferred using the 'expert' and 'counterpart' model, but this model is not the appropriate one for a development organisation:

> Sida prefers to use the concept *development of knowledge* in order to show that learning requires active processing of knowledge and that solutions are developed in a process of give and take between several parties
>
> (Sida 2000: 7)

The document on capacity development is clear that there are different conceptualisations of knowledge, and that these are intimately connected to theories about the state, the market and human potential. Thus, a belief in the market as the decisive factor in development, and the need for minimum regulation, would have one kind of effect on any knowledge economy. By contrast, a belief in the enduring importance of institutional frameworks supporting values, laws and policies would have another. Equally the rise of democratisation, world-wide, should also have an impact on the role of capacity development.

Sida reaches a conclusion that the role of knowledge in development is inseparable from institutional health, strengthening and sustainability:

> The ultimate objective is to create conditions for the professional sustainability of institutions and organisations, including national systems of education, training and research.
>
> (Sida 2000: 2)

Despite the recognition that knowledge should be Sida's most important resource in capacity and institution development, there will inevitably be many examples of the old ways of working still present, and probably ongoing tensions between Sweden's role as an exporter of competitive expertise on the one hand, and its role as collaborative creator of knowledge on the other (Wieslander 2000). It is nevertheless a salutary recognition that national or international knowledge policies are neither developed in a vacuum nor received in one.

What is critical in Sida's approach to learning and capacity development is not very different from what was traditionally the hallmark of several of the agencies and foundations that have supported research in the developing world for decades – a powerful conviction that knowledge and scholarship existed in the South, and that Northern funding could assist in their exploration (Gmelin, King and McGrath 2001).

New frontiers for knowledge sharing: the GDN and the Gateway

Are these lessons being learned? Consider two examples: first, the Global Development Network, and its associated web vehicle, GDNet; and second, the Global Gateway. Both are World Bank-led initiatives.

GDN and GDNet

Resonating on a larger scale with some of these same ideas about the value inherent in knowledge development in the South would be the genesis of the Global Development Network (GDN). The growth of this network of initially seven regional think tanks or fora from the non-OECD regions of the world has been taking place over the same period that knowledge management and sharing has been explored by several development agencies. During 2000, a further two nodes were identified – in the Japan Bank for International Cooperation, and in the Bonn-based Centre for Development Research. Since May 2002 there has been a tenth node based in the United States.

What had been encouraged with the initial support from the World Bank was a set of nodes – some well-established, some very recent – that would play a role in generating, sharing and applying knowledge to policy in their respective regions. The identification of these regional hubs outside the North, and at least initially without the presence of major Northern research and policy networks, is at variance with the predominantly Northern sources of influence and of reference on knowledge management and knowledge sharing that we have analysed in the first part of this chapter.

One of the key elements in the GDN statement of mission is to 'build up research capacity in developing nations'. Like the mission of the International Development Research Centre (IDRC) in the 1970s and the Swedish Agency for Research Co-operation with Developing Countries (SAREC) a little later, the assumption had been that for research to be influential in the South, there must be national or local generation of knowledge and not just the down-loading of 'global' knowledge sourced from the North. In the keynote speech at the formal launch of GDN in Bonn in December 1999, Stiglitz, former Chief Economist in the World Bank who had supported the GDN concept, underlined the centrality of the re-creation and re-invention of knowledge in local contexts.[2] Intellectual confidence and self-reliance were necessary to avoid becoming a knowledge recipient (Stiglitz 1999).

An essentially dynamic role for knowledge generation in the South, Stiglitz argued, must be a critical dimension of any truly global knowledge network. This emphasis on the process of creating knowledge in the South parallels what we noted for the Sida document on capacity development through 'knowledge development'. Equally, Stiglitz was concerned with the 'tacit knowledge' which we noted was so central to the thinking about communities of practice in Northern knowledge firms and development organisations. But, applied to the emerging GDN concept, the recognition of the tacit dimension in all learning provides an important health warning to any simple notion of technology and knowledge transfer, North–South. It is also salutary, in all the discussion about global knowledge facilities, to be reminded of the essential requirement for knowledge to be rooted and embedded in specific national or social contexts. Or in the words of Lyn Squire (Squire and Giszpenc 2000), the Director of the GDN secretariat, still temporarily housed in Washington:

> GDN supports local knowledge that is locally generated. In keeping with the times, GDN aims to support that knowledge generation with communications technology so that local development can benefit from global knowledge – and global development from local knowledge.

But the acknowledgement of this very specificity in turn provides one of the key challenges to the initial seven regional networks in the South: – how can a single contact point for sub-Saharan Africa, or for South Asia, or for Latin America and the Caribbean really act on behalf of so many diverse research environments within each of those regions? This issue of the representativeness of seven regional groupings that are primarily composed of economists to represent their wider social science communities was raised very seriously at the launch of GDN. But it continued to be a concern in the online discussions in the year after Bonn, and right through to the Second Annual Meeting of the GDN in Tokyo in December 2000. On the other hand, the very focus on the Southern capacity-building side of GDN would appear to have been vital in maintaining donor interest (GDN 2000; GDNet Web Strategy Advisory Group 2000). The readiness to look 'Beyond Economics' (in the title of the GDN 2000 conference in Tokyo) and to emphasise the mechanisms for institutional strengthening (of the South) have in combination been important in assisting the legitimation of the GDN as concerned with a narrowing of the knowledge divide between North and South (see further McNeill in this volume).

However, one of the fascinating outcomes of the Tokyo conference of the GDN was to underline the fact that there were, for a time, two sides of the Southern knowledge base of this new organisation. On the one side, there was the GDN governance structure, still with the seven original regional hubs along with new hubs in Japan and Europe. These nodes were still felt to be predominantly concerned with the discipline of economics, and, despite the Tokyo theme, there were continuing doubts about the capacity of most of these to represent the wider policy research interests in their respective regions. On the other side, there was the GDNet which was an online community that had been an outgrowth of the Bonn meeting. Coordinated from the World Bank Institute (WBI), it had taken a very firm stand on the need at least for the Internet architecture of the GDN to reflect the breadth of social science institutes and think tanks in the South. Rather than waiting for this vision of 'beyond economics' to be debated in Tokyo, the GDNet proactively visited regions such as South Asia and East and Southern Africa in order to encourage their participation and presence in the online policy research community.

The result, for a time, was that while the governance structure of the GDN seemed somewhat constrained by the choice of the initial institutes and networks, the online GDNet community consisted of almost 2,000 institutes and some 9,000 individual researchers, many of which were from disciplines such as education, sociology, environment, gender studies, planning, etc. The mechanism which allowed the GDNet to break through to a much more inclusive version of a policy research community had been to build on the expertise of a major database in the North but then populate a new GDNet community deliberately with researchers, institute profiles and documentary resources from the South which have traditionally been relatively inaccessible. There is no doubt that without the proactivity of the World Bank Institute and the support of the Department for International Development (UK) specifically to this GDNet initiative, the actual knowledge base and knowledge reach of the GDN would not have grown so rapidly in its first 12 months.

Arguably, however, the open-access structure of GDNet was an implicit criticism of the core GDN concept and of the constrained knowledge architecture of the GDN's governance. This eventually led to the withdrawal of WBI support to GDNet, and the reconsolidation of the GDNet and GDN into a single entity.

It is still far too early to say whether the GDN will play a substantial role in implementing the vision of developing countries being involved in all phases of knowledge creation. However, it is clear that this is the intention and that there is within the GDN a growing sensitivity both about the relationship between knowledge and policy, and about the dominant role of economics and economic rationality.

The Development Gateway

We have left till last the largest and most ambitious knowledge management and sharing project of them all – the Development Gateway (DG – originally the Global Development Gateway). In its sheer scale and diversity, it dwarfs everything we have discussed thus far. In its inclusiveness, it could provide a compelling location to place many of the KM initiatives of the individual agencies we have analysed. There will be few communities of practice that might not think it valuable to be linked to what could become the world's largest development portal. At the same time, the breathtaking comprehensiveness of the project has raised understandable competitive concerns amongst those who are already Internet providers of development information, and amongst those who are anxious about the overall impact of such a degree of knowledge centralisation.

In brief, the Gateway (GDG 2000a) will afford an entrance to development knowledge through three entry points: community (e.g. private sector, government, or civil society); topic (e.g. education, law and justice) and country. The five components of the Gateway include an aid effectiveness exchange (which links to the lessons being learned across the aid community, as well as providing a forum for development practitioners); a Civil Society Forum; a Marketplace (aimed at the private sector, and specifically at foreign direct investment, and small and medium enterprise development); a Government Forum (providing policy knowledge, services and procurement opportunities at every level of government); and finally Country Gateways (which parallel the range of the other four elements but involve local ownership and multiple stakeholders, and use local and international languages).

In a word, at its outset the DG appeared to be the world's most comprehensive development project, and like much World Bank activity, it proved controversial because it would not be satisfied with merely linking users to existing sites, though there would be much of that. In many different ways, it was feared that there would be attempts to add World Bank value, analysis and judgement.

For instance, in one example related to the topic of this chapter, knowledge-based aid, there has already been some rapid progress in the integration of development project databases under the project called Accessible Information on Development Activities (AIDA). At a later stage, there will be an attempt to work with agency partners to derive lessons from all bases simultaneously. Finally, there could be an advisory service to provide tailor-made support on lesson extraction related to specific contexts (GDG 2000a: 7–8).

Compared to the communities of practice, where knowledge from a single agency was being analysed, the ambition in the Gateway to derive lessons at a meta-level from across the entire agency world, but fitted to a particular context, is going to be very demanding. And the resulting lessons are likely to be powerfully affected by the technology associated with the meta-level sorting and synthesis.

But precisely because the Gateway's potential knowledge sources are from every conceivable supplier (public, private and civil society), and the potential recipients likewise – from the smallest community-based organisation in Bangladesh to a top aid agency official in Japan – it will be very difficult for the various sectoral professional bodies not to take a proprietary interest in what treasures are revealed when one clicks on the topic area closest to their hearts.

There will be different crucial decision points for the private sector marketplace or the sourcing of advice to governments, but for all the main topic areas from education to energy, and from population to poverty, the most central knowledge management role is associated with a person who is being termed a 'Topic Guide' (GDG 2000b).

We shall look in some detail at the initial plan of work for the Topic Guide, since the original conception touches on many of the worst fears of those who saw in the Gateway when it was first developed a potentially massive centralisation of development knowledge. But we shall end by suggesting such fears may, in the practical working out of the Gateway, have been exaggerated.

'Guide' is a very user-friendly term, but a closer look at the original terms of reference for 'The role of the Topic Guide' would suggest an individual with quite exceptionally demanding knowledge and research requirements. It would seem that the Topic Guide would need to be a very unusual combination of knowledge manager, net-worker, reviewer, disseminator, synthesiser, policy analyst, and – last but not least – scholar.

In creating and maintaining the Guide Page on a particular theme on the Gateway, one of our concerns would be how easily a specialist Guide could be identified who could fulfil all the following necessary conditions, and whether as a result the digital divide between North and South in educational policy analysis could be in any way affected.

Here are just a few of the conditions of this crucial knowledge management position. Inescapably, there are massive challenges lying behind the adjectives used to describe some of these characteristics, like 'credible', 'best available', 'broadly acceptable', 'highest quality', 'proper' and 'international'.

First, the Topic Guide must convene 'a network of credible information sources … pulling together the best available resources, and fostering an exchange of ideas within the topic community'. In other words, the Guide must work with a community of practice, but not in the narrow sense we have been using it, of a thematic group in an agency. This is, rather, a community of practice world-wide. How wide? The Topic Guide, it is suggested, 'must be sufficiently familiar with their subject matter and know enough of the key players in their community to be able to establish and maintain a network of contacts that represents a broadly acceptable range of opinion and resources'. Again, almost impossibly demanding for a single person. But there is more to come.

The Guide 'at a minimum [must have] a deep understanding of the topic from both technical and policy perspectives [and must have] international experience or a demonstrated interest in understanding the international aspects of the topic'. 'International' is of course one of the most problematic words in the development directory. In this context it would be essential that the Guide had expertise on the developing world, as well as on trends in OECD countries, but would clearly need superior networking skills and contacts with what the terms of reference suggest should be 'a broad and credible network of information resources in the field'.

But the purpose of these quality linkages with the world of education (in this example) is so that the Guide can – on at least a weekly basis – produce on the Guide (web) Page a series of Spotlights; Key Issues; Questions from the Community; Selected Links; and Community Contributions. These are to be aimed at the core target audience of 'informed generalists, policy makers and researchers, as well as technical experts and specialists in the field as well'.

The Topic Guide would have to seek to achieve for a world audience what we have suggested is difficult enough to achieve even for a single agency. A whole series of succinct summaries of best practice, lessons learned, as well as a compilation of basic concepts and key issues that lie at the heart of the community's long term and current interests.

But the most challenging demand of all, perhaps, was that the Guide was meant to select linkages to some 20 to 30 websites that would provide more information on the topic. We have suggested in our discussion of the GDN and GDNet that there is likely to be a constant tension between the established sites of expertise in OECD countries and the GDN mandate deliberately to build Southern research and policy capacity. In the same way, the Topic Guide could be faced with a very tough policy choice between linking to the kinds of high quality external websites which have already become partners of some of the thematic groups of the World Bank on the one hand, and some way of creatively and proactively providing access to emerging Southern institutions on the other.

In this connection, it is interesting to note that it was suggested that the Topic Guide could have a category called: 'Community Contributions' – sources that do not quite make the quality credentials for the Topic Page.

> These are documents, web sites or other resources that have been submitted by users and reviewed by the Guide, but that are not deemed of sufficient quality to be included in the Selected Links or other sections [encouraged to] craft commonly posed questions about the topic and to provide possible responses 'from a balanced range of resources'.
>
> (Global Devt Gateway 2000b)

This is already quite a sensitive selection procedure, but then it is also suggested that the Topic Guide would select, down the right hand side of the web page a whole series of Community Resources – a set of linkages which should be as inclusive as possible, but the Guide may highlight or recommend from among them. These would include: professional communities, databases, directories, discussion forums, event calendars, etc.

There is a great deal more on this original outline of the multiple tasks of the Topic Guide, much of which deserves serious critical commentary, but we should end this section by noting that the Guide should have 'a commitment to spend a minimum of 20 hours a month on Guide Page activities'! (GDG, 2000b)

We have spent time on what may be thought a mere detail in what is a hugely exciting challenge to the development community. But, in fact, it is precisely the detail of who are the co-funding partners of the Gateway, and who are the Topic Partners who are 'co-branded' on individual Topic Pages that will be crucial to the image and influence of the Gateway. If it is to be owned by the world and if it is to play a crucial role in making information available for the reduction of poverty, then the websites of the poorer countries of the world must not only be found on the Country Gateways or on the Community Contributions of the main topic guide page.

Evaluating what has happened to this initial conception of the role of the Topic Guide over the last three years in all the different sectors of the Gateway would be a research project in its own right. But in a small scale analysis of just one sector of the Gateway, what is conspicuously absent is the kind of strong analytical work that has been associated with many of the Bank's policy papers and WDRs in different sectors over the last twenty and more years. The sector examined gives, rather, the sense of a smorgasbord, with a series of possibly tasty dishes, but without a menu or any coherent guide to its contents.

Of course this may not be true of all sectors, but for those organisations that were very worried about the possible Bank domination of the global development discourse via the Gateway, this is probably good news. These Topic sites may well turn out to be more concerned with information than with knowledge (King 2001).

Conclusions

We shall conclude this analysis of the intriguing world of knowledge management in the agencies by pointing to a number of issues for further research, and a few challenges to those directly involved in the area of knowledge sharing.

By far the largest intellectual hurdle we have noted as the agencies scramble to become learning organisations is what we have termed the agency-centricity of their knowledge preoccupations. With just a few exceptions, we would argue that this initiative is being carried on for the immediate advantage of the agencies, and only down the line might it incorporate the natural partners of aid organisations in the developing world.

We have hinted that in some cases the reason for this misplaced focus on the agency has been the temptation to regard the development agency as just another multinational firm rather than as a unique organisation mandated to develop something other than itself.

The result has been that the agencies have not started with the dramatic knowledge deficits of the South, nor with the key question of how knowledge management could assist knowledge development in the South. A continuation along their present trajectory will arguably be counter-productive; it will make agencies more certain of what they themselves have learnt, and more enthusiastic that others should share these insights, once they have been systematised.

The agencies' current knowledge focus has not been systematically evaluated, nor have the various assumptions underpinning their KM and KS strategies been seriously interrogated. An alternative approach is still eminently possible, since the exercises in knowledge management are still very much at the exploratory stage in many agencies such as JICA and DFID. But progress would really consist of turning the present approach on its head.

Instead of asking yet more questions about how lessons learned by the agency could be further synthesised, a start could be made at the other end and it could be asked how might joint involvement in agency projects better build knowledge in the South. To do this effectively, it would be essential to have a much more elaborate account of knowledge bases and knowledge systems in the South.

Instead of wondering how to ensure that Northern research and policy directories, databases and training systems could be placed more conspicuously on agency webs, agencies, with their special mandate to develop the South, could ask many more conditioning questions about how Northern expertise could be obliged much more symmetrically to partner the South.

This is a question that has not been systematically applied to the enormous Northern resources on the South. And these are not just the agency databases but also the very considerable NGO resources of knowledge on the South. How can they be leveraged more effectively so that knowledge development occurs in the South or jointly with the South?

The missing condition of Southern involvement in the agencies' knowledge management could be extended and applied to much else that the agencies have undertaken in recent years. For instance, it could be asked of the key policy objectives of the OECD/DAC – the International Development Targets (IDTs) – which have become so central to JICA and to DFID policies, to what extent are they really in any sense owned by the nations of the South? And it could also be asked of the many hundreds of evaluation reports by the agencies, which are set to become one of the key sources of lesson learning in agencies' knowledge management strategies, did any of these really succeed in incorporating the joint participation of the South in the evaluation process?

It is still perhaps not too late, therefore, to seek to ensure that the knowledge management being initiated now in many OECD capital cities genuinely becomes a form of knowledge developed jointly with those with whom it is most centrally concerned. If this were to happen, then the knowledge management revolution could really become a gateway to 'a new way of working' and not just one more passing fashion of the agency world.

Notes

1 An earlier and much longer version of this chapter appeared in King (2000).
2 The origins of the GDN go back at least to 1997, but there was clearly a series of strands that came together in the final proposal. See for more detail King (1999) and also Johnson and Stone (2000). The GDN is sometimes presented without any historical context of some 40 and more years of agency support to research in the developing world. The earliest players were Ford and Rockefeller followed by IDRC and SAREC. Many of the 'tools' or 'knowledge products', such as research competitions and awards, now associated with the seven regional hubs in the South, have historically been used by these research foundations.

References

APQC – American Productivity and Quality Centre (1998) *Knowledge Management and the Learning Organisation: A European Perspective.* Houston: APQC.

Beguin, J. B. and Estrada, J. A. (1999) *IDB Knowledge Exchange Network.* Washington, DC: The InterAmerican Development Bank.

Bellanet International (2000) *Report of the Knowledge Management for Development Workshop.* Ottawa: Bellanet. Available online at htpp://www.bellanet.org/km/km2.

BMZ (2000) *The Potential and Future Role of Knowledge Management for the German Development Co-operation System.* Bonn: BMZ.

European Commission (2000) 'Proposal for the Creation of an EC Knowledge Exchange for Development'. Draft for Discussion, 23 August 2000. Brussels: DG Development.

GDG – Global Development Gateway (2000a) 'Global Development Gateway: Harnessing Knowledge and Technology for Sustainable Development and Poverty Reduction'. Project Proposal, Draft, June 19. Washington: The World Bank.

GDG – Global Development Gateway (2000b) 'The Role of the Topic Guide'. Working paper. Washington: GDG.

GDN – Global Development Network (2000) 'Summary of Interim Donors' Meeting' Brussels, June 7, 2000.

GDNet Web Strategy Advisory Group (2000) 'Creating the Future of Development Networks ... the GDNet'. Washington: World Bank Institute.

GDNet is available online at http://www.ids.ac.uk/gdn.

Gmelin, W., King, K. and McGrath, S. (eds) (2001) *Development Knowledge, National Research and International Co-operation* Bonn and Edinburgh: CAS/DSE/NORRAG.

Johnson, E. and Stone, D. (2000) 'The Genesis of GDN' in D. Stone (ed.) *Banking on Knowledge: The Genesis of the Global Development Network*. London: Routledge.

King, K (1999) 'GDN: History, Process and Future' *NORRAG News* (25): 72–6. Available online at http://www.norrag.org.

King, K. (2000) 'Towards Knowledge-based Aid', *Journal of International Cooperation in Education*, 3 (2): 23–48.

King, K. (2001) 'Banking on Knowledge: The Old and New Knowledge Projects of the World Bank' Paper to the Oxford International Conference on *Knowledge, Values and Policy*. 19–21 September, 2001. Shorter version: Compare 32 (3): 311–26.

King, K and McGrath, S. (2004) *Knowledge for Development? Comparing British, Japanese, Swedish and World Bank Aid.* London: Zed Books.

Mathews, S. and Thornton, N. (2000) *'Doing the Knowledge' – How DFID Compares with Best Practice in Knowledge Management.* London: DFID.

McGinn, N (ed.) (1996) *Crossing Lines: Research and Policy Networks for Developing Country Education*. London: Praeger.

Nonaka, I. and Takeuchi, H. (1995) *The Knowledge Creating Company*. New York: Oxford University Press.

NORRAG (1999) Special Issue on '"Swapping Partners": The New Politics of Partnership and Sector Wide Approaches' NORRAG News (25). Available online at http://www.norrag.org.

O'Dell, C. and Grayson, J. with Essiades, N. (1998) *If Only We Knew What We Know: The Transfer of Internal Knowledge and Best Practice*. New York: Free Press.

Petillon, Y and Chartrand, M. (2000) 'Knowledge-sharing Networks Support Proposal' Human Resources and Corporate Services Branch, Hull: CIDA.

Sida – Swedish International Development Cooperation Agency (1997) *Sida Looks Forward: Sida's Programme for Global Development*. Stockholm: Sida.

Sida – Swedish International Development Cooperation Agency (2000) *Capacity Development as a Strategic Question in Development Cooperation: Policy and Guidelines for Sida*. Sida Working Paper No. 8. Stockholm: Policy Secretariat for the Sector Departments, Sida.

Squire, L. and Giszpenc, N. (2000) 'Back to the Future: Global Technology for Local Development' *Foreign Policy* (Summer). Available online at http://www.foreign policy.com/global2000/backtofuture.html.

Stiglitz, Joseph (1999) 'Scan Globally, Reinvent Locally: Knowledge Infrastructure and the localisation of knowledge', GDN Conference, December 1999, Bonn. This paper is reproduced as a chapter in Stone, D. (ed.) 2000 *Banking on Knowledge: The Genesis of the Global Development Network*. London: Routledge.

Swiss Development Cooperation (1999) *Towards Knowledge Management: The Vision of the SDC Swiss Agency for Development and Cooperation*. Bern: SDC.

Wieslander, A. (2000) 'When Do We Ever Learn?', in Wohlgemuth, L. and Carlsson, J. (eds) *Learning in Development Co-operation*. Stockholm: Expert Group on Development Issues.

World Bank (1998) *What is Knowledge Management? A Background Document to the World Development Report*. Washington, DC: The World Bank.

6 Knowledge networks and global policy

Diane Stone

A world scientific community is in the making, one dominated by the scientists of the rich industrialised countries ... Local, national, international and global research is increasingly densely networked.

(Messner 1997: 47–8)

Introduction

This paper explores the transnational features of knowledge networks. The focus is on the policy-related roles of university researchers and other experts, who may be based in consultancy firms, philanthropic foundations, independent research institutes and think tanks, and who all interact in global knowledge networks (KNETs). The following section introduces the idea of 'global knowledge networks' and how they connect to, but are different from, 'transnational advocacy networks' and 'global public policy networks'. The paper then locates the debate about KNETS within long-standing debates about the link between ideas and politics. There are three different foci of analysis: epistemic community, discourse coalition and neo-Gramscian network approaches. The final section discusses governance, addressing how knowledge/policy research relates to policy-making, and raising questions about transparency and representation in the global agora.

The main conclusion of the paper is that caution is needed in assessing the impact of networks. Some observers see networks as contributing to a greater role for civil society and to the democratisation of global policy-making. However, there are strong grounds for concern about access and power. The global agora is not a level playing field for networks. It is characterised by an uneven distribution of resources and a hierarchy of discourses in which relatively few can be public actors. Accordingly, the extent to which global and regional networks become a focal point of public affairs has meaning primarily for those who have the resources, patronage or expertise to enter and traverse the agora.

By way of introduction, the term 'agora' needs definition. The dictionary definitions of this Greek word differ to mean 'market-place' or 'place of assembly' or a 'public space'. In its contemporary meaning, the term is borrowed from Nowotny *et al.*, who refer to a social or public space in which science interacts and is constituted. In their words the agora is

the space in which market and politics meet and mingle, where the articulation of private emotions and meanings encounters the formation of public
opinion and political consensus.

(Nowotny *et al.* 2001: 183)

At global level, the agora is said to consist of a highly articulate, well-educated
population, 'the product of enlightened educational systems ... who face multiple
publics and plural institutions' (Nowotny *et al.* 2001: 204–05). It is an 'open
space' onto which social action, administrative practice and public institutions are
not fully writ. The term also captures the sense in which global and regional public space or market place are jointly constituted and inseparable.

The agora is characterised by growing political interconnectedness, inter-
locking sites of decision-making, and a 'thickening of global community' (see the
essays in Ougaard and Higgott 2002). Liberal and democratic cosmopolitan
thinkers see the rise of non-state actors in the agora as a progressive contribution
to a global civil society and to a new and more democratic global domain and
prospects for 'governance without government' (Held 2000; and for a critique,
Stevenson 2002). However, with its diversity of both actors and activity, the agora
may be an unequal environment. Rather than organisational density and diversity
disrupting hierarchies and dispersing power, they can also represent new constel-
lations of privatised power. Instead of being civil society manifestations of
bottom-up, non-statist globalisation, networks and other formations may be
viewed as 'mutually implicated' in the affairs of states and international organisations (Baker 2002: 936). The agora is then a much less comfortable space.

Knowledge networks

We are familiar with two other kinds of network, which need to be distinguished
from knowledge networks (KNETS).

The first is the 'transnational advocacy networks' (TAN – Keck and Sikkink
1998; Diani and McAdam 2003). TANs have the character of social movements.
They characteristically accommodate a range of non-governmental organisations
(NGOs) and activists. They are bound together by shared values or 'principled
beliefs' and a shared discourse where the dominant modality is information
exchange. They are called advocacy networks because 'advocates plead the
causes of others or defend a cause or proposition' (Keck and Sikkink 1998: 8).
Examples include the transnational campaigns surrounding issues like anti-
slavery, debt relief and 'blood diamonds'. TANs usually have a strong normative
basis for moral judgement in seeking to shape the climate of public debate and
influence global policy agendas. However, they are not well integrated into
policy-making and operate more like 'outsider groups'.

The second kind of network is the 'global public policy network' (GPPN) that
delivers or regulates global public goods (Reinicke, Deng *et al.* 2000). GPPNs are
trisectoral in character; that is, they are alliances of government agencies alongside international organisations as well as corporations and elements of civil

society. Official involvement gives a quasi-public veneer and 'insider' status. Actors invest in these communities to pursue material interest but have in common a shared problem. Their interactions are shaped by resource dependencies and bargaining. They tend to cohere around international organisations and governments that have entered into a policy partnership for the delivery of public policy. The transnational character of policy problems establishes rationales for co-operation. These problems have led to new forms of 'soft' authority recognised in these networks.[1] Examples include the Apparel Industry Partnership, the Roll Back Malaria Initiative, the ISO 1400 process and the Global Environment Facility. There are, however, many more networks. Over time the network may become institutionalised with the creation of formal arrangements such as advisory committees, consultation procedures and recognition by state and multilateral agencies in the implementation of policies.

A KNET is different. One of the few definitions of 'international knowledge network' is that of 'a system of coordinated research, study (and often graduate-level teaching), results dissemination and publication, intellectual exchange, and financing across national boundaries' (Parmar 2002: 13). This definition places greater emphasis on co-ordination and the transnational dimensions of knowledge generation and dissemination. However, two further considerations should be added. Although somewhat tautological, another characteristic of knowledge networks is that they engage in networking. Furthermore, they are often engaged in 'capacity building'; that is mobilising funds and other resources for scholarships and training, supporting institutional consolidation that facilitates both network regeneration and knowledge construction.

Knowledge networks (KNET) incorporate professional bodies, academic research groups and scientific communities that organise around a special subject matter or issue. Individual or institutional inclusion in such networks is based upon professional or official recognition of expertise as well as more subtle and informal processes of validating scholarly and scientific credibility. The primary motivation of such networks is to create and advance knowledge as well as to share, spread and, in some cases, use that knowledge to inform policy and apply it to practice.

Sometimes, knowledge networks are identifiable from their organisational composition. For example, transnational think tank networks have proliferated (see Struyk 2002). Examples of regional networks include the Open Society Institute policy related think tanks in Central and Eastern Europe (OSI 2001) and the ASEAN Institutes of Strategic and International Affairs – ASEAN-ISIS. The latter became particularly prominent in the 1980s and 1990s as the 'establishment academics' associated with ASEAN-ISIS were incorporated into a regional policy community that was coming to terms with resurfacing security tensions in a post Cold War context. Through 'track-two diplomacy' these experts and their institutes became influential in security dialogues that informed the development of the governmental ASEAN Regional Forum and the semi-governmental Council for Security Cooperation in the Asia Pacific (see Simon 2002).

Transnational knowledge networks can be classified by their issue orientation. For example, as discussed by Shirin Rai in this volume, the South Asian Research

Network (SARN) on Gender, Law and Governance is composed of feminist research groups from five countries. By contrast, the Evian Group conducts trade-related research and convenes high level dialogues on the future role of the WTO.[2] In a different arena, the Rural Development Forestry Network (RDFN) was created in 1985 under the auspices of the Overseas Development Institute, London's leading think tank on development issues, to conduct research on and raise awareness of forestry issues.[3]

Often networks have a strong ideological character, like the US based International Centre for Economic Growth (ICEG) whose member institutes adhere to liberal principles of economic and political organisation.[4] Knowledge networks can be permanent or temporary structures. An example of the latter is the Blue Bird project in South Eastern Europe.[5] Typical of many academic ventures, Blue Bird was a three year long research project composed of a cross-national team of researchers co-ordinated by the Central European University. The project assumed that the invention of the Southeast European region requires the construction of a common regional vision and the emergence of a regional public debate. Accordingly this knowledge network was about altering, indeed creating, new terms in which region is thought about in the Balkans. However, it is *ad hoc* and temporary in both policy objectives and research structure.

There are other distinctions between KNETs. At one extreme, groups such as the Global Development Network can be categorised as 'open assembly' in organisational style given that involvement is open to interested stakeholders (Struyk 2002). By contrast, at the other extreme, Evian is more exclusive and club-like. These examples of KNETs indicate the variety, different power bases and diverse motivations of networks. They create different images of the global agora and have local roots in dramatically different constituencies.

Many KNETs are engaged in the so-called 'disinterested pursuit and exchange of knowledge' – and this is a key feature distinguishing them from 'transnational advocacy networks' and 'global public policy networks'. However, KNETs can be drawn into policy development, business-related advocacy and civil society activism. KNET is not a pure type. Instead, these networks blur and blend with other network types. Knowledge networks are not in isolation or hermetically sealed from other networks. More often than not, KNETs overlap with, or sometimes collapse into, GPPNs and TANs in a 'web' of interactions that also intersect with official decision-making venues. Consequently, SARN has the features of both a KNET but also in some degree, that of a TAN given its advocacy of women's rights. The overlapping network styles also allow some knowledge actors to traverse scholarly/policy subject fields and sometimes to act as 'brokers' between insider and outsider communities.

In this role, and in the relative absence of formal institutions of governance and regulation, KNETs informally mediate and interpolate in the global agora. In other words, 'they manage the ideological operation of 'decoding', interpreting and reformulating socioeconomic reality in accordance with the sociocultural project of the global society' (Nahrath 2000: 44–5).

As a 'research broker', a knowledge network performs two broad functions. First, the transnational communication and dissemination of knowledge can be undertaken in a co-ordinated fashion with KNETs acting as intermediaries within and between national and local (social) scientific/intellectual communities. Networks also build common infrastructure for communication via websites, newsletters, reports and other publications as well as through meetings and conferences. Moreover, a network presents a united or at least a collective voice. Sometimes this collective voice takes the form of a 'policy narrative'; that is the highly persuasive programmatic cause and effect stories we highlighted in the introduction to the volume. In short, a network creates an internalised space for discussion, setting agendas and developing common vision regarding 'best practice', policy or business norms and standards. This can not only help prevent duplication of effort but also reduce the cost of maintaining the infrastructure of 'communication codes'.[6]

Second, and more as interlocutors with external audiences, networks can have greater ability to attract media attention, political patronage and donor support than an individual or single organisation. A network amplifies and disseminates ideas, research and information to an extent that could not be achieved by individuals or institutions alone. Moreover, a network mutually confers legitimacy and pools authority and respectability in a positive-sum manner where the network becomes perceived as a locus for scientific authority. Its critical mass of expert opinion and adherence to professional or scientific procedures of peer review gives its representatives some credibility in shaping problem definition, determining research agendas and posing questions for policy deliberation. Networks are a social technology to propel knowledge into policy deliberation.

Take an example. The World Bank has adopted the discourse of knowledge sharing in its development programmes. Indeed, one objective of the Sustainable Development programme of the World Bank Institute (WBI) is to 'build broad-based constituencies and partnerships for sustainable change and development *and promote knowledge networks*' by facilitating a learning dialogue and disseminating innovative approaches to sustainable development, primarily among policy-makers and opinion leaders.[7] This is to be achieved through, *inter alia*, intensified partnership within and outside the Bank, harmonising programmes with other multilateral institutions, and expanded use of distance learning technologies. One programme is the Water and Media Network designed to help journalists examine the social, environmental, regulatory and financial issues relating to water.[8]

There are many other examples. Knowledge networks are essential for the international spread of knowledge, norms and what is deemed international 'best practice' on matters such as privatisation, environmental sustainability or corporate citizenship emanating from global policy discussion venues (see Stiglitz 2000). International 'public sector' organisations and other multilateral initiatives require policy analysis and research to support problem definition, outline policy solutions, to monitor and evaluate existing policy as well as to provide scholarly legitimation for policy development. They contract think tanks, universities and consultant firms as sources of international policy analysis and advice.

Understanding KNETs

KNETs apparently represent an organisational form to co-ordinate the flows of research and analysis, and for more regularised interaction. But how can they be understood? There are three well known approaches.

Epistemic communities

The first approach is to analyse KNETs as epistemic communities. These are 'scientific' in composition and founded on 'codified' forms of knowledge (Haas 1992). Professional consultants, researchers, scientists share common ideas for policy and seek privileged access to decision-making fora on the basis of their expertise and scholarly knowledge. Epistemic communities assert their independence from government or vested interest on the basis of their commitment to expert knowledge. This concept builds in (social) scientific knowledge as an independent force in policy development. Epistemic communities have:

1   shared normative and principled beliefs which provide the value based rationales for their action;
2   shared causal beliefs or professional judgements;
3   common notions of validity based on inter-subjective, internally defined criteria for validating knowledge;
4   a common policy enterprise.

The status and prestige associated with the expertise of epistemic community members and their high professional training and authoritative knowledge regarding a particular problem is politically empowering and provides some communities limited access to the political system. This is especially the case in conditions of 'uncertainty' – conflict and crisis – where decision-makers are unable to make decisions on the basis of existing knowledge or past experience and approach expert groups for assistance.

Consequently, epistemic communities require political patronage in order for ideas or science to become policy relevant and often need to make alliances with TANs or enlist other sources of support. However, it is also the case that different networks compete, not only for political attention to institute their way of thinking but also for funding (Cooley and Ron 2002).

Although often a powerful force, (social) science is not inherently or automatically persuasive in policy debates. The neo-liberal orthodoxy on free markets and trade integration – such as that propounded by most members of the Evian Group – is founded upon neo-classical economic theories that are dominant in the economics discipline and within international financial institutions. However, this world-view is contested by NGOs, social movements and other intellectual communities. The Evian Group secretariat finds it an ongoing necessity to publicly challenge the discourses of 'protectionist forces'. For instance, in the 22 June 2002 email to members of the Evian Group 'Brains Trust', Jean-Pierre Lehman, Director of the Evian Group states the following:

There is now a coalition of NGOs know as Trade Justice Movement, which recently held a demonstration in London that was allegedly 'well received' by Tony Blair. The problem is that while they get it half-right, they are still biased on two fronts: (1) favouring protectionism in developing countries, (2) remaining viscerally anti-corporate. ... Two further points to bear in mind: (1) they are much more numerous – and much better funded!!!!; (2) public sympathy tends to be very much on their side. All this to continue to stress that we do have an important mission. ... Evian defined as 'a coalition for liberal governance' is especially relevant in the current context. Your active support remains critical as the Evian Group is one of the very few global vehicles that has the voice, the credibility and the respect required to continue the struggle for an open global economy and an open global society.

Discourse coalitions and communities

A second approach draws on the theory of 'transnational discourse community'. Essentially, it identifies symbols, language and policy narrative as a source of power. This framework emphasises firstly the transnational qualities of professional groups and secondly, the role of discourse.

Public sector professionals, traditionally expected to represent a specific national view on any issues in their international activities, no longer only do that. In fact, by fore-grounding their professional identity, they transcend the power of the nation-state system to impose its categories of identity upon them. They also tend to assume a global or regional rather than national outlook on key issues (Krause Hansen *et al.* 2002: 109).

On this reading, global networks are venues where national identities of researchers, donors and international civil servants are complicated by the professional commitment to questions of development or reform that are increasingly less questions of national determination under the impact of globalisation. Transnational identities are further enhanced by global and regional interactions brought about by face-to-face communication at international meetings as well as the communication advances wrought by information technology.

Second, drawing upon Foucault, the discourse community concept locates discourse at the interface of power and knowledge. Discourses generate 'effects of truth'; that is, naturalising specific ways of thinking and normalising certain ways of doing things. Furthermore, power and knowledge operate through discursively informed social and institutional practices such as networks:

> Professionals create a transnational community through a boundary drawing discourse that defines who and what is to be considered inside and outside the community, establishing a distinction between professionals and non-professionals, and between good and bad professionals. The specific vocabulary and jargon, the speech and meeting rituals etc. create possibilities for the professionals who master them.
>
> (Krause Hansen *et al.* 2002: 111)

Transnational discourse communities construct identifiable discourses which serve to establish the goals of reform, justify the necessity of change, describe the means to achieve better results and predict outcomes. Boundary drawing helps a community to canonise certain viewpoints at the cost of others, elevating them to unquestioned status and superior position.

A related literature makes useful distinctions between the formation of coalitions, the extent to which a coalition achieves discourse structuration, and finally, institutionalisation (Hajer 1993; also Fischer 2003). Discourse coalitions seek to impose their 'discourse' in policy domains. If their discourse shapes the way in which society conceptualises the world or a particular problem, then the coalition has achieved 'discourse structuration' and agendas are likely to be restricted to a limited spectrum of possibilities. If a discourse becomes entrenched in the minds of many as the dominant mode of perception, it can become distilled in institutions and organisational practices as the conventional mode of reasoning. This latter process is 'discourse institutionalisation'. The framework captures better how discourses are transformed in their articulation through the policy cycle.

(Dis)Embedded knowledge networks

Finally, knowledge networks can also be viewed as (anti-) hegemonic projects. Embedded knowledge networks are not dissimilar to institutionalised discourses. They are 'ostensibly private institutions that possess authority because of their publicly acknowledged track records for solving problems, often acting as disinterested 'technical' parties in high-value, high-risk transactions, or in validating sets of norms and practices for a variety of service-provision activities' (Sinclair 2000). The approach emphasises the importance of authoritative judgement making built and sustained through trade journals, professional associations and research departments (of investment banks) or consultancies. Credit rating agencies such as Moody's or Standard and Poor are one example.

This approach treats knowledge, discourses or ideas as a tool of power used by dominant interests in maintaining the capitalist order. Knowledge networks are part of the 'micro-politics of contemporary hegemony' and symptomatic of the 'war of position'. Think tanks, foundations, consultants and research institutes are one component of 'globalizing elites': that is, a 'directive strategic element within globalizing capitalism' (Stephen Gill quoted in Sinclair 2000: 494). Ideas do not have independent power (as implied in discourse approaches) but are closely related to social and political interests via networks.

Ideas are treated in a constructivist manner as intersubjective meanings that shape perceptions of social structure. However, the identification of the agents, innovators or carriers of knowledge and how they use ideas to legitimise policy is also important. What becomes considered to be the truth involves gaining control over material resources and this includes knowledge networks. The emphasis is on 'organic intellectuals' playing a central role in hegemonic projects where specific sets of ideas are funded, generated and disseminated by foundations, think tanks, publishing houses and NGOs. Consequently, global knowledge networks can be viewed as an evolving contemporary social mechanism to make certain ideas – put in league with particular social forces – more powerful and hegemonic. However, the global agora can also become a site of ideological contest.

Networks are often composed of contradictory knowledges or reflect discursive competition. Hegemony is incomplete and partial. The approach posits a degree of intentionality or purposiveness to knowledge agents and networks that is not necessarily the case. A grid-like complex of ideas shaping consciousness and dominating the global order gives little credence to alternative world-views and sites of intellectual resistance.

A related approach drawing upon subaltern studies and the critical feminist literature sees knowledge makers as 'those engaged in historical transmissions as well as those in defiance of dominant epistemological flows of power'. This perspective, developed by Shirin Rai in her chapter, loosens the hegemonic grid-like power of the neo-Gramscian approach. It also overlaps with discursive frameworks in that it draws on Manuel Castells to speak of 'communication codes' that help integrate and expand networks into flows of power and globalising capitalism.

These different understandings of networks provide conceptual tools to address the policy relevance of KNETs and their relations with international organisations and other actors in governance. This is not meant to force a conceptual synthesis, but to indicate the multiple styles of KNET connection to policy. The 'embedded knowledge network' framework stresses the role of ideas being connected and subsidiary to interests. KNETs represent a means for sustaining the neo-liberal capitalist order through the reproduction of ideas supportive of it. Consequently, policy becomes a battle of ideas and knowledge is a weapon in the service of material interests.

By contrast, the 'transnational discourse community' perspective allows scope for ideas to have independent force and inherent power, diffusing into consciousness. Discourse is less directed or strategic. The epistemic community framework is more rationalistic. Epistemic communities cohere around a preferred technical rationality and have a tendency towards technocratic policy-making.

Of the knowledge networks mentioned in this paper, some can be identified as epistemic-like in character. Notwithstanding internal disagreements among individuals, the Evian Group is supportive of neo-liberal order. It is informally connected to powerful social forces within the WTO, the EU and leading corporations such as Nestlé and Unilever. The academics, journalists and bureaucrats of this knowledge group play a supporting role in constructing the terms of debate, building consensus for open trade, clarifying concepts and writing technical papers on the implications of WTO rules that feed into the wider public discourse. But Evian is in competition to 'win hearts and minds' where other KNETs or TANs may construct more compelling or emotive narratives about free trade or story lines about the threats of globalisation.

Similarly, ASEAN-ISIS is epistemic-like and embedded. Over more than two decades, it has developed a relationship of trust with Southeast Asian governments through the processes of 'track two diplomacy' (Simon 2002).

Interestingly, the dominance of this group in regional policy debates on security and human rights has generated, in opposition, a regional TAN (Kraft 2002). The GDN also has epistemic community characteristics; however, it is a very broad and loose coalition of forces. Although the development discourse of economists is dominant, other social science narratives are audible. Given the nature of its sponsorship and political support, GDN might be considered as embedded. Yet, capacities to set policy agendas and structure public discourse is highly unstable and mediated by the considerable scientific competition within these networks as well as outside them.

ICEG is more like a discourse coalition. It was founded in 1985 in San Francisco as an organisation working with a network of policy research institutes dedicated to providing market-based solutions to economic reform problems. Today, ICEG has expanded both its mission and network to include more than 5,000 economists, central bank presidents, ministers, and former heads-of-state, in more than 300 member institutes in over 100 countries. ICEG discourse (if not the network itself) is challenged and opposed by another network, the Third World network. Its objectives are to engage in research and publication on economic, social and environmental issues pertaining to the South; and to provide a platform representing broadly Southern interests and perspectives at international fora such as the UN conferences and processes.[9] Notwithstanding their research interests, both networks have strong advocacy roles not dissimilar to the style of TANs.

The OSI is a much larger entity with diverse pursuits and has the features of a TAN with its discourse on the 'open society' and direct funding of policy advocacy institutes and citizen groups. However, in the OSI's 'engagement with globalization' and 'recognition of the critical significance of policy', some elements of OSI are evolving more towards a KNET by 'building its own policy advocacy capacity' (Palley 2003).

The specialist group RDFN has exhibited through its history characteristics of a discourse coalition. This lies in its role as having been a key agent in the mainstreaming of the importance of people in tropical forests over the last fifteen years through its research and activities on village tree planting and participatory forest management. RDFN co-ordinators use the term 'narrative' not only to account for the impact of the forestry network but also to signify the strategic approach of network research. Indeed, they claim they have 'established a new area of discourse'.[10] Now that the development agenda in this policy field has been 'set', the RDFN has a stronger research character. Indeed, a sign of its long term success is flagging interest from donors to support the network.

In ascertaining influence, the neo-Gramscian frameworks help identify knowledge networks lacking political influence or choosing to challenge dominant policy discourses. SARN and Blue Bird are 'dis-embedded'. Blue Bird is too disaggregated and short-term to fully develop and advocate a coherent policy discourse. It has a policy agenda – an alternative vision to reconstruct the terms in which we 'see' and comprehend South Eastern Europe – but this is more an intellectual endeavour undertaken by loosely connected individual researchers.

Similarly, SARN is a subaltern KNET. Notwithstanding their lack of policy or political influence, these networks perform wider societal roles of knowledge creation and capacity building.

KNETs cannot be fully independent or completely autonomous as they are reliant on funding support from donor agencies or governments. However, this is not to suggest conspiracy, centralised direction, or conscious global strategy of policy intervention and control. Instead, power is discontinuous. Where there is power, there is also resistance and this resistance is plural in form (Pal 1990). Power and knowledge are dispersed in the agora and take form – like SARN or Blue Bird – in local or regional institutions and networks. In 'sites of domination [knowledge actors can provide] unique information resources [and help form] alternative definitions of reality' (Conway 1990: 172, my insertions). However, the lesson for SARN and Blue Bird from the experiences of RDFN and ASEAN-ISIS is that changing perceptions and shifting policy agendas can take decades.

While Evian and GDN are synchronised with the bureaucratic interests of the WTO and the World Bank respectively, and the network of ICEG institutes is ideologically aligned with the neo-liberal orthodoxy, these networks are neither hegemonic nor unthinking mouthpieces for their funders and patrons. By the same token, networks that appear to have little policy impact or to be espousing unorthodox policy perspectives are neither completely ineffectual nor hopelessly marginalised. Instead, subaltern KNETs are symptomatic of how 'dominated people form identities through common language and understanding and mobilize resources in resistance' (Conway 1990: 172).

KNETs and global governance

Alternative visions of the world with competing ideological principles and policy positions are finding their way into public debate. Clearly, some KNETs are more powerful and better resourced than others, but new configurations emerge, new coalitions develop and with them, new constructions of knowledge. In global governance, however, of relevance is which discourse or knowledge is selected, where knowledge networks are politically patronised, by what groups and for what reasons?

First, the expansion of knowledge networks as 'sites of authority' potentially accelerates the 'normalisation of the dominant discourses of power' (see Rai, this volume). Networks systematise knowledge generated by diverse individual and organisational knowledge actors and impose a rationality that gives precedence to a particular conception of knowledge – usually of a codified, technocratic, secular, westernised variety. Participation is informally restricted and regulated through boundary drawing discourses by the network to exclude or devalue indigenous or protest knowledge that does not conform to techno-scientific criteria.

Recognising think tanks, law firms and research institutes as centres for expert, scientific and authoritative advice occurs not only because of the scholarly credentials of these organisations (and their self referential habits) but also because of the relationship with policy makers and donor groups that a network structure facilitates. Through their club-like tendencies, networks both accrue and accredit authority through the collective policy entrepreneurship of their members. As research brokers, KNETs draw their power and policy influence by combining epistemic, discursive and ideological practices.

Networks are not simply linking knowledge and policy arenas. Instead, the interaction of knowledge and policy is one of mutual construction:

> Thus, the seemingly mundane daily activities of scientists and bureaucrats engaged in the preparation of scientific papers or consultancy reports, the elaboration of models, participation in workshops, meetings or email discussion groups, and engagement in formal and informal policy briefings are a central part of the joint production of science and technology
>
> (Keeley and Scoones 2000: 7)

States as well as international organisations require the creation of persuasive reasoning of what constitutes 'public policy problems', and the widespread acceptance of such problem definition in society, as the basis of legitimate policy and just laws. Public institutions depend on groups of 'experts' whose views on such issues are considered authoritative. Knowledge networks or communities not only provide such expert interpretations and scientific narratives, they also create self-supporting structures of authority to incarnate as 'neutral' research brokers and intermediaries. That is, networks become a globalised locus of authority. In sum, KNETs do not simply 'crystallize around different sites and forms of power' (Held 2000: 19), the network is a site and form of power.

Second, when involved in global policy developments, knowledge networks – alongside other partnerships, alliances and private regimes – set in motion a structural dynamic that both excludes and opens up policy-making to certain groups: networks privatise knowledge as well as turn it into a public good. In principle, policy networks are a flatter and more horizontal structure (compared to public sector hierarchies) that are porous to participation of private and third sector actors. Yet, networks also privatise decision-making to stakeholders. Dominant epistemic or discourse communities attempt to harden the boundaries of a policy network. It is in their 'cognitive interest' to do so. That is, in their professional context, specific groups of knowledge producers – whether they are economists, anthropologists or statisticians – have a cognitive interest in the selective use of their mode of problem definition, methodological approaches and policy solutions. It becomes a self-reinforcing dynamic that encourages resistance to other perspectives or disciplinary approaches (Nustad and Sending 2000). Consequently, a network can develop a carapace, sometimes in the interests of internal network cohesion and unity, but also to exclude those who do not speak the same specialised language. Policy debate is not taken out of the public domain but it is cordoned off from those not deemed to be so-called 'stakeholders' or those without mastery of the communication code.

On the other hand, knowledge networks represent a means to protect and preserve the public status of knowledge; that is, a means to deliver a public good (Stiglitz 2000). The websites of knowledge groups and networks provide a wealth of information. Toward the Evian Group mission of educating and informing on economic governance, policy briefs are made available, a newsletter in circulation, meetings and conferences organised, and a guide to trade experts constructed. Similarly, TWN provides information on global economic governance from a very different perspective. Other chapters in this volume have described how networks have produced valuable knowledge in domains as diverse as fisheries management and the promotion of Roma human rights. What might be described as an inter-generational public good – the 'Young Evian' network – has been cultivated to communicate more effectively with younger generations. It is an indirect, long-term, non-guaranteed means to gain greater understanding and commitment for the multilateral rules-based system of global economic governance and to provide support to the next generation of leaders.

Even so, questions can be raised regarding the extent to which networks represent a dual dynamic for the concentration as well as dispersion of knowledge. The widening of the knowledge generation gap between South and North and between the countries of the South reduces the pool of institutions and individuals that can be drawn into knowledge networks. Researchers from developing countries characterised by weak enabling environment (such as inadequate political commitment) and the lack of a research culture are at a disadvantage in seeking to participate in networks even though the network may be effective in disseminating knowledge downwards. As such networks become transnational, further distancing can ensue. They are more likely to revolve around international research agendas and Northern policy concerns (see the essays in Gmelin *et al.* 2001). The lack of ownership and empowerment in shaping research agendas and donor driven intellectual priorities can establish a 'non-decision making' dynamic that sets up subtle modes of exclusion.

Network participation is resource intensive. Access to global public policy networks requires time, commitment and funds. Many developing country knowledge agencies do not have sufficient resources to devote to national policy deliberations let alone global dialogues. At other times, network participation can have perverse consequences. As indicated by one World Bank official: 'In Benin, we discovered there were more networks than scientists – this leads to no time to do their own jobs' (quoted in Keeley and Scoones 2000: 35). Indeed, their participation may be irrelevant in the absence of a 'communicative code' that is decipherable by all potential partners. The dominance of OECD actors in regional and global policy debates is notable. Accordingly, 'openness' and 'closure' is not an evenly balanced dynamic across networks. Instead, access and exclusiveness vary considerably across networks, over time and according to issue area or policy field.

Third, networks are becoming a mode of governance whereby the patterns of linkages and interaction are the means through which joint policy is organised. In short, there is a functional interdependence between public and private actors whereby networks allow resources to be mobilised towards common policy objectives in domains outside the hierarchical control of governments (Börzel 1999).

> Although the agora is a structured space, it is wrong to attempt to subdivide it again into sectors like markets, politics or media. ... these forms of differentiation are beginning to break down and to be replaced by fluid and dynamic (and pervasive) interlinkages. As a public space, the agora is shaped by the interaction of its actors/agents. Some are more visible, easier to identify and recognize and more powerful than others
>
> (Nowotny *et al.* 2001: 209)

Furthermore, the network logic itself is being diffused by international organisations with their advocacy of partnership and tripartite policy coalitions as method to deal with global problems (Brinkerhoff 2002).

Networks as mechanisms for the delivery of (global) public goods is most clearly drawn in the GPPN framework. In the absence of global or regional institutions, these trisectoral networks carve out new policy space as knowledge creators, service providers and standard setters. They also play a central role in policy monitoring and evaluation. Consequently, there is significant scope for policy entrepreneurs to mark out the ill-defined contours of the global agora and, as suggested in the epistemic community framework, respond to policy uncertainty and the institutional hiatus at the global level with policy solutions. For example, as noted by the organisers of RDFN:

> When new directions are first taken in a particular subject, there is often no obvious forum for new findings and nowhere to turn for comparative experience. This is what happened in forestry in the early 1980s, when concerns about desertification and fuel-wood shortages created strong donor pressure for tree-planting programmes with local people.[11]

The RDFN not only filled this 'knowledge gap' but interacted with donor agencies and researchers to put ideas into practice via the network medium.

Fourth, networks are part of global civil society. Networks with a strong advocacy character or directed towards the promotion of international norms like TANs are relatively permeable to broad societal participation. By contrast, epistemic communities and GPPNs are more elite and exclusive. The rich ecology of knowledge networks adds to the diversity and plurality of this civil domain. Some regard networks as effective at building trust, consensus or what has been called 'global social capital' helping to ameliorate the 'democratic deficit' in the global agora (Reinicke, Deng *et al.* 2000). For example, in discussing 'how the WTO can best function for the enhancement of global prosperity' the Evian Group seeks to build 'confidence between members of the global economic community'. But in generating trust and a consensus on the benefits of a liberal trading order, Evian also notes that 'multilateral corporations must exercise global responsibility commensurate with their knowledge and influence'.[12] And as one observer has noted:

'The more that tripartite networks of global governance are inclusive, their procedures and decisions transparent and subject to public deliberation, the more the democratic deficit of transnational governance can be tackled' (Risse 2002: 270).

Conclusion

The nature of the relationship of non-official experts, their organisations (think tanks, foundations, etc) and their coalitions with states and international organisations presents important questions about representation, accountability and legitimacy. These are questions relevant to any idea of a cosmopolitan order in the global agora. Nevertheless, global or regional networks are not 'public' entities – that is, accountable to formally elected representatives of the public or a sovereign authority. A network may be accountable to network members but these member organisations and individuals cannot be considered as entirely representative of the 'global public'.

Global or regional networks are usually private organisations (notwithstanding public sources of support or the production of public goods) and are not subject to the usual reporting and accountability requirements of public bodies in liberal democracies. The public – even the well-informed and politically literate of OECD countries – are still largely unaware of the roles, reach and influence of global networks. Newspapers and the electronic media do not treat bodies like the Evian Group, RDFN or ASEAN-ISIS as newsworthy. Combined with the technocratic character of many such networks, the public is excluded and political responsibility is undermined. As a consequence of the lack of transparency and mechanisms for public representation, and lack of knowledge about them, these networks act with relative autonomy and in some anonymity. In any event, they are more able to thwart challenges to their activities or calls for transparency by emphasising their non-state, private status. This tendency is compounded in knowledge networks that also stress their disinterested, scientific and politically neutral research endeavour.

Consequently, we should end on a cautionary note regarding the democratic potential and deliberative capacity of global (knowledge) networks. They may well be sites of social capital but this kind of capital has negative as well as positive implications.

Notes

1 See the working papers at http://www.globalpublicpolicy.net.
2 Further information at http://www.eviangroup.org.
3 RDNF disseminates research information on key issues in tropical forestry to 2900 members in 130 countries. It aims to influence policy and decision-makers (about 30 per cent of its membership) in both governments and international aid agencies. To do this it disseminates information provided by its strong base in the research community (about 37 per cent of its membership), which is validated by the day-to-day project experience of the Network's NGO and consultancy members (about 30 per cent of its membership). http://www.odifpeg.org.uk/network/index.html. Accessed 17 June 2003.
4 Further information at http://www.iceg.org.

5 Further information at http://www.ceu.hu/cps/res/res_bluebird.htm.
6 But networks also suffer from the Olsonian 'collective action' dilemma. Unless the number of members in a network is relatively small, rational self-interested members experience difficulty in achieving common group interest. Alternatively coercive measures or selective incentives may make members act in their common interest.
7 http://www.worldbank.org/wbi/sdenvmanagement/index.html. Accessed 17 June 2003. Up until late 2000, this WBI Division also co-ordinated Environmental Economics and Policy Network (EEPNET) which appears to have folded.
8 http://www.worldbank.org/wbi/sdwatermedianetwork/aboutus.html. Accessed 17 June 2003.
9 http://www.twnside.org.sg/twnintro.htm Accessed. 17 June 2003.
10 http://www.odifpeg.org.uk/network/history.html. Accessed 17 June 2003.
11 http://www.odifpeg.org.uk/network/history.html. Accessed 17 June 2003.
12 http://www.eviangroup.org. Accessed 17 June 2003.

References

Baker, Gideon (2002) 'Problems in the Theorisation of Global Civil Society' *Political Studies* 50 (5).

Börzel, Tanya (1999) 'Organizing Babylon – on the Different Conceptions of Policy Networks', *Public Administration* 76 (Summer): 253–73.

Brinkerhoff, Jennifer M. (2002) *Partnership for International Development Rhetoric or Results?* Boulder, CO: Lynne Reinner Publishers.

Conway, Thomas (1990) 'Background Reading: The Crisis of the Policy Sciences', in S. Brooks and A. G. Gagnon (eds) *Social Scientists, Policy and the State.* New York: Praeger.

Cooley, Alexander and Ron, James (2002) 'The NGO Scramble: Organisational Insecurity and the Political Economy of Transnational Action' *International Security* 27 (1): 5–39.

Diani, Mario and McAdam, Doug (2003) *Social Movements and Networks: Relational Approaches to Collective Action.* Oxford: Oxford University Press.

Fischer, Frank (2003) *Reframing Public Policy: Discursive Politics and Deliberative Practices.* Oxford: Oxford University Press.

Gmelin, Wolfgang, King, Kenneth and McGrath, Simon (eds) (2001) *Development Knowledge, National Research and International Cooperation.* Edinburgh, Bonn and Geneva: CAS-DSE-NORRAG.

Haas, Peter (1992) 'Introduction: Epistemic Communities and International Policy Coordination' *International Organisation* 46 (1): 1–35.

Hajer, Maarten (1993) 'Discourse Coalitions and Institutionalisation of Practice: The Case of Acid Rain in Great Britain', in F. Fischer and J. Forester (eds.) *The Argumentative Turn in Policy Analysis and Planning.* London: UCL Press.

Held, David (2000) 'The Changing Contours of Political Community: Rethinking Democracy in the Context of Globalization', in Barry Holden (ed.) *Global Democracy: Key Debates.* London: Routledge.

Keck, Margaret and Sikkink, Kathryn (1998) *Activists Beyond Borders: Advocacy Networks in International Politics.* Ithaca NY: Cornell University Press.

Keeley, James and Scoones, Ian (2000) *Environmental Policy-making in Zimbabwe: Discourses, Science and Politics.* IDS Working Paper No. 115.

Kraft, Herman (2002) 'Track Three Diplomacy and Human Rights in Southeast Asia: The Asia Pacific Coalition for East Timor' *Global Networks* 2 (1): 49–63.

Krause Hansen, Hans, Salskov-Iversen, Dorte and Bislev, Sven (2002) 'Transnational Discourse Communities: Globalizing Public Management', in R. Higgott and M. Ougaard (eds) *Understanding the Global Polity*. London: Routledge.

Messner, Dirk (1997) *The Network Society: Economic Development and International Competitiveness as Problems of Social Governance*. London: Frank Cass.

Nahrath, Stephane (2000) 'The Power of Ideas in Policy Research: A Critical Assessment', in D. Braun and A. Busch (eds) *Public Policy and Political Ideas*. Cheltenham: Edward Elgar.

Nowotny, Helga, Scott, Peter and Gibbons, Michael (2001) *Re-Thinking Science: Knowledge and the Public in an Age of Uncertainty*. Oxford: Polity Press.

Nustad, Knut G. and Sending, Ole J. (2000) 'The Instrumentalisation of Development Knowledge', in Diane Stone (ed.) *Banking on Knowledge: The Genesis of the Global Development Network*. London: Routledge.

Open Society Institute (2001) *Open Society Institute Related Public Policy Centres: Activity Report, June*. Budapest: Open Society Institute.

Ougaard, Morten and Higgott, Richard (eds) (2002) *Approaching the Global Polity*. London: Routledge.

Pal, Leslie A. (1990) 'Knowledge, Power and Policy: Reflections on Foucault', in S. Brooks and A. G. Gagnon (eds) *Social Scientists, Policy and the State*. New York: Praeger.

Palley, Thomas (2003) 'The Open Institute and Global Social Policy' *Global Social Policy* 3 (1): 17–18.

Parmar, Inderjeet (2002) 'American Foundations and the Development of International Knowledge Networks' *Global Networks* 2 (1): 13–30.

Reinicke, Wolfgang, Deng, Francis *et al.* (2000) *Critical Choices: The United Nations, Networks and the Future of Global Governance*. Ottawa: International Development Research Centre.

Risse, Thomas (2002) 'Transnational Actors and World Politics' in Walter Carlnaes, Thomas Risse and Beth A. Simmons (eds) *Handbook of International Relations*. London: Sage Publications.

Simon, Sheldon. (2002) 'Evaluating Track Two Approaches to Security Diplomacy in the Asia-Pacific: the CSCAP Experience' *Pacific Review* 15 (2): 167–200.

Sinclair, Timothy J. (2000) 'Reinventing Authority; Embedded Knowledge Networks and the New Global Finance' *Environment and Planning C: Government and Policy* 18: 487–502.

Stevenson, Nick (2002) 'Cosmopolitanism and the Future of Democracy: Politics, Culture and the Self' *New Political Economy* 7 (2).

Stiglitz, Joe (2000) 'Scan Globally, Reinvent Locally: Knowledge Infrastructure and the Localization of Knowledge', Diane Stone (ed.) *Banking on Knowledge: The Genesis of the Global Development Network*. London: Routledge.

Struyk, Raymond J. (2002) 'Transnational Think Tank Networks: Purpose, Membership and Cohesion' *Global Networks* 2 (1): 83–90.

7 Creating the Global Development Network

An exercise in institutional theory and practice

Sarah Clarke and Lyn Squire

Introduction

Imagine that it is early 1999 and Joseph Stiglitz, then Chief Economist and Senior Vice President at the World Bank, has asked you to create a worldwide organization or association to strengthen socio-economic research institutes throughout the developing world. Imagine that you have also recently come to know and appreciate the marvellous ideas of Nobel Laureate Douglass North. As a result, you have fully internalized the notion that the rules, formal and informal, that constitute both the skeleton and the nervous system of economies have significant implications for the internal design of organizations and for their ultimate impact in the world at large. In reading this chapter, take what your imagination tells you and apply it to the actual development of the Global Development Network (GDN), in particular to the activities that the Network supports in the hope of building research capacity, influencing policy formulation, and, in a small way, improving the world.

No doubt, questions are already popping into your mind. Perhaps you are asking what already exists that serves this function. You might think of some of the efforts to build research capacity in Africa such as the African Economic Research Consortium (AERC) or in the Middle East such as Economic Research Forum (ERF) or wherever your own regional experience lies. You would surely ask how such an association is to be governed. By the researchers themselves? By the donor community since funding is an inevitable issue? Or by the international development community through the World Bank or another multilateral agency? And of course you would ask what constitutes the research domain. Does it include all scientific endeavour related to development? Or is it confined to certain disciplines and if so which ones? Finally, you would ask perhaps the single most important question: what should the association actually do? How could such an association help to build research capacity and more effective policy?

For better or for worse, all of these questions have been confronted and answered by mid 2003. To provide you with the background to assess the answers that were given to these questions and to devise your own solutions where necessary, this chapter begins by recapping some of the key messages emerging from Douglass North's views on institutions and development. This draws heavily on his recent work and especially the presentation that he made at the Second Annual Global Development Conference held in Tokyo (North 2000).

The next section provides a brief history of the Global Development Network. It covers four years: from the meeting held at the World Bank in May 1999, where some of the first decisions regarding the association were taken, to the meeting of GDN's governing body held in May 2003, where important issues regarding funding, legal status and location were debated. While the intention is to be as factual as possible, the history also tries to explain the thinking behind the various developments. The task of the reader is to see whether North's insights have been adequately captured and, if not, how things might have been done differently. In addressing this question, the reader should bear in mind Professor North's emphasis on path dependency, a phenomenon that inevitably limits the scope for decision making.

The penultimate section is perhaps the most important as it describes some of the activities currently supported by GDN. The key question is the following: given what we know about institutions and the performance of economies over time, are the activities currently being supported by GDN well chosen? Will they in fact contribute to better development? This is, unfortunately, a very difficult if not impossible question to answer because, as Douglass North makes clear, our knowledge of the factors governing the performance of economies is inadequate in many respects. Nevertheless, decisions have to be made and activities have to be selected. Your views on the choices that have been made are solicited. And your suggestions for future directions are also sought. To this end, the concluding section of the chapter recalls the key tenets underlying GDN's development to date.

Institutions and performance

We know from experience around the world that the same policy implemented in two different countries can lead to two quite different outcomes. Douglass North, along with others working in the field of New Institutional Economics, has stressed the importance of institutions in influencing implementation and determining outcomes (North 1990). For North, institutions constitute the formal rules, the informal rules and the enforcement mechanisms that govern the functioning of economies. Policy is the prime example of a formal rule, but a change in policy can leave all the related informal rules and enforcement mechanisms unchanged. As these informal rules and mechanisms differ across countries or over time, the outcome of a particular policy change can be quite different in different places and at different times.

Over recent years, scholars have increasingly come to recognize the significant role that institutions, defined as both the formal and informal rules of society and enforcement mechanisms, play in obstructing or facilitating economic activity. Authors working in this field have studied the great variety of structures that are erected formally at both the national and international level or that emerge informally. Thus, knowledge of institutions potentially provides a valuable key in the process of policy formulation: understanding existing institutions is essential if policy is going to be effective in responding to the world we live in. Since the Global Development Network is meant to be an organization that builds research capacity to inform policy decisions, an understanding of institutions is critical to the design of the network itself and to the selection and implementation of activities supported by GDN.

Douglass North provides a framework that allows us to conceptualize economic change. This understanding helps us to develop an organization designed to generate knowledge and influence economic change for the better. He effectively describes the role that institutions play outlining how the rules, norms, conventions and beliefs that constitute institutions are constructed according to our perception of reality. Over time, as perceptions of reality change, actors seek to alter these institutional frameworks in order to improve their competitive position. The paper explores economic change and institution building, and examines some of the obstacles that this process faces.

North explains that humans hold beliefs regarding the reality of the political–economic systems, and the dominant beliefs in a society determine the structure of institutions which govern economic and political performance. The belief systems that we hold evolve from a learning process. This learning process can provide us with a set of concepts or it can go further and change the structure of our concepts and mental models. From this learning process, a belief system evolves that will induce political and economic entrepreneurs to erect frameworks dictating what skills and knowledge are perceived to have the maximum pay-off. This incentive structure will ultimately shape micro and macro economic performance. Three important conclusions flow from this analysis.

First, any number of outcomes is possible due to the numerous perceptions and mental constructs held by individuals from different backgrounds making different choices. Thus, even agents with the same preferences can arrive at different decisions because of their differing experiences and perceptions of reality. This surely implies that the readers of this chapter, even if they all share the goal of building research capacity and influencing policy, will probably arrive at different ways of achieving that goal which are also different from those actually chosen by the architects of GDN.

Second, the learning process and how learning is shared within a society is an incremental process. Even if we are all in perfect agreement about the knowledge generating and sharing activities that GDN should support, their ability to change beliefs and perceptions will be limited. And since changes in belief systems and perceptions of reality are crucial to institutional change, such change will be overwhelmingly incremental and path dependent. GDN, at best, will be only one of many forces seeking to increase our knowledge about development and, in the current age of electronic communications, it will be only one of many agents spreading knowledge around the world at ever decreasing cost.

Third, the likelihood that an action or policy change achieves its intended purpose depends on the accuracy of policy makers' perceptions of reality. Those perceptions in turn depend on policy makers' individual experiences and systems of belief. To the extent that beliefs emerging from the learning process coincide with 'reality', there is some prospect that ensuing institutions and policies will produce the intended results. North points to the former communist countries where a belief in the command economy and central planning was based on a flawed understanding of human behaviour. This would eventually prove fatal and led to disintegration of European communism in 1989.

These three conclusions, complex and intricate in their own right, are complicated further by the observation that we live in a world of constant change that evolves as a result of natural and human induced alterations to our surroundings. This produces revised perceptions of reality and new systems of belief. As a result, political and economic entrepreneurs are obliged to constantly seek new approaches to improve their competitive position. At the same time, policy makers are constantly driven to reformulate policies and refashion programs to improve the functioning of economies. Ultimately, by pursuing improved economic performance, actors bring about a process of institutional change. But, path dependency and the slow speed of institutional change raise multiple challenges that plague institution building and policy formulation.

North provides us with an in-depth examination of the challenges we face if our institutions and policies are to effectively address the needs of the changing world. This highlights two important points that bear directly on the issues raised in this chapter regarding the design and purpose of GDN. First, with respect to design, there is a need to build flexible institutions that are capable of responding effectively to their environment. Second, with respect to purpose, there is a need for constant, ongoing learning and quality research to inform our perception of the world we live in. These represent two essential ingredients as we strive to respond to our surroundings and build a better world. The following sections draw on these conclusions to look at the process of institutional change and development within GDN and how GDN works to support the process of institution building and learning in partner organizations.

Global Development Network: goal and design

The Global Development Network emerged from a series of discussions, meetings and conferences over several years. Apart from the direct request from Joseph Stiglitz noted above, the initiative was prompted by two additional developments. One was the advent of new electronic means of communication that make the goals of capacity building and knowledge sharing much easier to realize. The other was the progress achieved by the World Bank and many other agencies in supporting regional research institutions such as AERC and ERF.

In March 1999, the World Bank assembled interested parties to consider the possibility of forming an association of some kind to foster high-quality, policy-relevant research in developing and transition countries. Representatives of three broad groups were present: the 'southern' research community, including representatives of the Indian Centre for Research on International Economic Relations (ICRIER) and the Latin American and Caribbean Economic Association

(LACEA); the 'northern' research community; and other multilateral institutions such as the United Nations Development Program (UNDP).

The meeting quickly endorsed the basic idea of a global association devoted to supporting research in the developing world. In addition, it recognized that broad participation in the design of the association was critical both to achieve the best possible format and to ensure legitimacy. To this end, the meeting endorsed the idea of a worldwide electronic discussion to publicize the initiative and solicit inputs from as many interested parties as possible. The global discussion culminated in a conference at which the emerging association was formally launched and the next steps in its design debated.

The meeting also reached two other decisions that, with the benefit of hindsight, had important implications for the immediate future of the association. The first was to conduct a survey of research institutes throughout the developing world to learn from them what kind of support would be most useful. In the end, the World Bank in collaboration with the International Economics Association (IEA) surveyed more than 500 research institutes of various kinds covering all regions of the developing world (GDN 1999). The second decision was to immediately initiate one activity that would give the new association a presence. The association would build on a research project already under way in Africa to better understand the factors contributing to, or hindering, growth and development.

Inaugural conference

GDN was formally launched at a conference in Bonn in December 1999. This conference, 'Bridging Knowledge and Policy', introduced many of the features that have been preserved in subsequent GDN conferences (Tokyo, December 2000; Rio de Janeiro, December 2001; and Cairo, January 2003). Included among these are: provision of an international forum for researchers from around the world with a special emphasis on younger, promising researchers from developing and transition countries; an effort to ensure policy relevance captured in the title of the conference and the presence of policy makers at the conference; exposure of GDN's goals and activities to critical comment by participants at the conference in what has now become GDN's annual meeting; and involvement of donors and other supporters in both the general sessions and special sessions designed to secure donor input and support.

The spirit of the conference was well captured in the closing remarks of Kofi Annan when he said

> we realize more and more that knowledge is what makes the difference: knowledge in the hands of those who need it, and of those who can make best use of it. You are all scholars, committed to truth and objectivity in the search for knowledge. But you also understand the importance of conveying that knowledge to those who take decisions – in the private sector and civil society as well as in governments and international organizations. Which means you have to interact with them, and understand their needs. Even more

important, you have understood how vital it is that knowledge should be more fairly distributed around the world. Used imaginatively, your network can help overcome the knowledge gap – and so provide those imprisoned in poverty with the key to the gates of their prison.

(Annan 1999)

While the Bonn conference was both well attended (500 participants) and well received, various issues arose. Prime among these was the question of governance. As a World Bank initiative, GDN had been managed by a small secretariat in the Development Economics Vice Presidency of the World Bank. However, it had become clear, both before and during the conference, that many of the intended beneficiaries of the association, that is, researchers in developing and transition countries, felt that their interests would be served best by an independent organization. The point was recognized and internalized by senior management of the World Bank. However, the question remained: how is an appropriate governance structure to be determined and what gives it legitimacy? This of course is a classic example of the chicken-and-egg problem. One needs a process to determine the governance structure, but, in the absence of a governance structure, who or what decides on the process? Clearly, some arbitrary decisions had to be made albeit with as much consultation as possible.

Governance: defining a constitution

Under the chairmanship of Enric Banda, Director General of the European Science Foundation, a session at the Bonn conference devoted to the issue of governance decided that a working group, consisting of eight members drawn from around the world, should be established. The group comprised four members of the global research community: Bina Agarwal, University of Delhi; Kwesi Botchwey, Harvard University; Randolph Filer, Centre for Economic Research and Graduate Education – Economics Institute (CERGE-EI); and Dani Rodrik, Harvard University. And it included four representatives of national or multilateral development institutions: Ishac Diwan, World Bank; Kaoru Hayashi, Japanese Bank for International Cooperation (JBIC); Inge Kaul, UNDP; and Lyn Squire, World Bank. This group was charged with the task of consulting widely and arriving at a broadly endorsed governance structure before the next annual conference arranged for December 2000. Implicit in this decision was the need to embrace the perceptions and belief systems of as many people as possible while retaining flexibility that would allow adjustment to a changing world.

The first activity undertaken by the working group was to hold a series of electronic discussions on several different aspects of governance. The survey of research institutes conducted in 1999 contained a section specifically addressing the question of access to the Internet and e-mail. This revealed fairly widespread access at the level of institutions (GDN 1999). For example, two-thirds of the responding institutions reported that more than half of their staff regularly used the Internet. Indeed, this proved an effective method to gather a wide range of input and generate a broad-based exchange of ideas. The electronic discussion format served to overcome time and travel constraints, not to mention budget concerns, and enabled a broad spectrum of participants to voice their opinions.

The 'governance' discussions lasted a month and concluded with a total of 87 messages posted from 27 countries. The discussions allowed many to participate, even more to observe, and responses revealed a wide range of views. Based on this input, the working group was then given the responsibility of developing a formal constitution for GDN. This was captured in a report outlining matters such as principles of governance, scope, legal status, membership, and the role and procedures for the governing body and secretariat. This proposal was resubmitted to worldwide scrutiny and comment on the Web before being finalized in early October for presentation at the Tokyo conference, December 2000 (GDN 2000a).

The governing body

The October draft of the constitution served to establish the responsibilities that would fall to the governing body. It was agreed that the governing body's principle tasks would include broad direction of GDN and selection of the activities to be supported. Membership on the governing body would include representatives from the diverse communities which GDN serves: seven members nominated by the research community in the developing world, three members nominated by the research community in the developed OECD countries, two members nominated by international agencies, three members nominated by international professional associations (only one of which was selected in initial round for reasons explained below), and two-at-large members (also left open in this initial round).

The constitution also served to establish a nomination process for the governing body. Ideally, a totally open election would have been the most appropriate process. However, practically speaking such a process would have been impossible both administratively and financially. Instead, partner institutions such as the Organization for Economic Cooperation and Development (OECD), the Economic Education and Research Consortium (EERC) in Moscow, the African Economic Research Consortium (AERC) in Nairobi and the South Asia Network of Economic Institutes (SANEI) in Delhi were asked to form selection committees and carry out a transparent nomination process to determine their choice to serve on the governing body. Successful candidates needed to be highly respected members from the communities they were to represent and willing and able to give time to realizing GDN goals.

The governing body was introduced and met for the first time at the Second Annual Global Development Conference held in Tokyo in December 2000. To complete the move to independence the governing body took two decisions. First, the network should be legally separate from the World Bank. GDN was formally incorporated as a not-for-profit agency on March 16, 2001. Second, the secretariat should be physically separate from the World Bank. The secretariat moved to 2600 Virginia Avenue in Washington, DC in July 2001 on a temporary basis, and, at the Fourth Annual Global Development Conference held in Cairo in

January 2003, New Delhi was selected as the preferred, long-term home for GDN. The move to New Delhi is expected to take place in 2004 or 2005.

Multidisciplinary research

Other matters required consideration by the governing body. Throughout the electronic consultation and especially at the Tokyo conference, concern was raised about the apparently excessive focus on economics within GDN. GDN had run into a conflict identified in Professor North's framework. Recall that North points to change as being incremental and path dependent: systems of belief and perceptions are based on many years of accumulated experience and, as a result, are slow to change. The importance of this observation lies in the fact that many of the organizations participating in the development of GDN have an economics base. The reality of path dependence meant that the strong focus on economics had produced a certain orientation in GDN activities.

However, as North points out, individuals committed to the same goal can have very different systems of belief and perceptions and consequently arrive at different decisions. This emerged clearly in Tokyo where conference participants from many different backgrounds were present. Participants at the conference, especially those representing European donors, voiced their support for a multidisciplinary approach to research on development. These calls reflected the divergent approaches to development that exist within the GDN community and the belief that a more complete understanding requires input from a range of disciplines.

An immediate task for the governing body, therefore, was to consider how and to what extent GDN could more effectively promote research in all social sciences, moving away from a bias towards economics. At its meeting in May, 2001 in Washington, the group listened to a series of presentations and debated the issue at some length. Finally, the governing body requested that the Secretariat prepare a report laying out the rationale for addressing this concern by pointing to the specific contributions of multidisciplinary research and setting out GDN's position on the matter.

The subsequent report, endorsed by the governing body, made three points (GDN 2001). First, the governing body agreed that the involvement of multiple disciplines 'allows the exploration of research questions which would not otherwise arise within the boundaries of a single discipline and therefore is closely connected to originality in development research' (Jackson 2001). Second, the governing body felt that different social science techniques 'are required to tackle different problems, and a combination of techniques will frequently yield greater insight than one used in isolation' (White 2001). This observation was made with particular reference to the use of quantitative and qualitative research. Finally, it was argued that

> Good scholarship must involve a tension between 'discipline' and 'anti-discipline' … one of the most fruitful ways of maintaining this tension is through

deep immersion in a discipline, combined with subjecting of knowledge deriving from the discipline to that developed by others.

(Harriss 2001).

In other words, researchers must, on the one hand, be well versed in the techniques and accumulated knowledge of their own disciplines, but must not be blindfolded to the insights and inputs of other disciplines.

To turn these conclusions in to action, the governing body made two sets of decisions. The first set dealt with personnel. It was agreed that if GDN was to be truly multidisciplinary, representatives of different disciplines had to be placed in the key, decision-making and implementing agencies of GDN. To this end, four new members were invited to join the governing body. During the nomination process slots had been left open in the initial round so that these slots could be used to correct any imbalances with respect to, say, gender or discipline, emerging from the decentralized process of nomination. Since the process was decentralized there was no way to ensure a balance in all these dimensions. Thus, the governing body called for representatives to be selected by the International Political Science Association and the International Sociological Association. It used the two at-large slots to select a demographer and a political scientist. In like manner, a political scientist has been added to the staff of the secretariat.

Another set of actions dealt with GDN supported activities including: agreement that future Global Research Projects focus on topics that lend themselves to multidisciplinary research; that the themes for future annual conferences be chosen to encourage multidisciplinary participation; that the topics for future rounds of the Global Development Awards allow ample scope for multiple disciplines; and that in the next round of regional competitions, the regional research networks be asked to choose broad topics that promote multidisciplinary research and will be asked to use review panels drawn from several disciplines. Progress on this front was intended to clearly demonstrate GDN's inclusion of practitioners from outside the economics tradition in all activities and projects (GDN 2001).

Governance: part II

By the time of the Fourth Annual Global Development Conference held in Cairo in January 2003, many of GDN's initial issues had been dealt with successfully. Independence from the World Bank, establishing a governance structure, and embracing multidisciplinary research were either completed or well in hand. New issues were, however, beginning to appear. Prime among these was the question of GDN's legal status that arose naturally in connection with the relocation of the secretariat to a developing country. Since GDN is currently incorporated as a non-profit organization in the US, a similar status in the intended new location (India) is an obvious option. An alternative, however, is to consider changing GDN's legal status to that of an international organization thereby making it 'independent' of any single country.

This issue was first debated seriously at the meeting of the governing body held in conjunction with the Cairo conference. Initial reactions were mixed. Some saw the benefits in terms of stature, voice, and ability to mobilize funds that would accompany international organization status. Others saw the risk of political interference from the governments that would sign the charter making GDN an international organization. All considered the issue too important to be decided quickly. Consequently, the secretariat was charged with the task of preparing an analysis of the costs and benefits of international organization status relative to that of a non-profit organization incorporated in a developing country. The secretariat was also asked to redraft, with appropriate legal assistance, the draft charter to address the concerns regarding political interference. The matter was then tabled for discussion at the governing body's next meeting scheduled for May 2003 in Washington.

Based on the material prepared by the secretariat including a revised version of the charter, the discussion of international organization status at the May meeting saw progress to the point where the governing body felt that it had enough understanding of the issues and sufficient background material to seek the views of the of the GDN community at large. Recall that the original governance structure for GDN had emerged from a worldwide, electronic discussion designed to capture the views of the diverse community that GDN sought to reach. The governing body felt strongly that the same degree of participation would be important before any decision on the issue of international organization status could be finalized. Accordingly, the secretariat organized a global electronic discussion in early July 2003.

The response was overwhelmingly in favour of GDN moving to international organization status – almost 95 per cent of those responding supported the idea. Moreover, this discussion attracted more contributors than the initial discussion on GDN's governance structure (an increase of more than 20 per cent) and a greater share was from developing/transition countries (more than 75 per cent compared with 50 per cent for the initial discussion). Based in part on this very strong showing of support for international organization status, the governing body decided by electronic vote at the end of July to move forward with the idea of transforming GDN into an international organization. Many issues remain to be resolved, including finalization of the charter and the selection of signatories, but the process is now underway.

This completes the early history of GDN and outlines the efforts undertaken to ensure that the foundations for this new global association were, and continue to be, laid through a highly participatory process. The ultimate goal was to establish an inclusive and flexible organization capable of responding to the great diversity of communities that it serves. Hopefully, the reader is now in a position to assess whether the insights of the New Institutional Economics – path dependency, the recognition that individuals with the same goals will not necessarily arrive at the same decisions, the need for flexibility in a world of constant change, and so on – have been adequately reflected in the original design of GDN and its subsequent evolution.

GDN in action

In addition to its own process of institution building, the Global Development Network seeks to build the capacity of partner institutions. These partners represent an essential link to local realities and provide the tools necessary to respond to the process of economic change. By building capacity to undertake high-quality research, GDN provides an essential building block in the formulation of responsive and effective policy. Thus, GDN attempts to address two of the shortcomings identified by North. First, GDN's support and capacity building efforts contribute towards deepening our understanding of developing and transition country polities. Research provides the cornerstone on which our perceptions of reality in these countries are based. Second, since our notions of reality change from one economy to the next and over time, learning needs to be a constant and ongoing process. Consequently, GDN's activities support research and learning as an ongoing process that needs to be constantly adapting and improving.

In deciding what activities to support, GDN considered what gaps needed to be filled by asking: what do research institutes in developing and transition countries want in order to produce better research and better policy? What are donors currently supplying and how effective is it? What do local policy makers want from the research community in order to improve policy formulation and effectiveness? Answers to these questions came from specially designed surveys and evaluations mostly undertaken under GDN auspices.

To answer the first question, GDN undertook a survey of 500 research institutes throughout the developing/transition world. The survey revealed a strong interest in an annual conference, better access to data, and more funding opportunities. Interestingly, the vast majority of respondents claimed to seek to influence policy. In fact, 74 per cent of respondents indicated that on a scale from 1 (not at all important) to 7 (extremely important), influencing policy was ranked 5 or higher (GDN 1999). Thus, GDN's goal of supporting research that influences policy makers is shared by many research institutes throughout the developing world. The survey also revealed the considerable access that research institutes in all parts of the world have to e-mail and the Internet, a fact that led to GDN's reliance on the Internet (GDNet) as a key tool for sharing information and building a worldwide community of researchers.

To answer the second question, GDN undertook an empirical assessment of support for research provided by the donor community (GDN 2000b). Among other findings, this report noted that most research funding is for specific topics, with the topics being identified by the funding agency. Since a large part of research in developing and transition countries is funded by the international donor community, it follows that a large part of the research agenda in the South is set by donors in the North. This is unlikely to stimulate good research or build capacity, and indicates that there is a need to support indigenous research initiatives. The same report also identified a phenomenon that can best be described as 'proposal mania' where significant effort is allocated to the review of proposals for funding, but little support is provided during the implementation of the research when the scope for capacity building is greatest.

Finally, a survey undertaken by the World Bank of 271 policy makers in 36 developing and transition countries found that 68 per cent wanted more input from local researchers (unpublished World Bank Survey 1998). Even if high-quality research is produced by international agencies or scholars in the OECD countries, southern policy makers are well aware of the significance of the local institutional context and the key role that this plays in the success or failure of policy implementation. North's assertion that effective policy implementation depends on the accuracy of perceptions about reality has, apparently, already been internalized by many local policy makers.

These surveys provided an indication of the current capacity gaps in the area of development research and policy formulation and were the basis, in concert with widespread informal consultation, for the selection of activities to be supported by GDN. The following subsections describe several (but not all) GDN activities, providing a flavour of GDN's approach to building research capacity and bridging the gap between research and policy.

The Regional Research Competitions

One of GDN's principle activities is to fund research competitions within each of the seven participating regions. Support for these competitions meets two goals: on the one hand, it provides an activity that builds the operation and procedures of partner institutions; on the other hand, the capacity of developing and transition country researchers to undertake policy-oriented research is also developed. These annual and semi-annual events represent an open, competitive allocation of funds to which all interested parties can apply. The intended outcome of the competitions is to further build regional research capacity and elevate the quality of research produced.

The competitive process prompts actors to improve their skills and abilities. The competitions serve to build not only the capacity of individual researchers but that of regional institutions capable of engaging in and sponsoring quality research. While funds are provided by GDN, regional research institutes are responsible for organizing and carrying out the competitions. This begins with selection of research topics. Typically, the regional research institute selects five to six topic areas and sets a timeline for papers to be submitted. This is in sharp contrast to the practice of many donors and puts the regional research networks firmly in control.

While competition raises overall quality, there is, however, a danger that the strongest, most well-established research institutions and experienced researchers will inevitably win the competition to the exclusion of those truly in need of support. This tension between quality research and capacity building runs through all GDN activities. It has led GDN to support a variety of activities with differing emphasis on high-quality research and capacity building in an effort to strike a balance between the two. For example, funds have been earmarked for countries in South East Europe and Central America in an attempt to reach less well-known and less developed institutions. Also, a special effort is made to give opportunities to younger researchers and link them to more experienced researchers. This can be done quite effectively at the review stage when the selection committee might be dealing with as many as seventy different proposals in a single round and can match more and less experienced researchers interested in a common topic.

The regional research competitions also provide a convenient vehicle for supplying another ingredient essential to successful capacity building: research expertise. Notwithstanding a rigorous, competitive and well refereed review process, research funds can still be wasted if the researchers, especially the younger and less experienced ones, receive no support as they conduct their research. Rather than promoting 'proposal mania', the research competitions all rely on mid-term reviews to provide guidance and mid-course redirection if necessary. The recent review conducted by the East European Network at CERGE-EI, for example, subjected all proposals awarded funding in last year's round to the comments and critiques of internal and external experts. Support from experts includes in-depth knowledge of the subject matter being explored and significant skill and experience in carrying out research. This combination of funds *and* research expertise appears to be crucial for successful capacity building.

The Global Research Projects

The Global Research Project provides another example of an effort that seeks to balance the need for quality research and capacity building and again features the critical combination of financial and human support. As with the Regional Research Competitions, much of the administration of the project is devolved to the regional networks in the interests of capacity building, but this time the topic is chosen centrally, albeit with considerable consultation. This capacity-building vehicle responds to one of Douglass North's principal concerns, namely, that we often develop universal models based on the understanding of one economy at one point in time, whereas different economies will function differently and change over time. Global Research Projects are well suited to address this concern because, as we shall see, they involve case-study research in numerous countries. Building understanding at the country level means that policy makers can then go on to identify where countries share similarities and learn useful lessons from other countries around the world. This has the added benefit of encouraging networking among researchers from all over the globe.

The first Global Research Project, 'Explaining Growth', extended a project that was initiated by AERC to explore the disappointing growth experience of Africa. Completed in 2003, the project sought to provide a comprehensive examination of growth experiences throughout the developing world, examining the growth experience in six regions: sub-Saharan Africa; the Middle East and North Africa; South Asia; East Asia; Latin America and the Caribbean; and Eastern Europe and the Former Soviet Union. While the project explores growth patterns around the globe, research focuses on the unique experience of different countries. This effort is intended to deepen our understanding of the unique circumstances and paths adopted by individual countries.

Key to this effort is the facilitation of high-quality work by local authors in partnership with each other and with development specialists from around the world. This reflects a belief that the understanding necessary to guide countries' destinies must be informed by local knowledge of a global calibre. To this end, more than 100 researchers from all over the world congregated at a workshop immediately after the Third Annual Global Development Conference in Rio de Janeiro in December 2001 to share the results of their country studies. This is when networking and capacity building truly come to the fore.

The Global Research Project puts primary emphasis on the importance of context specificity. As North highlights, different historical and cultural backgrounds, not to mention the ongoing process of economic change, mean that no single model of growth can fit all countries. Instead of relying on cross-country regressions which seek to establish universal models, the project relies on country case studies. At the same time, by creating a network of researchers, it allows for the sharing of lessons, specific experiences and methodological approaches across countries.

Linking research and policy

More recently, GDN has begun work in a third area that strives to make better use of research to produce well-informed and effective policy. It springs from the realization that quality research offers a key to understanding the world we live in. At the same time, policy provides the instrument with which we respond to this world and tackle the challenges that it presents. However, between research and policy there is often only a tenuous link which means that policy formulation is seldom informed by quality research and the contribution of research in the policy process remains weak.

It is possible to point to a number of factors that account for this weakness. Policy makers often fail to commission appropriate research or they may ignore and subvert results they are given. On the other side of the equation, researchers may pursue their own interests that do not always coincide with policy imperatives. It is likely that both sides will fail to communicate effectively regarding their activities. This is obviously an undesirable state of affairs since research institutes surveyed by GDN claim that they want to influence policy, and policy makers in developing and transition countries claim that they want more input from local researchers. Moreover, as North has argued, the likelihood that policy realizes its intended purpose depends on the accuracy of perceptions regarding the real world in which policy unfolds.

In response to this situation, GDN, along with other concerned partners, initiated a 'Bridging Research and Policy' programme intended to link research and policy. The main goal of the project will be to identify case studies where research has contributed effectively to the policy formulation process. This project will help identify approaches that could improve the research–policy linkage and broaden our understanding of how and when research can make a difference in the policy-making process and meet the needs of decision makers.

The project focuses on capacity building to help policy makers identify, commission and absorb appropriate research while assisting researchers to improve their ability to communicate findings. To this end a number of initial activities have been undertaken including three workshops at the University of Warwick in July 2001, at GDN in October 2002, and at the Cairo Conference in January 2003. In addition, a website devoted to the project (RAPnet) has been established. Based on initial work conducted in 2002, a work programme was prepared and a call for proposals was made in July 2003. Over 360 proposals were received, an indication of the enormous interest in this topic.

One major area of focus in the call for proposals is for case studies that explore how research has been successful in influencing policy formulation. This emphasis on effective policy implementation reflects recognition of the constraints posed by path dependency and context-specificity necessitating a large number of case studies. It is envisioned that work in this area will serve to build our ability to effectively link research and policy. The end result will be research which addresses the challenges facing policy makers, and policy making which effectively addresses the world we live in.

Looking to the future

In this chapter we have tried to convey some of the thinking that went into the design of GDN itself and into the selection of the activities to be supported. We hope the reader now has a firm basis to respond to the question posed in our opening paragraph. Readers will undoubtedly find instances where they would have followed a different course simply because different backgrounds will result in different decisions even if the objective is the same. Douglass North's point is well taken. That said, GDN is now itself subject to the laws of path dependency. Therefore, in thinking how you would change GDN, keep in mind where GDN has come from and where it now stands. This implies that suggestions for change that can be accommodated within the established framework will be much easier to implement than those that call for a return to the drawing board, and suggestions for new activities will probably be the easiest to implement.

To help crystallize your thoughts, we offer in this closing section four key factors governing much of the decision making to date. The first two deal with GDN's main objectives: building capacity and influencing policy. And the second two respond to North's admonition for flexibility in a constantly changing world and for attention to the experience of different economies at different times.

First, an important issue in designing programmes to build research capacity in developing and transition countries is the tension between realizing high-quality research in the short run and building capacity for the long run. The various activities supported by GDN such as the Regional Research Competitions and the Global Research Project resolve this issue in different ways. There is no guarantee that either is right and other vehicles may well be preferable. A central and common element, however, is the combination of financial and human support.

Second, understanding the process through which research influences policy and finding ways to strengthen that link is high on GDN's agenda but an extraordinarily difficult issue to tackle in any systematic way. In such circumstances, case studies emerge as the obvious research tool. There may well be other methods that should demand our attention and there are of course alternative ways of conducting case studies.

Third, Douglass North tells us that change is incremental. But he also says that change is constantly occurring. Therefore, the relevant question here is whether the governance structure of GDN allows sufficient flexibility to modify GDN itself or change the activities it supports. We offered two examples of GDN's flexibility to date: namely, its effort to ensure a multidisciplinary approach to the understanding of development by, among other things, changing the composition of the governing body; and its exploration of alternative legal structures as it readies itself for its move to a developing country. It is for the reader to judge whether these examples provide sufficient evidence that GDN will be able to adjust to future changes in the environment.

Last but not least, GDN has taken the view that local, context-specific knowledge is critical to the success of local policy making. Knowledge flowing from the developed countries to the developing ones and across developing countries clearly has an important role to play. By itself this knowledge can never be sufficient. Building local capacity to address local problems is at the centre of GDN's rationale. While GDN sees the local policy maker as the primary recipient of the new knowledge emerging from that local capacity, such knowledge can also inform the international development community and, as local material accumulates, lead to an improved understanding of development at a more general level.

In looking to its own future and development, GDN has drawn on the new institutionalism of Professor North regarding the importance of building flexible institutions and the need to incorporate ongoing learning from one location to the next and over time. These are keys that will enable developing and transition countries to respond effectively to the challenges they face. GDN has tried to embody these principles in its own formation and in its work with partner institutions. We hope this will be borne out in activities such as the Regional Research Competitions, the Global Research Projects, efforts to bridge research and policy and steps to support multidisciplinary research. It is up to the reader to assess how well we have put North's theory into practice and whether the path we have chosen will indeed build capacity to undertake learning, promote effective policy and ultimately lead us to a better world.

References

Annan, Kofi (1999) 'Message to the First Conference of the Global Development Network' *Bridging Knowledge and Development*, Inaugural Global Development Network Conference, Bonn, December 5.

GDN – Global Development Network (1999) *Researching the Researchers*. Available online at http://www.gdnet.org/pdf2/surveys/researching_researchers.pdf.

GDN – Global Development Network (2000a) *Governance Structure*. Available online at http://www.gdnet.org/about_gdn/history/statement_gov.html.

GDN – Global Development Network (2000b) *Report of the High Level Committee*. Available online at http://www.gdnet.org/pdf2/surveys/high_level_com_report.pdf.

GDN – Global Development Network (2001) *The Promotion of Research in All Social Sciences*. Available online at http://www.gdnet.org/pdf2/policy_docs/promotion_ research_social_science.pdf.

Harriss, John (2001) 'The Case for Cross-disciplinary Approaches in International Development', Presentation to the governing body of the Global Development Network, May 14–15.

Jackson, Cecile (2001) 'Disciplining Gender', Presentation to the governing body of the Global Development Network, May 14–15.

North, Douglass (1990) *Institutions, Institutional Change and Economic Performance*. Cambridge: Cambridge University Press.

North, Douglass (2000) *Institutions and the Performance of Economies over time*. Saint Louis: Washington University.

White, Howard (2001) 'Combining Quantitative and Qualitative Approaches in Poverty Analysis', Presentation to the governing body of the Global Development Network, May 14–15.

World Bank (1998) 'Survey of Policymakers'. Internal document. Washington, DC: The World Bank.

8 Networking across borders

South Asian Research Network (SARN) on gender, law and governance

Shirin M. Rai

Introduction

Key institutions and actors in the international knowledge networks are too often assumed to be development agencies, foundations, think tanks and consultancy firms, as well as individual experts and academics who are engaged with these institutions. This is evident also from the way knowledge networks are spoken of interchangeably as transnational policy research networks. Much of the literature on 'knowledge' and 'knowledge networks' is therefore framed within the context of engagement with institutions of power whether at the international, global or national levels. Such a focus emerges from dominant discourses of power/knowledge as well as the economic underpinnings of the 'knowledge industry'. References to the agency of subaltern actors and institutions, and to the work of academics who are engaged with these institutions, remain few and far between.

This chapter focuses on a different approach to networks – a subaltern perspective – by examining the setting up, and the early functioning, of the South Asia Research Network (SARN) on Gender, Law and Governance. I have been involved in setting up this organisation and the analysis of knowledge networks in this chapter reflects this experience. The chapter will reflect very briefly upon the construction of discourses about 'knowledge' and 'knowledge-makers' and issues of access that emerge as a result of these discourses and practice. It will then set out the experience of setting up SARN and the issues that the founding members of the organisation have been dealing with – examining our diverse starting points and political commitments. The chapter reflects upon three aspects of a 'politics of network(s)-ing': the politics of framing; the politics of process; and the politics of outcomes. The borders that we need to be aware of, it concludes, are not just national borders but borders of power.

The feminist organisations which are partners in SARN are largely research organisations. These are: Centre for Women's Development Studies (India), Intermediate Technology Group (ITDG) (Sri Lanka), Forum for Women, Law and Development (FWLD) (Nepal), Ain o Sailesh Kendra (ASK) (Bangladesh), National University of Juridical Sciences (India), Human Rights Study Centre, University of Peshawar (Pakistan), Hamdard Law University (Pakistan). Some of these organisations focus on legal issues. They provide legal aid to individual women and lobby governments on specific legal issues. Others work on a variety of women-related issues such as employment, violence and security. Almost all combine research with activism at both the grassroots and policy level.

Agents of knowledge, knowledge as power

A discussion of an 'archaeology of knowledge' needs to reflect upon both the material boundaries of epistemological power as well as the 'repertoires of collective action' in defiance of these boundaries (Cohen and Rai 2000). Knowledge and 'knowledge-makers' then can be acknowledged as those engaged in historical transmissions as well as those in defiance of dominant epistemological flows of power. Further, a subaltern perspective on knowledge and knowledge-makers would, in line with critical feminist theory, 'reverse the traditional relation of dependence, deriving criteria of rationality and knowledge from substantive ideals of solidarity and community, rather than vice versa' (Braaten 1995: 139).

Feminist and subaltern epistemologies

Much has been written about how traditional epistemologies exclude women as subjects and agents in knowledge production (Kemp and Squires 1997; Barwa and Rai 2002). Feminist critics have focused on how epistemological frameworks have been constitutive of the binaries of rational/emotional, universal/particular, objectivity/subjectivity. As Harstock has pointed out, 'the vision of the ruling class (or gender) structures the material relations in which all parties are forced to participate, and therefore cannot be dismissed as simply false' (1997: 153). However, feminist work has also been done on a more assertive project. As Alison Jaggar has pointed out, this has meant rethinking the relationships between these binaries so that the historical identification of emotions, particularity, and subjectivity with the subordinate or the subaltern is challenged by suggesting the mutually constitutive nature of these binaries (1997). Feminists have not only disrupted frameworks of epistemological power by challenging the socially constructed binaries, but have also developed what came to be called 'standpoint theory'. Drawing upon historical materialist accounts of knowledge, standpoint theory argued that the sexual division of labour provides two distinct epistemological perspectives. It has been argued that focusing on a standpoint allows us to examine 'the real relations among human beings as inhuman' and points to the historicity of relationship, which can be liberatory (Kemp and Squires 1997: 143). While this materialist account of epistemological power disrupts the dominant discourse of objective, rational and universal knowledge, it does not acknowledge fully the divided and dislocated nature of the Subject. As Gayatri Spivak has pointed out, while an economic mode of life might determine the class position of the Subject, it does not encapsulate the Subject, whose 'parts are not continuous or coherent with each other' but are fragmented and contradictory (Spivak 1988: 276; also see Liddle and Rai 1998).

Feminist concerns about dominant epistemologies are echoed in radical historiography. The starting point of Subaltern Studies lies in its critique of dominant historiography and anthropology: 'entire field of transgressions, disorder and violence remains outside the anthropologist's privileged domains of enquiry ... [who creates] order by eliminating the chaos that the introduction of the subject might create' (Das 1989: 310). By examining the stories of the marginalised through their struggles that were not recounted in the histories of dominant elites, the Subaltern Studies school makes an important contribution in 'establishing the centrality of the historical moment of rebellion in understanding the subalterns as subjects of their own histories' (Das 1989: 312). However, it is also critical to acknowledge that the Subject of colonial subaltern history is also a colonial Subject. The embeddedness within and engagement with the dominant legal and political frameworks of power at the same time show history as a 'moment of defiance [as it is] to construct the form of legal-rational domination' (Das 1989: 314).[1] However, while a subaltern perspective allows us insights into the Subject position of the subaltern in the moment of defiance of the dominant power relations, it also often imbues the Subject with qualities that sit ill at ease with his/her marginality. There remains an unanswerable tension in the dialectic of empowered and disempowered Subject which Subaltern Studies tries to answer by privileging agency at the same moment as it reminds us of the structural marginality of the Subject.

Those who were involved in setting up the South Asian Research Network on Gender, Law and Governance approached the project after reflecting upon some of these debates.[2] It was hoped that this network would facilitate a conversation across borders in a region where such cross-border contact has been largely the preserve of political elites. Through SARN new methodologies of agenda setting for research could also be developed which are not predominantly led by the funders but which emerge from the discussions of participants engaged in feminist research in Bangladesh, India, Nepal, Pakistan and Sri Lanka. And, finally, the hope was to keep under review the relations between the researchers and civil society, the researchers and the funders and between researchers and the end-product users. At every stage the acknowledgement of the power as well as a defiance of epistemological, political and historical boundaries was seen as critical.

Knowledge networks, nodal communications and democratic norms

If 'knowledge' is a contested term so is our understanding of networks. According to Manuel Castells, 'A network is a set of interconnected nodes' and 'within a given network flows have no distance, or the same distance between nodes'. Networks are, then, open structures 'able to expand without limits, integrate new nodes as long as they are able to communicate within the network, namely as long as they share the same communication codes'(Castells 1996: 470). Such an understanding of networks allows us, one could argue, to evidence both the democratic impulse of networks and also their exclusionary power. The language of politics and the politics of language of networks becomes critical here. Expansion and integration go hand in hand with recognition of 'the same communication codes'. The questions we need to ask here are: expansion to and for what? Integration with and into what? And how can communication codes be made more accessible, or how are these used to assert the dominance of these codes over others? In sum, how do networks legitimise and/or challenge flows of power? This is a difficult issue at the local level, but more so when we consider global networks operating on an epistemological terrain reflecting the material power of global capitalism.

In such a context, do networks provide an integrative function by 'linking up' the sites of dominant knowledges as well as the organisations and individuals that seek and/or obtain recognition within this communicative field? The expansion of networks, in this context, would also be the further normalisation of the dominant discourses of power – the example of Global Development Network (GDN) set up by the World Bank comes to mind here. The 'gateway to development knowl- edge',[3] through the incorporation of myriad local and global networks, then attempts to systematise the knowledges generated by the individual and organisa- tional actors that make up these networks. In doing so it seeks to impose a rationality that gives precedence to the 'conception of knowledge rather than ideals of community'. Expansion of networks is then integrated into the dominant development policy framework which legitimises the policy framework and ensures the communicative codes are not challenged.

Further, such systematising framework of knowledge integration also casts a light upon the (lack of) distance between different nodes within the network. From agenda setting to funding, the nodal density of Northern based organisations such as the UK Department for International Development (DFID), London-based think tanks like the Overseas Development Institute (ODI) or the Ford Foundation is far greater within integrative knowledge networks than of other constituent members. As Castells points out, 'network morphology is also a source of dramatic reorganisation of power relations. Switches connecting the networks ... are the privileged instruments of power' (1996: 471). These switches can be seen as the nodes of concentration of economic and political power, which can be used simply as a threat or be operationalised to deflect and undermine the defiance of the dom- inant communicative codes. The distance between nodes then cannot be assumed to be the same, and indeed reflects the material relations within which networks are embedded. However, as Sperling, Marx Ferree and Risman have argued, the resources that networks can garner are not only financial, 'but may also include access, reputation, influence and other intangible benefits' (2001: 1159). Indeed, reputation could be a resource as well as a marker of particular moral politics. This could lead to the recognition of the world of the 'moral entrepreneurs'[4] and allow subaltern networks to approach this world with 'their eyes wide open'. While at times the power of privilege conflicts or competes with subaltern local networks and activities, at others access to tangible and intangible resources of transnational networks supports particular mobilisations and helps inform and/or expand the effectiveness of local networks. The desire of networks to secure their own reputa- tion can therefore also be a resource for local networks.

These issues have been critical in the discussions leading towards the setting up of SARN. As outlined in the network terms of reference, the

> purpose of this network is three-fold. First, to allow a conversation regarding gender and governance to take place between organisations and researchers working in this area across national borders. This is important to share experiences both positive and salutary as women's groups and researchers make headway in individual countries. Second, to facilitate and strengthen the links between different groups within each participating country. This will allow for regular contact between researchers and activists for example, and consolidate the different but inter-related work on issues of gender and governance. Third, through these processes of conversing and networking we will undertake collaborative research on specific areas and aim to arrive at a regional perspective on issues of gender and governance.
>
> (SARN 2002)

All this occurs within a geopolitical context, which is diverse as well as historically anxious. The network comprises the already existing feminist research groups in the five participating countries of South Asia, but in their new configuration within SARN. Thus only elements of the existing research groups that are working in the area of law and governance make part of the network. Does this reflect the same distance between the network funders and the network partners?

The area of research (agenda setting) within SARN formed part of intense discussions. The Norwegian Agency for Development Cooperation (NORAD), the initial funding body supporting SARN, has a declared interest in the promotion of women's human rights and would have liked SARN to focus on this area. However, in order to define women's human rights a communicative code was needed that was decipherable by all the partners. If we read off the discourse of human rights from the UN Declaration, for example, many within the network would be placed at a much greater distance from that starting point than others would be. As the conversations about women's human rights in South Asia are informed by religions, political histories and specific gendered regimes of the law and of civil society, NORAD's broad commitment to human rights discourse was challenged by the experience of feminist activism and research in South Asia. The emphasis on law, in its broadest sense, then replaced a more pointed reference to human rights. A critical, subaltern discourse on the law and rights then became possible, as did the expansion of the communicative codes with which to converse across boundaries.

The 'diffusion of networking logic substantially modifies the operation and outcomes in processes of production, experience, power, and culture', writes Castells (1996: 469). In paying attention to this networking logic we can thus approach the process of production of knowledges from different and overlapping standpoints, ever aware of the material inequalities built into such production and at the same time of the defiance of the constraints imposed by these. More positively still, through this ongoing critical dialogue we encounter vocabularies that might enhance the quality of conversations, expand the lexicon of feminist writing, and that might constructively interact with each other and 'emerge significantly altered' (Sperling, Marx Ferree and Risman 2001: 1159). The permeability of communicative codes is thus moot here. However, embeddedness of networks is also reflected in the site of these conversations. I have already referred to the difficult geopolitical terrain upon which SARN is located. In the next section I wish to explore the meso-territory which SARN occupies, between the local and the global.

SARN as a regional network: working across political borders

Regional networks are important arenas for not only conversing across borders but also for doing so in contexts that are more immediate and familiar to all involved. The strength drawn from regional collaborations can feed back into both national and global participation of women's groups. The starting point for SARN was an acknowledgement of the common history of the region, and at the same time of the significant resistance to border crossing through state regulation.

Regionalisation from below

While the languages of nationalism and women's activism have long helped in creating communicative channels across borders in South Asia, keeping these channels open has not always been easy. It was also important to acknowledge that many activists and researchers that would form part of a regional network were already operating on a much wider global terrain. Globalisation in this case formed the backdrop of this regional network. If, we had to ask, our partners were already participating in global policy fora, what would be the purpose of a regional network? It was evident that the political debates on globalisation within the five countries involved in SARN had led to some communicative linkages on the ground. The 1990s saw a growing concern about women's work as well as women's political representation in all five countries. There was also some evidence that internationally supported strategies of women's empowerment, for example mainstreaming gender issues through institutional initiatives such as national machineries for the advancement of women, were also providing women's movements with a recognisable framework on the ground (UN 1996; Rai 2003). The Beijing Conference also pointed to the importance of global networking on the one hand, and the difference among women on the other. The spread of technology, especially e-mail, allowed for building upon the contacts made at international fora, but the lack of hardware on the ground also suggested the limitations of this strategy for networking.[5] Finally, the question of power differentials in global networking as well as national politics was also an important starting point for us. Would a regional, meso-level articulation of issues allow SARN to contribute to democratising debates at both the global and national levels, as it arguably has in other parts of the world?

Blacklock has argued that regional economic integration in Central America through the Central American Common Market poses questions for women at the regional as well as the national levels. It then allows for the regional Foro de Mujeres Para la Integracion (Central American Economic Integration Women's Forum) to engage the institutions of the common market as well as national states in debate (Blacklock 2001). No such regional integration exists in South Asia. Despite the framework of SARC (South Asian Regional Cooperation), South Asian states have not been able to overcome their considerable political differences to address the issues of globalisation through developing regional perspectives. While all the five countries involved in SARN are members of SARC, we could not therefore build on already operative regional perspectives. At the inaugural conference of SARN in August 2002,[6] members discussed whether developing a regional perspective on specific issues of law and governance might provide us with political resources to intervene more effectively in global fora and therefore to more effectively address the issue of power differentials among women's groups from the North and South. As Blacklock has argued in the context of CACM, 'Central American nation-states see in regionalization some potential to augment their power'(2001). SARN could contribute to the political processes of regionalisation in South Asia through creating common communicative codes, based upon co-operative research work, which might further enhance the common imaginings of/for the region. SARN could also contribute towards the augmentation of the relative power position of South Asian women's groups within international organisations through development of such a regional perspective on gender law and governance.

Democratic structures and practice: the setting up of SARN

Working together across boundaries – national and regional – poses distinct questions of democratic practice. Many issues of democratic structure and functioning of the organisation, together with the focus of its research, were discussed among SARN members at the inaugural conference. The structure of SARN reflects our attempts to address the issue of power differentials.

The network works through three principal bodies drawn from within itself: partner organisations, the conference committee and the co-ordination group. *Partners* have a commitment to participate in the network for a minimum of three years. The partners propose, discuss and assess the research agenda of the network at the annual conferences. They also propose specific projects to be undertaken within the agreed research agenda. This ensures that the responsibility and the power to shape the comparative work of the network rests not with the funders, or even the co-ordination group, but with partner organisations already involved in women's groups and contributing to debates in individual countries. The funders will thus be 'offering opportunities for … networking' but less so 'models for effective local action' (Sperling, Marx Ferree and Risman 2001: 1160), which will emerge from discussions and conversations of the partner organisations. I will address how the question of competing research and political agendas might be answered in the concluding part of this paper.

The *conference committee* of SARN comprises the partners who will host the conference in a particular year, and the co-ordination group. The membership of this group will therefore rotate annually, with the co-ordination group providing continuity. The committee will also provide the local point of contact for that year, and will be responsible for publishing and disseminating the proceedings and outcomes of the conference. One of the strengths of this model of organisation is that the conference committee will be able to draw upon the expertise and knowledge of local women's groups and to invite them to attend the conference. The potential for the extension of the network would also be enhanced. Such a rotation in the work of SARN in this management model will also allow for the sharing and transferability of technologies and skills. An important aspect of this rotation is that it addresses regional sensitivities. Dominance of bigger countries, who also have greater resources, will be avoided in terms of management of contact between partners.

The *co-ordination group* will continue to help secure funding and co-ordinate the projects of the network, provide a steer on the crossover between the theoretical and empirical elements of research and their policy relevance, and in the initial phase of SARN manage its website. A *panel of advisers* has also been established, which includes academics, activists and policy-makers from South Asia but also from other countries. The panel members will publicise the work of SARN and will also help to further international links of SARN. The role of the co-ordination group is both critical and sensitive in the organisation. The members of the co-ordination group are all, as yet, based in universities in the UK (Warwick). They also have the most direct contact with the funders on the one hand and the partners on the other. Issues of accountability of the co-ordinators will no doubt arise during the functioning of the network. While the group is a resource for partners on the one hand, it also occupies a more privileged position (switch/node) than the partners. However, the resources of the group are also based upon the co-operation of the partners and of their existing national networks. The partners in this case, while looking to enhancing their credibility at the regional levels, are already resource-stable organisations. This dialectic of privilege and dependence was discussed during the inaugural conference. The partners were convinced of the importance of having a co-ordination group outside South Asia to act as a catalyst as well as the organisational hub for SARN. The political situation on the ground, as well as the existing responsibilities of partners in their local spaces meant that none of the partners wished to dilute the role of the co-ordination group. However, the co-ordination group also suggested that eventually its membership needs to widen and change in the interest of stabilising the organisation.

The various bodies comprising SARN work through not only the annual conferences, but more routinely through the SARN website.[7] The website occupies a unique place in the structure of SARN – a virtual office, the site of the various databases developed by SARN, and a communicative space. In order to create a communicative space within which all partners feel empowered, an extensive questionnaire seeking their views was circulated prior to the inaugural conference.

The development of the website thus reflects the priorities of the partners and extends the possibility of developing democratic practice through working in a safe space.

Does such an organisational structure and methodologies of working together make SARN a non-hierarchical network? This is a difficult issue to address. As a research network one could argue it already occupies an elite position within the region. While there are national women's networks, these are largely activists or at least self-consciously occupy a dual space of activism and policy-oriented research. The partners either occupy this dual space (CWDS, New Delhi) or are clearly academic institutions involved in research (Human Rights Study Centre, Peshawar University). Second, the structure of SARN, though conceived of on a horizontal plane, is already marked by difference between the relative nodal power of the funders and the co-ordination group and the partners. Third, while the agenda setting process is envisaged as a 'bottom-up' project, it is as yet diffi- cult to predict whether the broadening of this agenda to address issues which the funders/co-ordinators or even some of the partners have not anticipated (a cross border peace initiative, for example) will result in conflicts of interests, and how these will be resolved. After the inaugural conference one can, however, say that the beginnings have been positive – different research agendas were discussed openly and passionately and a way was found to resolve issues of precedence and focus. Finally, there is the question of relations with nation-states and with global institutions. On the one hand, there is an expectation that national policy networks will be accessed by partner organisations with augmented regional authority gained through comparative work within SARN. On the other hand, SARN also expects to develop critical and subaltern perspectives on issues concerning gender law and governance, which might not support such an engagement with govern- mental organisations. This tension will need to be addressed, if not resolved, if the network is to be sustained over time.

'Critical and creative' research agendas

Much has now been written about the engagement of women's and feminist groups in the debates about globalisation as well as engagement with global eco- nomic and social institutions (Rai 2002; O'Brien *et al.* 2000; Marchand and Runyan 2000; Peterson and Runyan 1999). The literature has not only covered issues of discursive and economic power relations between women's organisa- tions and global institutions, but also the changing relations and differences among women's groups and movements. The process of engagement itself has been reviewed within the context of issues of access to policy-making institutions, agenda shifts, and the resources available to various groups in this process. I have argued, for example, that 'Attempts to leap-frog the nation-state by approaching multilateral organisations can also result in the undermining of democratic poli- tics or struggles towards a democratic politics on the ground' (2002: 176). Often such undermining occurs as a result of lack of resources of time, technology and money. NGOs often find themselves committing to the agendas and programmes of funders without enough discussion about the politics or processes attached to the funding in order to pursue goals of organisational sustainability (Cohen 2000; O'Brien *et al.* 2000). This lack of time to focus on the politics of projects becomes more difficult if organisations are working across borders, and do not have the technological and financial support to do so – project-based funding imposes a disciplinary framework which is often not conducive to democratic practice. These were also some of the issues discussed at the inaugural conference.

At the conference it was decided that SARN would contribute to the debate about the relevance of regional economic linkages on the one hand and the nature of these linkages on the other. These debates will necessarily include the question of peace across borders, as attempts to focus on economic and trade relations in favour of boundary issues between countries have thus far been unsuccessful. Issues of conflict and security then would form an important element of SARN's research and policy work. Definitions of conflict and security would have to be explored and expanded to include violence against women within and between communities, food security and women's contribution towards resolving these conflicts through both political participation in community organisations and through participation in food production and knowledge creation to support this role. Another area where we were able to map regional policy transfers from global/local perspectives was that of addressing women's under-representation in political institutions of the countries of South Asia. National machineries for women's advancements exist in all participating countries. Conversations across boundaries between members of these machineries as well as women's groups engaging with these machineries have already occurred on a regular basis and there is some evidence that these conversations can contribute towards a regional understanding of the constraints as well as the benefits of these institutions. Quotas for women in local institutions as well as national institutions is another area where there is some cross-fertilisation. The Indian legislation in this regard has led to debates about the efficacy of quotas as a means of addressing gender inequalities in panchayats in Pakistan, for example. A sharing of lessons learned from different experiences of a similar strategy could be a useful starting point for a South Asian contribution to this debate globally. Local governance then formed the third research focus for the first phase of SARN's work (SARN 2002). SARN will be the catalyst for exploring regional perspectives in these areas through the research of partners.

Network sustainability: the challenges before SARN

Scholars have identified three types of relations that go towards making a stable network and are crucial for the sustainability of social action. First, interpersonal networks, which facilitate recruitment and participation; second, links between individuals and organisations based upon their multiple allegiances; and third, inter-organisational links that allow for a degree of trust between the participants in a network (Bosco 2001). I would add here the importance of trust between participants and funders. In the coming together of SARN all these four have been operative, but also need to be continually nurtured and critically assessed.

Interpersonal networks have been crucial in the setting up of SARN. The crossing of national boundaries, which is at the heart of the network, was made possible through the members of the co-ordination group establishing close professional and then friendship ties. Two members are originally from India, one from Pakistan and one from Oslo. A common interest in issues of gender and governance was the basis of this relationship, as has been a commitment to the development of a regional perspective on these issues. Personal histories for transnational forced family migrations across borders at the time of the partition of India have contributed to this commitment (Rai 1997). Involvement in national politics as well as in women's movements has also secured interpersonal networks upon which SARN has been built. Academic contacts as well as collaborative projects between institutions and individuals have nurtured existing networks and allowed SARN a credibility base critical in the establishment of a new project. Finally, interpersonal networks have been used to draw upon the particular membership from among a rich tapestry of women's activist and research groups in South Asia. The challenge here is how to build upon these important interpersonal networks without personalising the long-term trajectory of the network. It would not do to create a sense of a club that hangs together through these interpersonal threads. We will also need to establish norms to guide us in the processes of expansion or reconfiguration of network membership. Issues of transparency and democratic accountability will have to be discussed and working procedures established in order for future recruitment to take place without necessarily the original interpersonal contacts being dominant.

The links between individuals and organisations within SARN are based upon their multiple allegiances – NORAD is not just funding SARN but a myriad of projects. While this project with its emphasis on governance is currently important to NORAD it might not remain so in the future. NORAD will need to communicate to the network the extent and length of its commitment, to help build resources which will be self-sustaining and engage SARN members in dialogue which will allow the development of sustainability strategies. SARN will need not only to establish its rules of organisation and functioning but also establish new organisational relationships through its individual members (partners, panel of advisers, new funding organisations). Though SARN Partners are committed to developing regional (rather than a comparative) research and political perspectives, this will not be easy. Most partners are grounded in their own countries. To gain a comparative perspective might be of great value and immediate relevance to the participating organisations. To engage in developing a regional perspective needs a further commitment of resources of time and effort, which will only gradually begin to bear fruit. Will the co-ordination group be able to provide a sustained focus to partners on this crucial issue? Its interpersonal skills and the trust of partners will be crucial here.

Different relationships will need to be secured through the development of trust. First, though partners have established a framsework of working with each other which is open, deliberative as well as respectful in order to sustain long-term collaboration, this will need to be nurtured – at a distance; face to face contact through annual conferences might prove critical here. Then there is the relationship between SARN members with NORAD, its initial funding body. How far can NORAD exercise agenda-setting influence without compromising the autonomy of the network? One example has already been provided about this in the context of human rights/governance focus of the network. Another area that we have struggled with is that of registration of the network. NORAD, together with many other northern funders, has strongly favoured that SARN be registered in a southern partner country, while being more sanguine about the registration of financial accounts in the north. While the political sensitivity necessitates this approach, responsibility and accountability issues for the co-ordinators of SARN make it imperative that institutional recognition through charity status recognition is gained in the UK where the co-ordination group is based. At the inaugural conference it was decided that SARN will not pursue a strategy of registration as a charity but instead it will concentrate on nurturing inter-organisational links between partners towards the sustainability of the network.

Conclusion: understanding the politics of knowledge networks

In this concluding section I reflect upon the politics of knowledge networks in three ways: first I examine the *politics of process* by assessing the possibilities of deliberative politics. Second, I examine the *politics of outcome* by reflecting upon issues of access and dangers of circularity of knowledge and policy networks. Finally, I examine the *politics of framing* by assessing the relevance of 'cosmopolitics' in understanding the global/local space that knowledge networks occupy.

Politics of process, outcome and framing

The politics of process is critical to building of trust and also to legitimising the outcomes of deliberation. Deliberative democracy has been put forward as one important model for addressing issues of process in decision-making (D'Entreves 2002; Elster 1998; Bohman and Rehg 1997). Deliberative democracy involves three elements – process, outcome and context. Its starting point seems to be that 'democracy revolves around the transformation rather than simply the aggregation of preferences' (Elster 1998: 1). Feminists have argued for a similar process/outcome based politics when they have spoken of 'rooting and shifting' or 'transversal politics', of situated deliberation leading to democratic outcomes as particularly suited to the way women do (or are predisposed to do) politics (Yuval-Davis 1997). Equality is a central theme in the deliberative democratic argument. Having reflected upon the need for equality of distance among network nodes on the one hand, and the undermining of this parity through inequality of resources on the other, developing a process of deliberation is indeed a challenge for transnational knowledge networks such as SARN.

A second challenge to the stability and sustainability of SARN emerges out of the politics of outcome. I have already referred to the tensions that might arise between the roles of activists and policy advisers for SARN partners, and also between the focus on a comparative and a regional perspective. We have also reflected upon issues of agenda-setting and the power differentials between funders and the funded. The question of access here is of particular relevance. The terms upon which access to policy-making institutions is granted is crucial. Following Rounaq Jahan, I have argued elsewhere that most of the 'initiatives taken by these institutions under pressure from women's groups are often "integrating" rather than "agenda-setting"'(Rai 2002). Further, increasing evidence of women's engagement with policy-making institutions, especially international financial institutions suggests that such engagements do not generally favour women. Not only are there significant differences between policy-making institutions and women's NGOs or networks, the differences among women's groups and networks also suggest that different actors bear differential costs of (non-)engagement with policy-networks. Not only do these issues of difference go towards building or undermining trust within network, they also point to the dangers of circularity. Working against the grain can be difficult; access to influence can exact the price of losing control of agendas for research and around which to build a political argument. In this context, the processes of deliberation can lend themselves to legitimisation of outcomes – whether agenda setting, research or the choice of political campaigns. The seduction of influence can blunt the critical edge of subaltern politics. While SARN seeks a serious engagement with policy networks, its agenda is also to challenge and shift policy frameworks.

Finally, transnational networks are constituted by and constitutive of the politics of framing. The global space has become the terrain for transnational politics. This has become possible through the expansion of flows of information, resources, and technological change. This new (or old) politics has been captured in the discourse about globalisation. As discussed above, globalisation is, like most political phenomena, a contested concept. Gupta and Ferguson contend that

> Something like a transnational public sphere has certainly rendered any strictly bounded sense of community of locality obsolete. At the same time, it has enabled the creation of forms of solidarity and identity that do not rest on an appropriation of space where contiguity and face-to-face contact is paramount.
>
> (1992: 9)

However, more cautious voices warn us, 'the discursive spaces through which transnational actors move are socially structured' (Guarnizo and Smith 1998: 21).

A new form of politics beckons at the same time as we become aware of the enduring power of capitalist social relations that also frame this new political space. So, while Stone (2002) is correct in pointing to the discourse structuration of development economists, I would argue that this discourse is indeed embedded in the dominant social relations as is evident from the minimal shifts in macro-economic framework of development economic policy-making. The question then arises: what can subaltern networks do to produce not only a methodology of social practice but also outcomes that are democratic? A cautionary stance is important if networks are not to transform themselves into 'systems that create themselves' (Riles 2000: 173). The seduction of networks in providing a sense of agency against all odds, at times through emphasising the process over outcome, at others through emphasising 'empowerment' without the transfer of resources that denotes changes in power relations, also provide cautionary tales. Does this mean that networks are simply integrative? I am not suggesting any such thing. What I am arguing is that networks, like any other structure/agent, are implicated in the many nodes of power in our global society; that they are politically hetero-geneous. For subaltern networks to be sustainable not only of their organisation but also of their politics they need to be self-reflective. Without such critical self-reflexivity the consequences of network failure can be enormous not only to those directly involved but also to those who depend upon the work of such net-works.

Notes

1   For more on Subaltern Studies, see Guha (1982–94).
2   The initiative to establish SARN emerged at a meeting on gender and law at Peshawar University, Pakistan in 1996 (Rai 1997). At the time, of the three colleagues involved, one was based in Pakistan, one in the UK and one in Norway; all three are academics. Two carried with them histories of personal/political engagement in South Asia, and one a long experience in setting up a network on gender and law in southern Africa. Another colleague later joined the group in the UK, and the colleague from Pakistan also moved to the UK. So, now all three members of the co-ordination group of SARN are based in the UK, and the colleague from Norway is member of the panel of advisers.
3   See http://gdnet.org
4   Moral entrepreneurs are defined by Sperling, Marx Ferree and Risman as 'those who contribute to building organisations and discourses that have moral implications ... [and] in the process they develop a greater or lesser degree of international prominence and credibility' (2001: 1159). I would suggest that both transnational and local organi-sations can be moral entrepreneurs. For a discussion about 'knowledge management' as means for NGO accountability see Smyth (2002). Accountability here is to funders and investors, while knowledge management also contributes to securing reputations through cornering the market in specific areas of 'systems for learning', which could be either through activities in 'the field' or 'institutional learning' within the NGO sector.
5   In an interview with Brinda Karat the author ascertained that an all-India organisation of more than 100,000 women had to do with fewer than ten computers.
6   The conference was originally to take place in Peshawar University, Pakistan. The move to the UK was made because of the difficult political situation between India and Pakistan during the months leading up to the conference. At one stage there were no flights between the two countries, visas were being denied to citizens of the other coun-try, even war seemed imminent. While the move from Pakistan to the UK posed significant challenges for SARN members, it also underlined the need for cross-border co-operation in the region.
7   See http://www.sarn-glg.net.

References

Barwa, S. and Rai, S. M. (2002) 'The Political Economy of Intellectual Property Rights: a Gender Perspective', in P. Newell, S. M. Rai and A. Scott (eds) *Development and the Challenge of Globalization*. London: IT Publishers, pp. 41–56.

Blacklock, C. (2001) 'Regional Economic Integration and the New Regime of Governance: The Case of Central America', Paper prepared for the 42nd International Studies Association Convention.

Bohman, J. and Rehg, W. (eds) (1997) *Deliberative Democracy, Essays on Reason and Politics*. Cambridge, Mass.: MIT Press.

Bosco, F. (2001) 'Place Space, Networks, and the Sustainability of Collective Action: The Madres de Plaza de Mayo' *Global Networks* (1): 307–29.

Braaten, J. (1995) 'From Communicative Rationality to Communicative Thinking: A Basis for Feminist Theory and Practice', in J. Meehan (ed.) *Feminists Read Habermas: Gendering the Subject of Discourse.* London: Routledge.

Castells, M. (1996) *The Rise of the Network Society.* Oxford: Blackwells.

Cohen R. and Rai, S. M. (2000) 'Global Social Movements, Towards a cosmopolitan politics', in R. Cohen and S. M. Rai (eds) *Global Social Movements.* London: Athlone Press.

Cohen, S. (2000) 'Social Solidarity in the Delors Period: Barriers to Participation', in Catherine Hoskyns and Micheal Newman (eds) *Democratizing the European Union: Issues for the Twenty-first Century.* Manchester: Manchester University Press, pp. 12–38.

D'Entreves, M. (2002), *Democracy as Public Deliberation*, Manchester: Manchester University Press.

Das, V. (1989) 'Subaltern as Perspective', in Ranjit Guha (ed.) *Subaltern Studies IV, Writings of South Asian History and Society*. New Delhi: Oxford University Press.

Elster, J. (1998) 'Introduction', in Jon Elster (ed.) *Deliberative Democracy.* Cambridge: Cambridge University Press.

Guarnizo, L. E. and Smith, M. P. (1998) 'The Location of Transnationalism', in M. P. Smith and L. E. Guarnizo (eds) *Transnationalism from Below.* New Brunswick, NJ: Transaction Publishers, pp. 3–34.

Guha, R. (ed.) (1982–94) *Subaltern Studies I-V, Writings of South Asian History and Society*. New Delhi: Oxford University Press.

Gupta, A. and Ferguson, J. (1992) 'Beyond 'Culture': Space, Identity and the Politics of Difference' *Cultural Anthropology* (7).

Harstock, N. (1997 [1983]), 'The Feminist Standpoint: Developing the Ground for a Specifically Feminist Historical Materialism', in S. Harding and M. Hintikka (eds) *Discovering Reality.* Dordrecht: Reidel Publishing Company, pp. 283–305.

Jaggar, Alison (1997) 'Love and Knowledge: Emotion in Feminist Epistemology', in S. Kemp and J. Squires (eds) *Feminisms*. Oxford Readers. Oxford: Oxford University Press, pp 188–93.

Kemp, S. and Squires, J. (eds) (1997) *Feminisms*. Oxford Readers. Oxford: Oxford University Press.

Liddle, J. and Rai, S. M. (1998), 'Feminism, Imperialism and Orientalism: The Challenge of the 'Indian Woman' *Women's History Review* 7 (4): 495–520.

Marchand, M. and Runyan, A. S. (eds) (2000), *Gender and Global Restructuring, Sightings, Sites and Resistances*. London: Routledge.

O'Brien, R. J. A., Scholte, A., Goetz, M. and Williams, M. (2000) *Contesting Global Governance*. Cambridge: Cambridge University Press.

Peterson, V. S. and Runyan, A. S. (1999) *Global Gender Issues*. Boulder, CO: Westview.

Rai, S. (1997) 'Crossing Boundaries: Women's North–South Cooperation Seminar – A Report' *Journal of Gender Studies* 6 (1, March): 63–70.

Rai, S. M. (2002) *Gender and the Political Economy of Development: From Nationalism to Globalisation*. Cambridge: Polity Press.

Rai, S. M. (2003) *National Machineries for the Advancement of Women: Mainstreaming Gender, Democratising the State?* (ed. for the UN Division for the Advancement of Women). Manchester: Manchester University Press.

Riles, A. (2000) *The Network Inside Out*. Ann Arbor: University of Michigan Press.

SARN – South Asian Research Network (2002) Proceedings of the Inaugural Conference August 25–29, 2002. Available online at http://www.sarn-glg.net.

Smyth, Ines (2002) 'Slaying the Serpent: Knowledge Management in Development NGOs', in Peter Newell, Shirin M. Rai and Andrew Scott (eds) *Development and the Challenge of Globalisation*. London: IT Publishers.

Sperling, V., Marx Ferree, M. and Risman, B. (2001) 'Constructing Global Feminism: Transnational Advocacy Networks and Russian Women's Activism' *Signs: Journal of Women in Culture and Society* 26 (4): 1155–86.

Spivak, G. (1988) 'Can the Subaltern Speak?', in Cary Nelson and Lawrence Grossberg (eds) *Marxism and the Interpretation of Culture*. Basingstoke: Macmillan.

Stone, D. (2002) 'The "Knowledge Bank" and the Global Development Network' *Global Governance* 9 (1): 43–61.

United Nations (1996) *The Beijing Declaration and the Platform for Action*. Fourth World Conference on Women, Beijing, China 14–15 September, 1995. New York: Department of Public Information, United Nations.

Yuval-Davis, N. (1997) 'Women, Citizenship and Difference' *Feminist Review* (57) Special Issue on Citizenship: 4–27.

9 Confluence and influence

Building policy capacities in research networks

Fred Carden and Stephanie Neilson[1]

Introduction

IDRC's programmes and projects increasingly express the intent to support and generate research that has the potential to influence public policy. But what constitutes public policy influence? To what degrees, and in what ways has IDRC-supported research influenced public policy? What factors and conditions have facilitated or inhibited the potential of IDRC-supported research to influence public policy? We set out to answer these questions, focusing on three case studies, from a set of 25 field studies that IDRC has commissioned. The three cases are all examples of transnational research networks. They are the Latin American Trade Network (LATN), the Asian Fisheries Social Science Research Network (AFSSRN), and the Technical Support Service to the Group of 24 (G-24).

Networks have been key to the Centre's delivery of programmes (IDRC 2000; Gonsalves and Baranyi 2003). In theory, they are the institutional mechanism that supports North–South and South–South cooperation, linking people and institutions in order to advance and utilize knowledge (Bernard 1996). Many research communities in the South are small, fragmented and significantly under-funded. Networks should thus be useful and viable mechanisms that enable researchers to carry out their research as well as provide them with funding opportunities, information sharing and mutual learning, technical support, and training.

Conceptual framework

A conceptual framework was developed to guide the evaluation. Lindquist suggested that 'assessing policy influence is typically about carefully discerning intermediate influences' (Lindquist 2001: 23), in particular (a) expanding research capacities of chosen actors to relate to policy issues, (b) broadening networks of interaction and exchange, and (c) engagement of researchers with policy networks. This recognizes that research for development is located 'upstream' from any kind of actual development 'impact'.

Expanding policy capacities focuses particularly on improving researcher capacities to carry out and create use for policy relevant research. This includes, *inter alia*, supporting new research, the development of new fields of research, enhancing researcher capacities to work on problems or issues as distinct from carrying out disciplinary research, as well as enhancing their capacities to communicate knowledge and ideas to diverse audiences.

Broadening policy horizons again focuses on the perspective of the researcher. Generally, it has to do with increasing both the availability of knowledge, as well as the comprehensiveness of this knowledge. For example, the accessibility and completeness of knowledge increases through multi-country networks of researchers or through networks bringing together researchers and others in the policy community:

- increasing the stock of policy relevant knowledge;
- introducing new ways of thinking into the policy arena;
- making sure knowledge is available to policy makers in forms that make it possible for them to use it.

Essentially, broadening policy horizons is about the means and relationships that translate research into knowledge which policy makers can use to change policy.

Affecting policy regimes is about the actual use of research in the development of new laws, regulations or structures. It is typically considered 'real' influence and is often considered a key indicator of influence. However, it is the least common type of influence following from research although it is not unheard of. From our cases it would appear most common in emergent fields such as information and communication technologies (e.g. the development of national ICT policies).

We argue that all three types of influence are crucial because of the very long time frames needed in policy change and policy evolution (see also Neilson 2001). The preparation of a policy community to use knowledge effectively is essential to the ability of policy and decision makers to respond quickly when decisions need to be made and when judgment must be exercised. Flyvberg, who describes the expert in the field, echoes the reality of decision making:

> In normal, familiar situations, real experts do not solve problems and do not make decisions. They just do what 'works' ... When there is time, and when much is at stake, experts will also deliberate before they act. Their deliberation, however, is not based on calculated problem solving but on critical reflection over the intuition ... .
>
> (Flyvberg 2001: 17)

From this position, the most important role for research and researchers in the policy process comes normally at the earlier stages of drafting research findings. This also suggests it will always be the rare occasion when research can claim a direct instance of policy change.

By employing this typology in the case studies, the researchers were able to draw out very specific instances of what people perceived to be 'policy influence'. They were also encouraged to draw out instances of (perceived) policy influence that were not covered, or were not an easy fit, within this framework.

Most found the typology adequate and comprehensive enough to use as a mechanism to characterize the type of influence found within their case. Only with respect to the ICT cases did the framework merit some expansion in order to include the fact that ICTs in developing countries are relatively new to policy formulation processes.

Methodology

The principal methodology employed in this study was the development of rich cases for analysis. Since context is crucial when observing (potential) instances of policy influence, the case studies provide stories and narratives that are attentive to local conditions and historical circumstances. To encourage and support these contexts and conditions, the unit engaged local researchers from the regions to conduct the 25 case studies. A key part was the use of a common methodology and interview questions. Using a common framework encourages both depth and richness in each qualitative case, and still allows for the values of the qualitative work to be combined with cross-case analysis (Weiss 2003).

Because our intent is to understand how research influences policy, we asked Centre programme staff to deliberately select cases where they felt policy influence had occurred. To this end, we also requested that they consider those projects that had a longer time frame in relation to the action or activities that had taken place vis-à-vis the subsequent influence.

Another important feature was the multi-national focus (Weiss 2003). Since there is relatively little documentation and literature with respect to policy processes in countries of the South, a broad scope helps to initiate more reporting in this area. As well, the study needed to cover each of the regions of the South where the Centre has established programming and projects, and across all three broad programming areas: information and communication technologies, environmental and natural resource management, and social and economic equity.[2]

In carrying out case studies we adopt the stance proposed by Flyvberg (2001), that because of the importance of the particular and of the centrality of context dependent knowledge in the study of human affairs, the case method offers the key way to develop depth of understanding of social phenomena (where large samples of cases provide breadth of understanding). In an earlier work, Yin also notes that 'in general, case studies are the preferred method when "how" or "why" questions are being used, when the investigator has little control over events, and when the focus is on a contemporary phenomenon within some real life context' (1994: 1).

To achieve a learning-oriented approach, the project team engaged Centre staff in a series of consultations before the fieldwork was conducted in order to ensure that the key issues for staff and the researchers they support were included. Once the initial fieldwork was completed, workshops were held to carry out preliminary analysis of the findings. The workshops were focused on several key cases from a region and engaged staff from that region, together with Centre partners and the consultants who conducted the research.

Several strengths to this approach have been noted above, but deserve to be highlighted here. From the study's inception, there were well-defined users who were engaged in several ways throughout the study, and who continue to be engaged. The use of narratives, combined with a core framework and common questions, allows the stories to unfold within particular contexts, but also lends itself to cross-case analysis. Another methodological benefit that merits attention is the use of local researchers. This not only ensures local understanding and knowledge within each case, but also builds capacity to conduct this type of research. It has produced local knowledge that will help to build the theoretical understanding of research-to-policy processes, particularly from the perspective of the South, while continuing to make methodological improvements within the fields of evaluation and knowledge utilization (Weiss 2003).

Three case studies

The 25 field cases included in the Centre evaluation are quite varied. They include cases on applied research and demonstration projects that influenced ICT policy formulation in Africa, mining cases in Peru, research on education budget reforms for indigenous people and women as a component of the Peace Accords in Guatemala, amongst others. The three cases chosen are all networks and transnational in character: two are regional and one is global.

The Technical Support Service Project to the Group of 24 (G-24)

Since 1972, the Group of 24 (G-24) has represented developing countries and is organized to provide Third World input into issues of global financial reform. It was established as a representative group by the larger group of developing countries, the Group of 77. In order for them to provide input into the reform process, the G-24 quickly recognized the need to have a research function. IDRC became involved in 1988, after the initial period during which time the UNDP (United Nations Development Programme) supported the G-24 research programme. During its earliest involvement, the Centre worked with the group to create the 'Technical Support Service Project', administered by UNCTAD (United Nations Conference on Trade and Development). The Centre has supported the Technical Support Service project for 15 years, and has contributed nearly CAD$1 million. Unlike the other two network projects, the G-24 Technical Support Service project was not designed or established as a formal network structure, but came into being as an informal mechanism as a result of its collaborative, transnational research efforts.

Over the first four phases of the Technical Support Service project, there were two key research coordinators, each with their own vision of what the primary purpose of the technical support group was, who they targeted for the purpose of influence, and how this should be done. The first of these leaders saw the main objective of the G-24 research as providing a 'voice for the underdog' (Tussie *et al.* 2003: 8). This objective was sustained by the strong relationships between the first research coordinator and IDRC, as well as between the research coordinator and the G-24. Always keenly aware of the budgetary constraints of the Group, he took the approach of supporting a small number of high quality papers by renowned researchers on issues targeted to influence the research agendas of the International Financial Institutions (IFIs). This pushed the IFIs to pour money into research on these issues and topics.

Throughout his tenure, the first research coordinator targeted the Executive Directors (EDs) of the G-24 as the main audience of the research results. Much of the focus was on publishing the research papers through UNCTAD. Perhaps one of the most important internal factors affecting policy influence was the idea that 'the research agenda must come from the G-24 and be seen to come from the G-24, which is best positioned to know its own needs, which often arise unforeseen, and at short notice' (Tussie *et al.* 2003: 19). Some of the G-24 countries were sceptical of the research coming out of the World Bank and the IMF, so as the reputation of the G-24 researchers grew, some of the Country Directors requested research on issues of importance to developing countries from a developing country perspective.

The first research coordinator stressed the need to give a voice to the underdog, but on his retirement in 1999, his successor highlighted the need to 'bring about a paradigm change' in order to 'change the environment in which policies are framed' (Tussie *et al.* 2003: 11). As a result, the research studies were published with the intent to influence public policy at a global level. This resulted in a shift away from the EDs as the primary target audience to an effort to influence wider international discussions on financial and monetary issues in political and intergovernmental as well as academic circles (Tussie *et al.* 2003). Although this shift gave more focus to the technical support group, it also created tensions among some of the key actors involved.

Most policy makers and academics have discarded the linear notion of research directly influencing policies and policy processes. Yet, findings from Tussie's review indicate that some aspects of the G-24's influence on international finance were in fact linear in nature. This occurred primarily with respect to 'short-term influence via policy briefs on specific issues and targeted to policy makers with the ability to make decisions' (Tussie *et al.* 2003: 17). On the other hand, the enlightenment of policy makers is more often associated with 'more academically oriented papers on systemic issues intending to alter the prevailing paradigm over a longer period of time in which a constellation of other actors in the broader policy community are harnessed in parallel efforts' (Tussie *et al.* 2003: 17). In effect, the approaches of both the two former research coordinators have achieved some level of success in terms of influencing policy. Using Lindquist's framework the type of policy influence can, for the most part, be described as 'broadening policy horizons'.

Closely linked with 'enlightenment' as a means to influence policy, the resulting form of influence is often in terms of new concepts being introduced to frame debates, new ideas on the agenda, and researchers and others educated to take up new positions with broader understanding of issues.

[Some interviewees] especially highlighted the importance of this form of policy influence, as many finance ministers today are less critical in their analytical approaches [than previously] ... this has led to the belief that 'good economics' means that economics should be specific to the conditions in which they are to be implemented ... .

(Tussie *et al.* 2003: 18)

In the end, the reviewer contends that the influence the project researchers achieved was most effective by harnessing a range of other actors to carry their messages to the international financial reform discussions. They did this by influencing the research agendas of the IFIs, through the powers of persuasion of renowned researchers involved in the project as well as through the high quality of their research papers, and sometimes through the personalities and personal contacts of both the research coordinators. The G-24 has not broken the policy monopoly of the US. However, it is an institution that is successful in placing developing country concerns on the table and inserting developing country issues into the global financial reform agenda.

The Latin American Trade Network (LATN)

The Latin American Trade Network (LATN) was initiated in March 1998, and was formed in response to the increasing complexity of the international trade agenda. Initially, the main objective of LATN was to develop and establish a mechanism to help Latin American countries 'position themselves more effectively in international trade negotiation' (Macadar 2003: 14).

Central to understanding LATN is the notion that it is a network of individuals not institutions. It brings together researchers, policy makers and civil society organizations from several Latin American countries and international institutions that are interested in looking at trade issues from a Latin American perspective. Initially, the network was created with the premise of generating and producing knowledge; however, over the course of its initial phase this objective was refined and now its primary function concerns organizing, filtering and synthesizing existing research into a form that is more easily understood and digested by trade negotiators and policy makers (Macadar 2003: 17). By focusing on already existing research, the network enables researchers to provide policy makers with various different options and positions for negotiations.

Of particular note in relation to policy processes in Latin America is that individuals fulfil various roles (as researchers, negotiators, government advisers) 'either simultaneously or rotationally over time' (Macadar 2003: 8). Consequently, LATN's target audience is constantly changing.

At a given moment, the target person may be a researcher, at another moment he may be serving as an advisor to some important official, or he may even have become a senior official himself. Indeed, a single member of the policy-making community may combine all these roles.

(Macadar 2003: 26)

The rotational nature of the different roles for individuals can be useful for the purpose of gaining recognition and influence with senior level officials, since some of them actually become senior officials and hence can influence from within. However, it can also make targeting specific audiences and individuals extremely challenging as these targets constantly change. To address this challenge, the Coordination Unit chose to target 'middle management'. These individuals generally remain the same, even as governments come and go. And as the author points out, this points to a further interesting notion within the Latin American policy process – 'it is the middle ranks that control the data and process information, and this gives them important power, even with the Minister and his advisors' (Macadar 2003: 26).

The 'power of the negotiating bureaucracy' (Macadar 2003: 22) also means that, during times of instability and volatility, the middle ranks

> … also have the power to determine the policy formulation process. They exercise this power by throwing up obstacles, employing delaying tactics, and rewriting the final resolutions for implementing the decisions. They have a very high measure of discretion and, depending on the circumstances, they can even modify the principle decision in part.
>
> (Macadar 2003: 23)

By targeting the middle ranks, the network's Coordination Unit was able to have access to those who have the power to influence even during times of instability and changes in government. This targeting is central in a region where governmental instability is frequent thus making policy influence an enormous, and at times daunting, task.

The case finds evidence of all three types of influence as defined by Lindquist and also finds that uptake of the research and results are promising. Early indications of this include: evidence that various Latin American governments (e.g. Argentina, Paraguay, Peru, and several Central American governments) and organizations in the region have approached LATN for assistance on trade negotiations, the World Bank has worked with LATN to customize its policy training courses for the region, and UNCTAD and WTO representatives see LATN as a vehicle for organizational collaboration (Macadar 2003: 14).

The review asserts that one of the key factors to this influence is the 'LATN approach and its trademark' (Macadar 2003: 46) of independence. The regional approach to these issues addressed by the network's researchers and Coordination Unit is one that transcends governments, international agencies and national interests, which has 'helped to give it legitimacy' (Macadar 2003: 47) as well as providing a common vision for the region.

Asian Fisheries Social Science Research Network (AFSSRN)

The Asian Fisheries Social Science Research Network (AFSSRN) was established to address the overexploitation of fisheries and environmental degradation of coastal resources. The Centre supported the network for 14 years, from its inception in 1983 until 1996. It continues today as a branch of the Asian Fisheries Society, with support from the International Centre for Living Aquatic Resources Management – now known as the WorldFish Centre. It was established originally as a three-country network of three institutions, but later expanded to include more countries and many more institutions. When the network was initiated, fisheries faced many challenges throughout Asia. In spite of the importance of the fishery, the resources have been very poorly managed and fishers remain among the poorest people in the region.

Concerns in the region about environmental degradation and overexploitation of the fisheries were treated as biological problems. In the early 1980s, it was being recognized that the problems were more socio-economic, institutional and political in nature. There was serious concern because of an almost complete lack of social scientists working on fisheries issues, with no systematic programmes of economic and policy research being undertaken. Thus the overriding objective of the AFSSRN was to build national research capacity that enabled researchers to address important social science issues in the development and management of fishery resources in the region. This was achieved through the development of professional and graduate programmes in resources management and in fisheries and aquaculture economics.

In the first phase of support to the AFSSRN, the University Pertanian Malaysia emerged as the leader in building capacity. It developed the first graduate programme in the region on resource economics. The network funded graduate programme development, scholarships, research projects, training programmes and supported the building of professional working relationships. The primary focus of Phase I was building the stock of trained fisheries economists who could both carry out research and train others in the region.

In each of the subsequent phases, the network expanded to a larger group of institutions and also modestly expanded to include a fourth country, Indonesia. There was a deliberate choice by the network not to expand the number of countries but rather to secure membership among existing country-members. This was done by increasing the number of institutions involved within each country.

Building the network as a mechanism of exchange among researchers began to take shape by the third phase of activity. In Phase III (1988–93), there were 14 teams in the network from the four countries. It was only at this stage when there were sufficient active researchers that there was an understanding of the merits of the network to support knowledge generation and problem solving. At this stage the network began to function more effectively and to move beyond serving as a training network to operate as a network used by its members to address issues, to exchange ideas and to work on problems in their countries. As the network strengthened its capacities, it started to build linkages and relationships with non-network institutions. As a result, the network was able to develop and consolidate its identity and began to see itself as a force in the domain of fisheries and resources management policies.

The strength and value of the network was such that when Centre funding was terminated at the end of Phase IV, network members were determined to continue and found a means to function as a section within the Asian Fisheries Society. It did so with modest funding from its host institution – the WorldFish Centre – and continues today with a well-read column in their newsletter and in conjunction with other fisheries society meetings. In Phase IV and beyond, membership has spread from the four countries to include fisheries economists and resource management specialists from Viet Nam and Sri Lanka.

There was a clear focus on building capacity in the early stages of network development, and a clear understanding that until there was a stronger research and professional base, it would not be possible to conduct policy relevant research that would have legitimacy. It was not until Phase IV of support that the network developed explicit activities around policy relevant research. At that point, many of its members were seen as highly qualified and their views began to be sought by their governments. They contributed to expanding the range of issues taken into consideration in the formulation of fisheries policies. And researchers also became more adept at identifying issues of import to policy makers:

> Originally, I would just do research for research's sake. My audience was not the policy-makers. Now being in government I better understand the need for good research to inform my decision-making and I better understand why the AFSSRN was pushing through training, the need for us to do policy relevant research. I request our researchers, both in government and in academe, to do research which I can use to support or not support decisions.
>
> (Dr V. Nikijuluw, Ministry of Marine Affairs and Fisheries, Indonesia, quoted in Pomeroy 2002)

Key findings

Networks

The AFSSRN and LATN networks provide insights of how knowledge and innovation generated through their research was exchanged across borders within a regional setting. LATN illustrates how networks enable researchers to transcend national governments and international agencies to find regional solutions to regional issues. Both the AFSSRN and LATN cases also show how policy makers used the research, even if the research was conducted in a country other than their own, resulting in the exchange and transfer of ideas across national borders.

Networks as 'platforms for action' are emerging more frequently and provide individuals and institutions opportunities to 'create new alliances, policy spaces and ways of negotiating with both development and policy communities' (Bernard 1996: 14). Succinctly stated, they are transnational advocacy networks and are distinguished by the 'centrality of beliefs and principled ideas' (Keck and Sikkink 1998: 2) where 'advocates plead the causes of others or defend a cause or proposition' (Keck and Sikkink 1998: 8). An example of a transnational advocacy network can be found in the G-24 research programme. As stated earlier, the first research coordinator described his role as 'giving a voice to the underdog' (Tussie *et al.* 2003: 11) in response to developing countries' roles in global financial reform discussions. The G-24 was expressly designed to influence economic and financial policies by using research and incorporating ideas from the perspective of the South. As a transnational advocacy network, it goes beyond thinking about or using research as important information to persuade policy makers, to using information in a more strategic way since it is the 'interpretation and strategic use of information that is most important' (Keck and Sikkink 1998: 30).

The case studies presented here provide evidence that is consistent with earlier writings on the effectiveness of research, policy and advocacy networks as a means of influencing policy (Keck and Sikkink 1998; Stein and Stren 2001). Our findings also suggest a number of issues and implications for funders to consider when supporting research that has intent to influence public policy.

Capacity building

Both the AFSSRN and the LATN projects are networks designed to build national research capacity in Latin American and Southeast Asian countries. Yet, capacity building is not just about building the capacity of researchers to do research. It is also about building researcher capacity to carry out policy relevant research and to communicate the findings effectively to policy and decision makers. For example, the AFSSRN began as a network of institutions created to build the national research capacity in several countries in Southeast Asia but by its fourth phase, member researchers had shifted their focus to policy-oriented research and policy analysis:

> With this skill base in social sciences, maturity in conducting research, career advancement, confidence in themselves as researchers, and more acceptance of social science research by policy makers, Network members became more knowledgeable and experienced in how to conduct policy analysis and began to *influence policy*. This was especially true in Phase IV of the Network which emphasized policy analysis.
>
> (Pomeroy 2002: 39, emphasis in the original)

By first attending to the issue of building research capacity, the IDRC-supported network was able to strengthen the skills of the researchers and the quality of the research produced. As policy makers recognized the quality of the research they became more accepting of the findings and could see how to use the information for developing new policies. The Minister of Fisheries in Vietnam reported, 'the article helped him to better understand fisheries management issues in neighbouring Southeast Asian countries and assist in developing new policies in the Fisheries Sector Plan for Vietnam' (Pomeroy 2002: 39). This example also illustrates the transnational character of the research and knowledge generated of this particular knowledge network. Government officials from other countries in the region find the research useful, even if it is not necessarily carried out in the context of their own country.

Building the capacity of researchers and negotiators in Latin America was a primary goal for the Latin American Trade Network. As the author of this review explains,

> In the face of [some] challenges, the larger countries have some capacity of their own to undertake research and analysis as a prelude to adopting positions. On the other hand, the smaller and medium sized countries that have no such capacity could benefit from a regional mechanism that would provide them with an ordered set of ideas on the main issues of the multilateral agenda.
>
> (Macadar 2003: 15)

Yet despite the capacities of the larger Latin American countries, they 'were not organized or prepared to respond to the proposals of the North, which seemed to be backed by abundant research and strong political support' (Macadar 2003: 15). By supporting researchers throughout the region, the LATN project enabled researchers to strengthen both their skills as well as their positions in the debates.

Ownership

The notion of ownership is very closely linked to capacity building. The Centre supports programmes and projects that build the capacity of researchers and policy makers to use their own research/researchers. This encourages the uptake of research within, and therefore influencing policy from within. The G-24 illustrates a good example of local ownership since the demand for research to better inform the G-24 representatives came from within the G-24 member-countries. As Stiglitz explains,

> If the developing countries are really to be 'in the driver's seat', they have to have the capacity to analyse the often difficult economic issues they face. Local researchers, combining the knowledge of local conditions – including knowledge of local, political and social structures (with the learning derived from global experiences) provide the best prospects for deriving policies that both engender broad-based support and are effective. That is why locally based research institutions are so important.
>
> (Stiglitz 2000: 26)

'Ownership' of the research can also affect the perceived (potential) effectiveness of policy influence. In the G-24 case, under the leadership of the first Research Coordinator and with the support of IDRC, important steps were taken to 'increase G-24 ownership of the research program' (Tussie *et al.* 2003: 9). The first was that G-24 members began to contribute to the trust fund themselves in response to IDRC's request for parallel funding. The second was the creation and establishment of the Technical Group. These two mechanisms 'offered a more defined process for the functioning of the research project, [and] to some extent, it may have provided the G-24 with a greater sense of "ownership" of the programme' (Tussie *et al.* 2003: 9). Building on these mechanisms for effective policy influence, the G-24 representatives requested 'soundly argued policy briefs to influence the policy debate' (Tussie *et al.* 2003: 20).

The new research coordinator who was more focused on a longer term effort of changing the paradigm instead chose 'a style and strategy that targeted the broader policy community as a whole rather than the [Executive Directors] more particularly' (Tussie *et al.* 2003: 20). This created a tension in the group, particularly in terms of accountability: a different target audience led to the question of who is the research programme of the G-24 accountable to – the G-24 or UNCTAD? This is an important and significant question since it also touches upon ownership of the research agenda, which is currently managed by the G-24 representatives. The issue of ownership also suggests a challenge for donors in terms of their level of involvement and role within a project.

Persistence

Many projects in this study are long-term commitments by the Centre. For example, IDRC supported the AFSSRN for 14 years, and the G-24 has realized 15 years of support. The notion of persistence is strong within the Centre: building capacity to do research takes a long time. It is seldom considered complete within the framework of a single project; rather, it usually requires engagement over time and through a number of projects. Short term, rapid results are seldom seen. As illustrated by the AFSSRN case, persistent support over the years provided network members the experience, expertise and confidence to conduct policy analysis research.

Another aspect of persistence is the changing roles of researchers. As researchers gain skills and knowledge, and as they become more aware of and connected to the policy process in their field, demand for their input increases. Over and over, the evaluator of AFSSRN found evidence of researchers who had become policy makers and continued to use evidence in their policy decisions. Providing support to the research community to engage with policy does not always assume specific linkages; but rather, over time builds their capacity to engage.

Issues of policy influence go beyond single projects (the 'project trap'). Too often, donor agencies regard aid and investment as individual projects and then evaluate those projects in terms of 'success' or 'failure', rather than looking at the bigger picture of the collective strength of several related projects. (Lusthaus *et al.* 2002). As such, donors might also consider persistence in terms of strategic funding – looking for projects that collectively build upon each other and which aim at particular policies.

Intent

If influencing policy is intended, then policy influence should be part of the project design, not an add-on at a later stage. In both the G-24 project and the LATN project, the researchers and donors set out with the deliberate intention of funding research that would be of interest to policy makers. They sought ways to identify issues of importance, consulted with the policy and decision makers throughout the project, and tried to seize policy windows as they emerged. In LATN, a preoccupation is identifying issues that are likely to come to the fore so research is carried out before it is needed. Design with intent has some exceptions, of course. For example, as the AFSSRN illustrates, the first few years of support were oriented towards changing the mindsets of researchers with little direct regard to policy influence. Once the network was firmly established and the researchers were aware of the implications of the research they were conducting, two things happened: one was a felt need to translate this research into language and ideas which policy makers could use; the other was that some of the original researchers were offered, and accepted, positions of influence in the national governments where they could put into practice what they learned through their research with the network.

What the AFSSRN case illustrates particularly well is that transnational knowledge, and its use, has a cumulative effect. This takes time to develop – in the case of AFSSRN it was not until Phase IV of the project that the general interest in the relationship between research and policy could be turned into explicit intent to influence policy. It took this long to develop the capacities and to build sufficient reputation on those capacities.

Both G-24 and LATN are examples of projects designed expressly to influence policy and both cases reported 'success' in terms of achieving those ends. On the other hand, the contribution that AFSSRN made to policy influence occurred later in the project. Once the capacities were sufficiently instilled in several national systems, the researchers were able to think in terms of policy influence, both in how they defined their research, as well as in terms of what demands and expectations policy makers placed on them.

The challenge for funders is to understand more effectively what is their 'intent' in relation to 'influencing policy'? We know that projects, programmes and institutions need to be clear on intent. This requires a sophisticated understanding of what is meant by 'policy influence' and understanding that there is no one single definition or meaning but rather that it is variable. It also needs to be clear from the beginning what resources and budgeting requirements are needed in order to facilitate this process.

Communication and dissemination

Findings from our case studies are consistent with the well-documented difficulties researchers face in their ability to communicate their findings in formats that enable policy makers to easily understand and absorb the information.

Packaging, marketing and communicating solutions to complex problems and issues appears to be a skill that many researchers and development donors have overlooked. Yet researchers are expected to do more than just research: they are expected to be able to communicate and disseminate their findings to policy and decision makers. As was noted by a researcher at a workshop to discuss the LATN and G-24 case studies, we are now asking researchers to 'be like Erin Brokovich … you have to have the legs, the looks, you have to be smart, you have to do the research … dissemination work, strategy work, publication work … I said, come on, I'm a researcher' (Maessen 2003: 51). They have a background in research, not in the communication of ideas to different audiences. That shift needs to be accompanied by a new thrust in capacity building. This also posits the question: are donors willing and ready to fund and support these kinds of activities?

Communication and dissemination of findings and issues emerged in many different ways. First, the ability of researchers to communicate their findings and results in a way that is understood by policy makers was frequently reported as a problem for researchers. Second, the understanding of IDRC Programme Officers regarding the need to build communication and dissemination costs into programmes was found to be weak. Third, the range of relevant formats for information was not known. Fourth, the informal nature of policy influence is not well understood or accepted by many researchers. For some researchers this is a contamination of the research process: they see researchers who can achieve this as 'research entrepreneurs', a term that connotes a certain somewhat less 'rigorous' type of researcher who is willing to compromise research in the interests of influence. Fifth, the timing of financial support to communicate findings was raised as an issue and is discussed in more depth below.

Systems of support

Review of the cases to date has clearly articulated the non-linear nature of the influence of most research on public policy. What emerged is the disconnect between the way we think about the influences of research on policy and the way we design and fund research projects. The former is clearly seen as multi-path, uncertain and changing over time. The latter is still fundamentally linear in process. Inside the Centre, there has been an approach to project support that takes a linear view of the project and of policy influence.[3] That is, when a project is granted support, there is a tendency to 'wait and see' if the research is going to be of sufficient quality and then find the funds needed for communication and dissemination activities. The conservative approach, therefore, is to commit funds only when staff and partners know there is strong potential. As a result, dissemination is often too late for policy influence.

This approach comes from years of experience and the knowledge that in research and innovation not all efforts are going to be successful. But it is also the legacy of a project management approach that comes from infrastructure systems where first you build the infrastructure and then you use it. In the implementation of research for development the issues evolve over time and change as we proceed.

It is not a linear process of research–findings–dissemination–change. Rather, researchers need to be engaging with new methods of project support that need to be explored and which allow the elements of the research to be exposed to the relevant communities on an ongoing basis. This might be as simple as creating multi-year flexible budgets and making communication and dissemination funding available from Year One. But it is the mindset and assumptions behind the project management approaches in use that are much more complex to change.

The development of appropriate support systems and project management systems that ensure accountability but are also agile in their ability to seize opportunities as they emerge is not an easy undertaking. This is particularly true in the context of a capacity building organization: the primary focus of the Centre is in improving the interest in and ability to use evidence as a basis for policy – and we are particularly focused on the researcher side of that equation, not the policy maker side. This means that much of what we work on is very long term; by the time the interest emerges we may have moved to new areas of funding. This in itself is not necessarily a bad thing – we saw in the case of the AFSSRN that the ownership and commitment were so strong that the network made sure of its own survival. But it is a challenge: if we frame our mandate in terms of improving the ability to use evidence, then what is the obligation of the Centre to provide that support, and over what frame of time does that obligation hold?

Conclusion

Transnational research networks can and do influence policy. What we have found in our examination of IDRC-supported networks is that the influence is not straightforward, cannot be assumed from the beginning, and demands strong leadership and vision in research and research capacity building. 'Hurry up and wait' seems a good slogan. Be ready when the policy windows open by maintaining strong networks which pull in ideas from other policy regimes, be ahead of the decision makers in issue identification and build a strong cadre of researchers who understand and rally to these policy issues.

The challenge for the Centre, as well as for others who support and carry out research, is to deepen our understanding of the interrelated issues about capacity building, our view of project life cycles, and the intent to influence policy. At the beginning of this study, some Centre staff and management questioned whether or not there was a trade-off between building capacity and influencing policy. So far, our findings suggest that this is not the case – building the capacity of researchers to better understand policy- and decision-making processes leads to research that policy makers can use to make informed decisions, or use the evidence or knowledge produced in the formulation of policies.

But the question here may not be one of 'trade-offs' but rather timing – short-term duration of projects with one-time funding versus thinking of projects more strategically in terms of being a long-term investment. As the AFSSRN case illustrates so well, capacity building does have legitimate and valid policy influences, and can lead ultimately to policy changes; either through policy makers' better understanding of the issues and of the research, or through researchers becoming policy makers themselves.

There is no formula, no recipe for knowledge utilization in the policy process. Our focus in this study is on presenting stories because it is through a deeper understanding of approaches, contexts, relationships and events that we can draw ideas for the future. Sustaining networks requires considerable time, effort and resources. It also requires a membership that has a need for the network and is able to use it for some purpose. The challenge of the *use* of transnational knowledge is understanding its relevance across borders and across cultures.

Notes

1 The views expressed in this paper are the views of the authors and do not necessarily reflect the views of the International Development Research Centre.
2 The Centre supports research in the following six regions: Latin America and the Caribbean, West and Central Africa, Eastern and Southern Africa, North Africa and the Middle East, South Asia and South East Asia.
3 This issue was brought up for discussion at a two-day retreat that was held for the Advisory Committee (February 20–21, 2003).

References

Bernard, Anne (1996) *IDRC Networks: An Ethnographic Perspective.* Ottawa: Evaluation Unit, IDRC. Available online at http://web.idrc.ca/es/ev-26858-201-1-DO_TOPIC. html.

Flyvberg, Bent (2001) *Making Social Science Matter: Why Social Inquiry Fails and How it Can Succeed Again.* Cambridge: Cambridge University Press.

Gonsalves, Tahira and Baranyi, Stephen (2003) *Research for Policy Influence: A History of IDRC Intent.* Ottawa: Evaluation Unit, IDRC.

International Development Research Centre (2000) *IDRC In a Changing World: Programme Directions* 2000–2005. Ottawa: IDRC.

Keck, Margaret E. and Sikkink, Kathryn (1998) *Activists Beyond Borders: Advocacy Networks in International Politics.* Ithaca, NY: Cornell University Press.

Lindquist, Evert A. (2001) *Discerning Policy Influence: Framework For A Strategic Evaluation of IDRC-Supported Research.* Ottawa: Evaluation Unit, IDRC. Available online at http://web.idrc.ca/uploads/user-S/10359907080discerning_policy.pdf.

Lusthaus, Charles, Adrien, Marie-Hélène, Anderson, Gary, Carden, Fred, and Montalván, George Plinio (2002) *Organisational Assessment: A Framework for Improving Performance.* Washington, DC and Ottawa: InterAmerican Development Bank and International Development Research Centre.

Macadar, Luis (2003) *The Influence of Research on Public Policy: The Latin American Trade Network.* Ottawa: Evaluation Unit, IDRC.

Maessen, Odilia (2003) *The Influence of Research on Public Policy Workshop Report #2: Montevideo 5–6 December 2002.* Ottawa: Evaluation Unit, IDRC. Available online at http://network.idrc.ca/ev.php?URL_ID=31580&URL_DO=DO_TOPIC&URL_ SECTION=201&reload=1057860084.

Neilson, Stephanie (2001) *IDRC-Supported Research and Its Influence on Public Policy. Knowledge Utilization and Public Policy Processes: A Literature Review.* Ottawa: Evaluation Unit, IDRC. Available online at http://web.idrc.ca/fr/ev-12186-201-1-DO_TOPIC.html.

Pomeroy, Robert S. (2002) *IDRC-Supported Research and its Influence on Public Policy: A Case Study Analysis of the Asian Fisheries Social Science Research Network (AFSSRN).* Ottawa: Evaluation Unit, IDRC. Available online at http://network.idrc.ca/uploads/user-S/10552528310AFSSRN20Nov.doc.

Stein, Janice Gross and Stren, Richard (2001) 'Knowledge Networks in Global Society: Pathways to Development', in P. Aucoin (ed.) *Networks for Knowledge: Collaborative Innovation in International Learning.* Toronto: Toronto University Press.

Stiglitz, Joseph (2000) 'Scan Globally, Reinvent Locally: Knowledge Infrastructure and the Localisation of Knowledge', in D. Stone (ed.) *Banking on Knowledge: The Genesis of the Global Development Network.* London: Routledge.

Tussie, Diana, Riggirozzi, M. P. and Tuplin, T. (2003) *A Study of Policy Influence: The G-24 Technical Support Service.* Ottawa: Evaluation Unit, IDRC. Available online at http://network.idrc.ca/uploads/user-S/10552526220G24_Final_14_Feb.doc.

Weiss, Carol Hirschon (2003) 'Studying Research Utilization', Paper prepared for IDRC Workshop, Ottawa, March 2003. Available online at http://network.idrc.ca/uploads/user-S/10551892530C._Weiss_Presentation_to_IDRC.doc.

Yin, Robert K. (1994) *Case Study Research: Design and Methods.* 2nd edition, Applied Social Science Methods Series, Vol. 5. Thousand Oaks, CA: Sage.

10 Research for reconstruction in Africa

Challenges for policy communities and coalitions

Pamela K. Mbabazi, Sandra J. MacLean and Timothy M. Shaw

New African developmental issues and institutions: beyond states to non-state actors

The burgeoning range of 'new' developmental, ecological and strategic issues facing Africa at the start of the new millennium cannot begin to be treated by African 'states' alone, especially given their diminished status and resources after two decades of shrinkage under structural adjustment conditionalities. In particular, any prospect of enhanced, sustainable human development and security (UNDP 1999) requires innovative responses which are rarely the monopoly of any regime, in Africa or elsewhere. Therefore, creative responses have to be sought increasingly in association with non-state actors, both for-profit organizations such as corporations and not-for-profit international non-governmental organizations (I)NGOs, whether indigenous, intermediary or international.

Such 'triangular' forms of 'governance', embracing states (from local to national), companies (from local to global) and civil societies (likewise from local to global), pose challenges to orthodox analysis of 'foreign policy' as the former are no longer the only actor type which can claim to practice it. Companies and civil societies now also have their own 'international relations' involving both similar (inter-corporate) and dissimilar types of actors (company–civil society) (MacLean and Shaw 1999; Shaw and Nyang'oro 1999). Moreover, in Africa as elsewhere, the recognition and treatment of few issues today are the monopoly of any one type of actor. Almost all contemporary issues require policy coalitions and partnerships amongst a range of heterogeneous actor types to both identify let alone tackle these issues (Mbabazi and Shaw 2000).

Indeed, many of the continent's continuing developmental issues require such responsive 'mixed actor' *governance* at all levels: bio-diversity, corruption, drugs and gangs and guns, ecology, energy, gender, HIV/AIDS, land-mines and small arms, migrations and refugees, and viruses such as ebola (Parpart and Shaw 2002; Shaw 2004a; Shaw and Nyang'oro 1999). Whether diminished states can combine with emboldened civil societies and private sectors to reach and sustain a new division of powers and modus vivendi remains to be seen. Certainly effective, sustainable governance for human security so necessitates.

Furthermore, today such issues rarely get identified let alone prioritized without the active involvement of non-state actors. In the post-war period, typically new issues were put on the international agenda by politicians and scholars. Nowadays, they are increasingly recognized through the innovative analysis and advocacy of INGOs and global think tanks. For a variety of reasons – such as government cutbacks and funding formulas founded on tuition incomes – universities and their research institutes are rarely in the vanguard of identifying or prioritizing 'global issues'. Instead, major think tanks and leading NGOs with their own innovative policy departments (Grant, MacLean and Shaw 2003) are taking greater prominence (Pegg and Wilson 2003). Hence, the growing salience of national to global knowledge and policy networks (Stone 2000).

This reshuffling and re-ranking of policy animators/initiatives is not confined to the traditional world of 'development' but applies likewise to that of 'new' security challenges. Indeed, post-bipolarity, issues of development and conflict, governance and security have increasingly come together (Duffield 2001). This chapter is unusual in that it *juxtaposes these two genres*, even 'disciplines' or 'solitudes', of 'development' and 'security'. Today, these are increasingly interconnected, however uncomfortably, around questions of the international political economy of conflict (Collier 2000; Grant, MacLean and Shaw 2003). In the divisions of global to local labour, there has been a move from more traditional 'peace-keeping' to more robust 'peace-making' – along with the variegated roles of state and non-state actors at different levels of diplomacy in security as well as development policy and practice.

Think tanks and policy networks have not often been considered along with questions of peace-keeping/-building/-making yet in fact, given the structural sources of such tensions and conflicts, any superficial or ahistorical analysis will not be persuasive, let alone effective in terms of informed policy responses. Rather, the roots of conflicts and their resolution or at least amelioration need to be pondered and fathomed. In turn, this means going beyond established rather superficial forms of either strategic or economic analysis: to the messy world of the informal and illegal – that is, mafias and militias around diasporas, drugs, money-laundering, small arms trade and so forth (Cilliers and Mason 1999; Naylor 1999; Reno 2000).

Traditional (realist) state-centric 'track one' modes of official diplomacy have not overcome the difficulties with which states in Africa and elsewhere have been faced in responding effectively to a range of new security threats in the post-Cold War era. However, through more informal and semi-official modes of track two diplomacy, a variety of non-state actors has been increasingly able to establish and then widen their roles in peace-keeping and reconstruction (Cawthra and Luckham 2003; Cliffe 1999). If track one diplomacy is orthodox inter-state and track three non-state, then the intermediate track two involves state officials and others in their personal capacities. It is an ambiguous meso-level policy practice that can inform and reinforce the other two levels.

Contemporary peace-building would be inconceivable without the involvement of NGOs like CARE, Médecins Sans Frontières (MSF), Oxfam and Save the

Children Fund (SCF): that is, non-state track three mediation and negotiation. Indeed, they increasingly agree on divisions of labour amongst themselves (that is, between 'tracks') in terms of such subcontracting roles – children, conversion, education, habitat, health, infrastructure, redeployment, redevelopment, refugees, etc. – all of which have traditionally been considered to be so-called 'low politics' issues (Beman and Sams 2000; MacFarlane *et al.* 2004). By contrast, arriving at mutually agreeable governance arrangements with the African state over time is much more problematic.

In addition to such functional, programmatic activities, elements in civil society, from local to global, increasingly play advocacy roles (Stone 2002). These are of considerable importance in terms of new security issues like land-mines and 'conflict' diamonds. They are also increasingly salient in terms of continuing roles over conflict prevention and reconciliation. As such, track two diplomacy essentially consists of quasi-official albeit private discussions of mixed groups of actors from NGOs, business and the research community and especially people acting in their personal capacities, even if they are formally employed by a state. Such informal, personal interaction has begun to develop in Africa around regional conflicts such as Congo, the Horn, Southern and West Africa. Indeed, given the shrinking of the state on the continent over the last two decades, track three, exclusively non-state, diplomacy might be expected to develop even further in contemporary Africa than in Asia (Shaw 2004b).

Governance for human development/rights/security? Onto multiple 'tracks'?

Established, albeit fluid and multi-layered, policy communities are increasingly turning to 'networks' to get their message across and to exert leverage in decision making. Post-bipolarity, this also increasingly necessitates attention to tracks two and three diplomacy and communication rather than just the traditional mode between states. The possibility of the evolution of track two or track three style diplomacy in Africa, rather than the perpetuation of the 'African state socialist' style of track one, is a function of the development over the last decade of a series of non- or semi-state think tanks. This is particularly the case in South Africa, where many of them grew out of the anti-apartheid struggle – for example, the African Centre for the Cooperative Resolution of Disputes (ACCORD), the Centre for Conflict Resolution (CCR) and the Institute for Global Dialogue (IGD). The appendix lists some of these, and their websites.

All of these institutions are, to a greater and lesser extent, engaged in research as well as advocacy and network to share ideas about advancing policy development. They arrange conferences, networks and workshops where problems of issues such as blood diamonds, drugs, debt, landmines or small arms are debated. They produce policy briefs and make recommendations to both governments and non-state actors with the aim of influencing policy agendas and governance processes.

The new breed of policy institutes (Mkandawire 1998; Stone 2002) interacts mostly with 'like-minded' NGOs over current issues, such as mercenaries and private security, peace-keeping, small arms and landmines, diamonds and coltan, and corruption, to facilitate more transparent processes of energy and mineral extraction.[1] These groups often network through conferences (organized by the institutes or the NGOs) and their electronic facilities enable them to participate in old and new security networks advancing both national and human security[2] (Nation 1999).

Two examples follow, illustrating rather different but not necessarily incompatible aspects of the new human development and security agenda. Blood diamond and debt relief networks are not often juxtaposed, as they treat different issue areas and in this case vary from the global to national levels respectively. Yet, in fact, they are interrelated, as the Ugandan and other African cases illustrate. Furthermore, and conceptually, they reveal distinctive patterns of coalition formation, participation and practice (Grant, MacLean and Shaw 2003). They both illuminate changeable varieties of track one to three diplomacy amongst a range of heterogeneous actors at the turn of the century on these two issues.

The first concerns the international coalition of forces around the global/continental 'blood diamonds' issue, and illustrates the development of a transnational advocacy network (Keck and Sikkink 1998). The second concerns the national response to debt in Uganda, and illustrates the development of a largely national 'epistemic community' (Haas 1992). Despite their heterogeneity, together these advance analysis and practice around sustainable human development and security. Non-state sectors have become increasingly central to the identification and processing of novel issues at all levels, particularly the global, through innovative forms of tracks two and three diplomacy rather than the exclusive or hegemonic use of the traditional track one.

Blood diamonds: the development of a transnational advocacy network

This case began to attract international attention when a small NGO, Partnership Africa Canada (PAC), with offices in Ottawa and Addis Ababa, commissioned a three-person team led by well-known NGO advocate, Ian Smillie (Smillie *et al.* 2000) to research and write a report on the real (economic) causes of the continuing conflicts and traumas of Sierra Leone (Hirsch 2001). In association with other analysts and activists especially in Africa and Europe, it succeeded in generating a snowball effect over the production chain of 'blood' ('conflict' or 'dirty') diamonds. Interacting in a coalition, this NGO was better able to raise publicly the possibility of sanctioning the informal and/or illegal sectors at certain chokepoints either in Liberia or in Antwerp and Tel Aviv (Stein 2001). This small partnership (of the International Peace Information Service in Antwerp and Network Movement for Justice and Development in Freetown with PAC) helped create a wider transnational advocacy network on conflict diamonds. It is now supported, as an indication of its resonance and salience, by a variety of foundations and donors. The PAC report (along with those from the UN and reinforced by analytic contributions (see Reno 1998; Marysse 2003)) helped to inform and encourage parallel debates in a variety of organizations, leading to a 'diamond summit' in Kimberley in May 2000 (*Other Facets* 2001).[3]

The Kimberley meeting brought together a very diverse range of mixed actors who constituted the central stakeholders – labour groups and representatives from cities as well as governments and companies, notably de Beers. The meeting was part of ongoing attempts to contain and reverse any negative impacts of such dirty diamonds from West Africa's informal sector for either human development and security, resulting in a global agreement in early 2003 to regulate the production and movement of rough diamonds. This is less than comprehensive and authoritative but should serve to reduce the flow of arms for uncertified diamonds. Seventy countries are participating, although only half meet the criteria of the Kimberley Process Certification Scheme. Some NGOs worry that without independent monitoring of national controls, credibility and effectiveness will be compromised (*Other Facets* 2001; Smillie 2003). In short, as always with international 'law', there is no authoritative centre to enforce agreements and codes of conduct. Instead, continued attention and pressure from global and local civil society associations will be imperative if the Kimberley agreement is to be effective in practice in the early 2000s.

An epistemic community? Debt relief in Uganda

By contrast to the above example of an extensive transnational coalition around contemporary conflict on the continent, we turn to a more national network. Nevertheless, this national network has 'transnational' connections, to advance HIPC in Uganda, with wider implications for the Great Lakes Region (GLR). As Christiansen with Hovland (2003) indicate, this is a very interesting case of research informing policy and practice, in part because of close professional relations between national, global and NGO leaders and analysts: an epistemic community? (Haas 1992).

Despite the painful contemporary history of Uganda, relatively few NGOs or think tanks have yet emerged which concentrate on human security or peace-building, other than those which treat some consequences or symptoms such as orphans. By contrast, there are several which focus on ecology, gender and HIV/AIDS, and especially debt (Dicklitch 1998 and 2000). The Uganda Debt Network (UDN) has a very interesting genesis that illustrates the importance of determination and coalition (Gariyo 2002; Reno 2002). It grew out of Uganda's 'star' status, which encouraged the donors to be relatively generous in terms of aid amounts and terms. Yet, as the debt grew, an NGO coalition drew attention to its negative developmental consequences, leading to the development of a creative and effective 'epistemic community' (Callaghy 2001: 15–20). This community was advanced by eminent international NGOs like Oxfam and Eurodad, and reinforced by pressure from the global Jubilee 2000 campaign for debt relief. The 'consensual knowledge' of this community, based on a mix of global and national analysis, is that the high cost of debt mitigates against sustainable development, which can only be realized if export incomes go into development projects rather than interest on debt, hence sustained pressure for debt elimination and not simply reduction.[4]

In response, in the mid-1990s, the Uganda Multilateral Debt Fund generated discussions and analyses which led to Uganda being one of the first developing countries to qualify for HIPC and HIPC II terms (Callaghy 2001; Reno 2002). The latter requires NGOs to both help design and effect a Poverty Reduction Strategy Plan (PRSP) based on a set of think tank derived Poverty Reduction Strategy Papers for particular sectors and regions. Organizations such as UDN, UNICEF, World Vision and UNDP (which itself regularly researches and publishes national human development reports) (UNDP 1998, 1999) and partners have become part of the continuing debt and development governance process, with all the ambiguities and complications that it entails (Christiansen with Hovland 2003).

Indeed, Callaghy (2001: 23) suggests that at times international NGOs have become part of the Uganda's development and foreign policy apparatus in advocating relief, with the Ugandan Debt Network in effect becoming an intermediary between local and global communities. In other words, due to the relative vacuum in state capacity, UDN has been shifting between levels: from tracks three to two and sometimes even one. As Callaghy (2001: 31) notes: 'For the international financial institutions and the creditor countries, this process also quietly shifts important responsibility to the international and African NGO community.' To be sure, a combination of a new World Bank President and the Asian crisis facilitated the rethink so that HIPC II constitutes an advance on HIPC, reflective of the persuasive lobbying of the national and transnational epistemic communities:

> The UDN continued to grow and increase its capabilities. By late 2000 it had more than 60 institutional members as well as strong ties to the Uganda Joint Christian Council and business, student, and labour organisations. The Catholic Church gave it particularly strong support. It held several campaigns in Uganda to raise the level of awareness about debt relief, as well as participated in Jubilee 2000's international activities, especially lobbying about HIPC II treatment of Uganda. It launched a major anti-corruption drive to make sure debt savings are used properly and lobbied parliament about future debt levels. Above all, however, it was becoming very active in coordinating civil society participation in the PRSP process, which it was doing with the help of Northern NGOs. Lastly, it had improved its own organisational capabilities and was running its own independent website.
>
> (Callaghy 2001: 33)

In short, the production of a series of PRSPs has augmented think tank research and policy roles in Uganda with important implications for the sustainability of autonomous analysis and advocacy at national and regional levels. As a consequence, effective tracks two and three diplomacy become a more realistic development.

However, it does need to be said that many threats remain which might erode such optimism (Griffiths and Katalikawe 2003). For example, an increasing debt

burden despite HIPC, donor fatigue, unhelpful foreign policies of the bigger powers including multiple conditionalities and high non-tariff barriers, rampant
corruption and embezzlement, HIV/AIDS, ecological decay and vulnerability,
massive poverty and increasing insecurity in the Great Lakes Region. These
issues are all the focus of attention of local to global think tanks as aspects of the
'new security agenda' whereby global research and advocacy networks overlap in
an embryonic regional security community which allows interaction with more
action-oriented NGOs on the ground.

Conclusion: implications for analysis and practice

Regrettably, too much of the burgeoning discourse about both shorter and longer
term 'peace-keeping and -building' in Africa still ignores the active roles of both
African and non-African non-state actors (Beman and Sams 2000; Mekenkamp *et
al*. 1999; SAIIA 2000), especially think tanks, and their emerging roles in effective tracks two and three diplomacy. This chapter has suggested that the 'agency'
of NGOs and think tanks, especially when aggregated through global networks,
needs to be recognized in terms of their capacity to both identify and respond to a
range of 'new' contexts and issues. Otherwise, we cannot begin to understand, for
example, the ability of transnational advocacy networks around, say, blood diamonds, to evolve into an epistemic community such as that centred on UDN over
Uganda's debt.

We conclude by returning to the imperative of juxtaposing a trio of solitudes or
genres relevant to African security communities. These situate the emergence of
networks or partnerships and relate to the tension between advocacy networks and
epistemic communities and so advance creative track two or three *peace-building
governance*. Together they present a series of rather serious challenges to prevailing state-centric analysis and practice both on and off the continent.

First, the emergence of such new forms of governance and coalitions confronts
established assumptions still prevalent in political science about state-centric government. The incorporation of diverse non-state actors into 'triangular' forms of
governance in Uganda as elsewhere challenges orthodox notions of 'development
administration' or 'public policy' as the prerogative of states alone (MacLean,
Quadir and Shaw 2001). Likewise, notions of 'transitions' and redirection, let
alone conversion and redeployment, have to incorporate continuous roles of
MNCs and NGOs in GLR as has been the case with NGOs in Eastern Europe and
Central Asia. The growing diversity of think tanks in such areas and cases has
begun to identify a range of specific and distinctive catalysts among regions and
time-periods. In turn, their roles raise 'old-fashioned' issues of accountability and
transparency around their own burgeoning operations, as they seek to bridge the
boundary between civil society, the corporate sector and the state (MacLean and
Shaw 1999; Murithi 1998).

Second, as Smillie *et al*. (2000) assert, prevailing established orthodox versions of either realism or capitalism, international relations or economics, cannot
explain continuing conflicts in West (or Central) Africa. Both have to incorporate

new actors and issues into their perspectives if they are to inform contemporary peace-keeping or -building: that is, non-state actors and non-formal issues. On the ground, mixed actor coalitions around diamonds, gender, HIV/AIDS, land-mines and small arms challenge state-centrism (Tomlin *et al.* 1998). At the global level, increasingly extensive informal economic relations undermine the formal market and prospects for regulation and monitoring via arms bazaar, blood diamonds, drug sales, smuggling of humans, the world of off-shore banks or money-laundering. These are the other aspects of 'globalizations' (Mittelman 2000).

Furthermore, the related 'political economy of conflict' perspective (Reno 2002) not only challenges prevailing notions of peace-keeping and -building but also established assumptions that conflict is bad for business. Instead, the Fowler (2000), Harker (2000), Smillie *et al.* (2000) and other reports indicate that conflict can be positive for a minority of shorter-term economic interests even if negative for the majority over the longer-term. Hence the imperative of NGO analysis and advocacy to both get new issues on the global agenda but also to articulate and advance them through tracks two and three diplomacy. Once momentum is built, then issues like blood diamonds and debt relief can be placed on the agenda of inter-state track one institutions and turned into international or national 'law', albeit under the watchful eye of participants in the other two tracks, in case states backslide from hard-won agreements with non-state actors.

Finally, then, the literature on African conflicts and peace-building needs to bring in notions of tracks two and three leading towards peace-building governance rather than assume that defining and realizing a security community (Adler and Barnett 1998) is the function of governments alone at the level of so-called track one (MacLean, Harker and Shaw 2002). The proliferation and recognition of expert bodies of actors – whether these be think tanks, universities or NGOs – is an important development in the post-apartheid and post-bipolar continent (Shaw 2001a; 2001b). It is leading to enhanced prospects for both advocacy networks and epistemic communities around a variety of issues like debt and conflict central to human development/security whether more established scholars and traditional schools of analysis have so realized or not (Dunn and Shaw 2001).

Appendix: Useful websites on think tanks and track-two diplomacy in Africa

http://www.accord.org.za
http://www.africa-research-bulletin.com
http://www.africa-confidential.com
http://www.alliancesforafrica.org
http://www.ccrweb.ccr.uct.ac.za
http://www.cdnpeacekeeping.ns.ca
http://www.copri.dk
http://www.copri.dk and ipra
http://www.diamonds.net

http://www.euconflict.org
http://www.gdnet.org
http://www.globalknowledge.org
http://www.globalpolicy.org
http://www.humansecurity.gc.ca
http://www.idrc.ca
http://www.idsnet.org
http://www.igd.org.za
http://www.iiss.org
http://www.icg.org
http://www.ipacademy.inter.net
http://www.isn.ethz.ch
http://www.iss.co.za
http://www.jubileeplus.org
http://www.mwengo.org
http://www.nsi-ins.ca
http://www.oneworld.org
http://www.pacweb.org
http://www.prio.no
http://www.sipri.se
http://www.sn.apc.org
http://www.un.org and depts and eca
http://www.unrisd.org
http://www.unesco.org and securipax

Notes

1 For example, 130 NGOs including the Open Society Institute and Global Witness participate in the new Extractive Industries Transparency Initiative (http://www.publish whatyoupay.org).
2 See http://www.mwengo.org and http://www.sn.apc.org.
3 See http://www.partnershipafricacanada.org.
4 See http://www.jubileeplus.org.

References

Adler, Emmanuel and Barnett, Michael (eds) (1998) *Security Communities.* Cambridge: Cambridge University Press.
Beman, Eric G. and Sams, Katie E. (eds) (2000) *Peacekeeping in Africa: Capabilities and Culpabilities.* Geneva and Pretoria: UNIDIR and ISS.
Callaghy, Thomas M. (2001) 'Networks and Governance in Africa: Innovation in the Debt Regime', in Thomas Callaghy *et al.* (eds) *Intervention and Transnationalism in Africa: Global-local Networks of Power.* New York: Cambridge University Press, pp. 115–48.
Cawthra, Gavin and Luckham, Robin (eds) (2003) *Governing Insecurity: Democratic Control of Military and Security Establishments in Transitional, Democracies.* London: Zed.

Christiansen, Karin with Hovland, Ingie (2003) *The PRSP Initiative: Multilateral Policy Change and the Role of Research.* ODI Working Paper No. 216. London: Overseas Development Institute.

Cilliers, Jakkie and Mason, Peggy (eds) (1999) *Peace, Profit or Plunder? The Privatisation of Security in War-torn African Societies.* Halfway House: ISS.

Cliffe, Lionel (ed.) (1999) 'Special Issue: Complex Political Emergencies' *Third World Quarterly* 20 (1, March): 1–256.

Collier, Paul (2000) 'Greed for Diamonds and Other Lootable Commodities Fuels Civil Wars'. Washington: IBRD.

Dicklitch, Susan (1998) *The Elusive Promise of NGOs in Africa: Lessons from Uganda.* London: Macmillan.

Dicklitch, Susan (2000) 'The Incomplete Democratic Transition in Uganda', in Remonda Bensabat Kleinberg and Janine A. Clark (eds) *Economic Liberalization, Democratization and Civil Society in the Developing World.* London: Macmillan, pp. 109–28.

Duffield, Mark (2001) *Global Governance and the New Wars: The Merging of Development and Security.* London: Zed.

Dunn, Kevin C. and Shaw, Timothy M. (eds) (2001) *Africa's Challenge to International Relations Theory.* London: Palgrave.

Dwan, Renata (2000) 'Armed Conflict Prevention, Management and Resolution', in *SIPRI Yearbook 2000.* London: Oxford University Press, pp. 77–134.

Fowler Report (2000) 'Report of Sanctions Committee on Violation of Security Council Sanctions against UNITA. Robert Fowler, Chair'. New York: United Nations.

Gariyo, Zie (2002) 'Civil Society and Global Finance in Africa: the PRSP process in Uganda', in Jan Aart Scholte with Albrecht Schnabel (eds) *Civil Society and Global Finance.* London: Routledge, pp. 51–63.

Grant, J. Andrew, MacLean, Sandra J. and Shaw, Timothy M. (2003) 'Emerging Transnational Coalitions around Diamonds and Oil in Civil Conflicts in Africa', in Marjorie Griffin Cohen and Stephen McBride (eds.) *Global Turbulence: Social Activists' and State Responses to Globalization.* Aldershot: Ashgate, pp. 124–39.

Griffiths, Aaron and Katalikawe, James (2003) 'The Reformulation of Ugandan Democracy', in Sunil Bastian and Robin Luckham (eds.) *Can Democracy be Designed? The Politics of Institutional Choice In Conflict-torn Societies.* London: Zed, pp. 93–119.

Haas, Peter M. (1992) 'Introduction: Epistemic Communities and International Policy Coordination' *International Organization* 46 (Winter): 1–35.

Harker Report (2000) 'Report to the Minister of Foreign Affairs on "Human Security in Sudan: Report of a Canadian Assessment Mission"'. Ottawa: Department of Foreign Affairs and International Trade.

Hirsh, John L. (2001) *Sierra Leone: Diamonds and the Struggle for Democracy.* Boulder: Lynne Rienner for IPA.

Keck, Margaret and Sikkink, Kathryn (1998) *Activists Beyond Borders: Advocacy Networks in International Politics.* Ithaca: Cornell University Press.

MacFarlane, Neil *et al.* (eds) (2004) *In Search of Human Security in and for Africa.* Tokyo: UN University Press.

MacLean, Sandra J and Shaw, Timothy M. (1999) 'The Emergence of Regional Civil Society: Contributions to a New Human Security Agenda', in Ho-Won Jeong (ed.) *The New Agenda for Peace Research*. Aldershot: Ashgate, pp. 289–308.

MacLean, Sandra J., Quadir, Fahim and Shaw, Timothy M. (eds) (2001) *Prospects for Governance in Asia and Africa: Globalizing Ethnicities*. Aldershot: Ashgate.

MacLean, Sandra J., Harker, John and Shaw, Timothy M. (eds) (2002) *Advancing Human Security and Development in Africa: Reflections on NEPAD*. Halifax: Centre for Foreign Policy Studies.

Marysse, S (2003) 'Regress and War: The Case of the DRCongo' *European Journal of Development Research* 15 (1, June): 73–98.

Mbabazi, Pamela and Shaw, Timothy M. (2000) 'NGOs and Peace-Building in the Great Lakes Region of Africa: States, Civil Societies and Companies in the New Millennium', in David Lewis and Tina Wallace (eds) *New Roles and Relevance: Development NGOs and the Challenge of Change*. West Hartford: Kumarian, pp. 187–97.

Mekenkamp, Monique *et al.* (eds) (1999) *Searching for Peace in Africa: An Overview of Conflict Prevention and Management Activities*. Utrecht: European Platform for Conflict Prevention and Transformation with ACCORD.

Mittelman, James H. (2000) *The Globalization Syndrome: Transformation and Resistance*. Princeton: Princeton University Press.

Mkandawire, Thandika (1998) 'Notes on Consultancy and Research in Africa' #98.13. Copenhagen: Centre for Development Research.

Murithi, Timothy (1998) 'NGOs and Conflict Resolution in Africa: Facilitators or Aggravators of Peacekeeping?', in Furley and May (eds) *Peacekeeping in Africa*. Aldershot: Ashgate, pp. 265–86.

Nation, Fitzroy (1999) 'Africanets: No Boundaries', in Mekenkamp *et al.* (eds) *Searching for Peace in Africa*. Utrecht: European Platform for Conflict Prevention and Transformation, pp. 45–51.

Naylor, R. T. (1999) *Patriots and Profiteers: On Economic Warfare, Embargo Busting and State-sponsored Crime*. Toronto: McClelland and Stewart.

Other Facets (Ottawa: PAC, occasionally, starting April 2001)

Parpart, Jane L. and Shaw, Timothy M. (2002) 'African Development Debates and Prospects at the Beginning of the Twenty-first Century', in Patrick J. McGowan and Philip Nel (eds) *Power, Wealth and Global Equity: An International Relations Textbook for Africa*. 2nd edition. Cape Town: UCT Press for IGD, pp. 296–307.

Pegg, Scott and Wilson, Alissa. (2003) 'Corporations, Conscience and Conflict: Assessing NGO Reports on the Private Sector Role in African Resource Conflicts' *Third World Quarterly* 24 (6, December): 1179–89.

Reno, William (1998) *Warlord Politics and African States*. Boulder: Lynne Rienner.

Reno, William (2000) 'Internal Wars, Private Enterprise and the Shift in Strong State-Weak State Relations' *International Politics* 37 (1, March): 57–74.

Reno, William (2002) 'Uganda's Politics of War and Debt Relief' *Review of International Political Economy* 9 (3, August): 415–35.

SAIIA (2000) Special Issue on 'War and Peace in Africa' *South African Journal of International Affairs* 7 (1, Summer): 1–137.

Shaw, Timothy M. (2001a) 'African Foreign Policy in the New Millennium: From Coming Anarchies to Security Communities? From New Regionalisms to New Realisms?', in Kevin C. Dunn and Timothy M. Shaw (eds.) *Africa's Challenge to International Relations Theory*. London: Palgrave, pp. 204–19.

Shaw, Timothy M. (2001b) 'Peace-building Partnerships and Human Security', in Rob Potter and Vandana Desai (eds) *Arnold Companion to Development Studies*. London: Arnold, pp. 449–53.

Shaw, Timothy M. (2004a) 'Africa', in Mary Hawkesworth and Maurice Kogan (eds) *Encyclopaedia of Government and Politics.* 2nd edition. London: Routledge, pp. 1184–97.

Shaw, Timothy M. (2004b) 'Prospects for Human Development and Security in Asia', in Marika Vicziany, David Wright-Neville and Pete Lentini (eds) *Regional Security in the Asia Pacific: 9/11 and After*. Cheltenham: Edward Elgar, pp. 40–50.

Shaw, Timothy M. and Nyang'oro, Julius E. (1999) 'Conclusion: African Foreign Policies and the Next Millennium – Alternative Perspectives', in Stephen Wright (ed.) *African Foreign Policies*. Boulder: Westview, pp. 237–48.

Shaw, Timothy M. and Nyang'oro, Julius E. (2000) 'African Renaissance in the New Millennium? From Anarchy to Emerging Markets?', in Richard Stubbs and Geoffrey R. D. Underhill (eds) *Political Economy and the Changing Global order.* 2nd edition. Toronto: Oxford University Press, pp. 275–84.

Smillie, Ian, Gberie, Lansana and Hazelton, Ralph (2000) 'The Heart of the Matter: Sierra Leone, Diamonds and Human Security'. Ottawa: Partnership Africa Canada.

Smillie, Ian (2003) 'Motherhood, Apple Pie and False Teeth: Corporate Social Responsibility in the Diamond Industry'. Ottawa: Partnership Africa Canada.

Stein, Nicholas (2001) 'The De Beers Story: A New Cut on an Old Monopoly' *Fortune* 143 (4, March): 80–95.

Stone, Diane (2000) 'Think Tank Transnationalisation and Non-Profit Analysis, Advice and Advocacy' *Global Society* 14 (2, April): 153–89.

Stone, Diane (ed.) (2002) 'Special Issue on Global Knowledge Networks' *Global Networks* 2 (1, January): 1–93.

Tomlin, Brian *et al.* (eds) (1998) *To Walk without Fear: The Global Movement to Ban Landmines.* Toronto: Oxford University Press.

UNDP (1998) *Human Development Report on Uganda*. New York: UNDP.

UNDP (1999) *Human Development Report 1999.* New York: UNDP.

11 From civil society development to policy research

The transformation of the Soros Foundations Network and its Roma policies

Andrea Krizsán and Violetta Zentai

Introduction

The policy making process is not the monopoly of the State. In all stages of the process, from agenda setting and decision making, through implementation to monitoring and evaluation, tasks can be shared by state and non-state actors. This is very much true for the case of the transition countries of Central and Eastern Europe (CEE). From the beginning of the 1990s, these countries had not finished the reform of their state structures when they faced new policy challenges. Indeed some of these were newly occurring challenges, others were problems with a long history, which came to be recognized or redefined following the 45 years of socialist regime. These states have done better in addressing the challenges in some fields, but done notoriously badly in other fields.

Some of the especially sensitive policy fields, however, which are of major importance to a well functioning democracy, are still considerably undeveloped, and in need of conceptually sound, efficient and consistent public policies. Experience, and frequently expertise, in research, definition, implementation, and monitoring of appropriate policies are often not available to the policy makers. Health care, education, reform of the judiciary and law enforcement mechanisms, policies relating to vulnerable groups of the population, including different national or ethnic minorities, women, and the mentally disabled are policy areas of this sort.

In these sensitive areas, the activity of state agencies is often complemented by other players, most notably international organisations and the non-governmental sector. Several countries in the region have recently become new members of the European Union (EU). The possibility of accession has been a strong incentive for the harmonisation of their public policies with EU standards. Other international organisations (World Bank, the International Monetary Fund, the United Nations Development Programme – UNDP, and the United States Agency for International Development – USAID) have also played important roles in defining and implementing sound policies in most of the above mentioned fields, however contested those policies often appeared. Non-governmental organisations have also become crucial policy players in the respective policy areas.

Our paper will focus on one of the most important non-governmental actors in the countries of the region: the Soros Foundations Network. We argue that the network played an influential role throughout the region during the last decade in promoting policy research, evaluating policy options, initiating and disseminating best practices, and monitoring policies in several of the above mentioned sensitive areas. The network functioned as a mechanism of bridging knowledge production and policy and thus influenced transnational and national policy processes. We make our case through the example of the network's involvement in Roma policies in Central and Eastern Europe.

The Soros Foundations Network and its policy 'awakening'

The international financier and philanthropist, George Soros, has been actively involved since the mid-1980s in supporting the dissident movements in some of the countries of the region. The aim of his support was to transform these closed societies into open ones, inspired by the theorem of Karl Popper on 'open society'.

> Unlike closed societies dominated by the state, open societies are characterized by a reliance on the rule of law, the existence of a democratically elected government, a diverse and vigorous civil society, respect for minorities and minority opinions, and a free market economy.
>
> (OSI 1994: 5–6)

By 2000, 'national foundations' were established in almost all countries of Central and Eastern Europe, the states of Former Soviet Union, and several other places elsewhere in the world. What we call today the Soros network consists of a number of national (local) foundations, the Open Society Institute, Budapest (OSI), established in 1993 as a regional centre, the Budapest-based Central European University established in 1991, and the Open Society Institute, New York. At the end of the last decade, the whole network embraced 1,000 people in fifty offices across more than thirty countries.[1] From the end of the 1990s, the network has also started to engage itself in various debates regarding global transformations and as a consequence, ventured to reach out to new regions of the world. Combining East–West, West–East, and East–East transport of ideas, the programmes of the network critically examine thorny issues of late modern and emerging democracies not only in a post-socialist but in a global context. Such issues include the loss of trust in various political institutions, the controversial impacts of the enhanced power of media, the crumbling of traditional welfare structures, tensions evoked by cross-national movement of people, and ethnicisation of social cleavages.

How does the network operate? Network-wide missions and programmes are determined by central decision making bodies in New York and Budapest; however, the locally embedded national foundations are always given a broad autonomy in setting their own objectives and mastering implementation themselves. George Soros conceives of his local partners as talented *bricoleurs* who generate a variety of institutions from principles that they commonly respect. He views the foundations all over the region as microcosms of open society. Accordingly, foundations are self-organized units with substantial autonomy in making decisions and taking responsibility for these decisions. In short, the Soros Foundations Network is a transnational network of independent organisations held together by personal philanthropy drives, the initial organisational philosophy embodying the principles of the 'open society' and the diverging convictions in the best programmatic responses to the challenges of post-socialist transition and globalisation.

In Soros' mind, the early goals were defined in terms of the Communist menace. In the early 1990s, the mission was refined: in particular, those spheres of social and cultural practice were marked as the ones in need of financial support that could not easily benefit from the emerging market economies. Thus, the Soros Foundations Network pursued individual grant making for scholarly research, academic advancement of the local expert communities, and enhancing diversified civil societies and independent media. For example, the Soros Network Foundations in Hungary awarded one-year fellowships for dozens of young academicians every year to pursue post-graduate studies in Western schools, multi-year grants for developing innovative multi-disciplinary programmes in the humanities and social sciences, major support to develop libraries and special colleges with extra-curriculum activities. Conference participation abroad was supported financially to encourage personal networking among new elites and intellectuals. The Foundation also supported grassroots non-profit organisations directly by institutional grants and indirectly by sponsoring 'incubator houses' and NGO training and support centres. Another well-respected funding activity of the foundation was to support the mushrooming critical journals and periodicals that helped in building a new public space in the country. The Soros Foundation in Hungary was not unique with this portfolio: other foundations in the region also invested heavily in generating a new elite, to enhance the freedom of thought and speech, and build a strong NGO community.

From the mid-1990s, a step-by-step redefinition of mission has taken place in the network. On the one hand, in crucial areas of open society development, the idea of *institution building* received primary attention in addition to supporting individual initiatives, one-time campaigns, and advocacy actions. On the other hand, Soros recognized that:

> If there is any lesson to be learned, it is that the collapse of a repressive regime does not automatically lead to the establishment of an open society. An open society is not merely the absence of government intervention and oppression. It is a complicated, sophisticated structure, and deliberate effort is required to bring it into existence.
>
> (Soros 1997: 10–11)

As a consequence, the network started to examine providing support for state institutions in the CEE and Former Soviet Union region in defining, implementing, and monitoring of their *public policies* in some key policy areas such as education and public health policy, legal reform, especially human rights issues, and media free-dom. As Aryeh Neier, the president of the Open Society Institute New York wrote:

> Now … in each country where we operate we have to concentrate on a few areas that we consider particularly important and where we think that we can make a difference; and we have to ensure that efforts that must endure can be sustained without us.
>
> (Neier 1998: 15)

With these developments in mind, the OSI Foundations Network has some features that might identify it as a regional 'transnational advocacy network'. However, unlike the South Asian Research Network identified by Shirin Rai in this volume, the Soros Foundations Network is a more formal and institutionalised network with an established bureaucracy, relatively secure funding and gradually centralis-ing structure. Given the interest in policy implementation, capacity-building and improved delivery of public services, the Soros Foundations Network also has some features in common with (global) public policy networks. Yet, the network is protective of its autonomy and independence and while it engages in partnerships, it does not seek sustained, semi-official tri-sectoral ties with governments, interna-tional organisations or business.

From the end of the 1990s, capacity building for facilitating policy reforms has become an explicit goal of the network. The national foundations have started to build policy research and policy making capacities by giving support to the emerging think tanks, higher education courses in relevant areas, associations of policy experts, pilot projects implementing policy innovations on national and sub-national levels, etc. The 'network programs' – transnational issue-driven ini-tiatives within the umbrella of the OSI-Budapest and OSI-New York – have generated comparative policy research in a number of areas (for example educa-tion, judiciary and penitentiary reform, decentralisation of government systems, media freedom and broadcasting regulations, minority protection, just to name a few). Dissemination of research results has targeted international, national and sub-national actors, who strive to articulate opinions in domestic policy debates. Network programmes have also continued their institution building activities, tar-geting both governmental units responsible for policy analysis and non-governmental groups engaged in research and advocacy. These efforts have become tied to the legacy of the previous network mission of promoting civil society development. Another important instrument used by the Soros Foundations Network for improving the policy processes is to support interna-tional NGOs – such as the European Roma Rights Centre or the Civic Education Project – of significant knowledge and reputation mobilized to the benefit of local parties. Cooperation among national and sub-national governments, interna-tional organisations, and locally rooted think tanks, professionals, and NGOs has become crucial in most of the newly defined policy fields.

Within the framework of the Public Policy Initiative of the Local Government and Public Service Reform Initiative, the network started to provide support for the creation and the networking of policy research centres across the Central and Eastern European region (LGI 2002b). The overall mission of the initiative was 'to increase the capacity, profile and standards for policy analysis in Eastern Europe and to foster the creation of international support links and networks for think tanks'.[2] The activity of the initiative consists of:

- professional support for policy advice by generating resource databases and networks of specialists and experts
- capacity building for think tanks
- support and training in procurement and fundraising
- fostering partnerships for selected think tanks
- encouraging the setting up of professional associations across the region
- animating a mutual support network for Soros related policy centres.

The nature of a shifting mission within the network can be grasped in areas in which the network has traditionally put significant resources, such as education policy. Throughout the first years of operation, education was the most important and the largest area of actions within the organisation. (In 1998 30 per cent of the total network expenditure was spent on education programmes – OSI 1998: 97). In 1998, a Budapest-based Institute for Education Policy was established to support other network programmes and national foundations in creating a coherent policy framework, and thus to inform and guide this large array of activities. At the centre of activities in the field of education policy was 'the recognition that one of the main obstacles to effective education change in the region has been a highly centralised, top-down approach to education planning, which has excluded major stakeholders from education policy development'. Some countries were seen to be in need of support in finding appropriate reform solutions. Other countries introduced reforms, but problems occurred in the implementation and follow-up process of these reforms.[3]

Assistance to the national foundations in developing large-scale education programmes implied an analysis of the relevant countries' educational systems, identification of issues relevant to the foundations' missions, and the development of approaches ensuring maximum impact, leverage, and sustainability. In 2002, large-scale educational policy reform projects were in progress, in the Albanian, Bulgarian, Georgian, Mongolian, Romanian and Russian national foundations. At the core of the encouraged reforms is an approach to education that emphasises teaching and learning developing human potential, systemic change, cost-effective and sustainable solutions, a focus on equity and quality, and democratic governance. Assessment and monitoring of educational systems and programmes currently in place, development of good practice initiatives, and formulation of recommendations for policy change are all based on policy research commissioned either by the network program or by the education programmes of the national foundations.[4]

In 1998, OSI, Budapest set up an International Policy Fellowship (IPF) scheme to identify and support innovative policy projects initiated by the next generation of young open society leaders in Central and Eastern Europe. Fellows (40–45 of them in each term) carry out individual research projects of strategic interest to the Soros Foundations Network. Beyond funding, the scheme provides a 'hot house' policy training programme in Budapest, which is meant to enhance the policy competency and research communication strategies of fellows as well as promote networking among them. The IPF scheme is seen as a crucial input for the development of the already existing and newly formed Soros Foundations Network programmes. The programme targets the development of individual capacities for sensitive and innovative thinking irrespective of institutional background. In the last three years, however, more and more applicants came with a major commitment either to acknowledged local think tanks, governmental bodies and task forces. In spite of the diverse research topics and uneven quality of final products, the scheme often discovers and launches reputable experts in different localities who induce exemplary impacts on the policy debates or sometimes on decision making processes in their respective countries.[5] After completing their research projects, fellows often become acknowledged policy researchers, thinkers, and occasionally, they are appointed to government positions (advisers, senior executives, etc.). Equally important is the influence, often transnational in nature, that fellows have on each other's understanding of the policy context in the region and of the potentials of 'cross-sectoral' policy thinking.

The growing policy awareness in the network has led to establishing new programmes with missions novel to the network. One of these new programmes has called for systematic efforts to build a particular knowledge in the organisation. The EU Accession Monitoring Program (EUMAP), launched in 2000, aims at examining the performance of the accession countries[6] along the three political criteria defined in Copenhagen in 1993: implementation of minority rights, independence of the judiciary, and transparency of governance (fighting against corruption). The programme has also supported an independent initiative of the Network Women's Program and the Open Society Foundation-Romania to monitor equal opportunities for women and men. EUMAP works in its monitoring efforts together with local NGOs and civil society organisations to encourage a direct dialogue between governmental and non-governmental actors.

This regular examination of performance is a specific form of policy knowledge, often called *monitoring*. In this case, monitoring is performed with the coordination of the EUMAP on a transnational basis, and thus underscored by a commonly shared conceptual frame and methodology. The indicators allow the use of different qualitative and quantitative methods and give a relatively large autonomy of local experts to explain the local contexts shaping the values of the indicators. In other words, the transnational method is sufficiently flexible to be modified by local knowledge. Another specific characteristic of this monitoring knowledge is that it deliberately builds on the expertise of local independent NGOs, think tanks and networks of researchers to ensure a critical approach both to monitored state policies and – although in a more cautious way – to guiding EU norms.[7] Policy recommendations addressed to governments, EU institutions and NGOs are part of each EUMAP report.

In some instances the reports contributed to opening up constructive dialogue between EUMAP report contributors and high profile national level policy makers. For instance, the reporter for EUMAP's 2002 report on the situation of Muslims in the UK met with British Home Office Minister Lord Filkin on several occasions as a follow-up to the OSI report launch, as well as with the UK Equal Opportunities Commission to discuss the report's recommendations to that body. A regular dialogue has been established between OSI and Home Office representatives on UK and EU enlargement issues. This has included briefing meetings between HO representatives and the editors of the Judicial Capacity and Corruption reports on the situation in EU candidate countries (EUMAP 2003). Given that EUMAP clearly targets EU institutional policy making, the reports were formally presented in Brussels. The programme has been invited to a number of important international human rights and rule of law forums; NGOs started to refer to it for methodological guidance and for support in advocacy.

In retrospect, we argue that even the 'traditional' grant-giving and civil society development activities of the Soros Foundations Network generated knowledge that informed policy thinking. General NGO capacity enhancement, institution building in education and other policy arenas and support for watchdog organisations often highlighted the empirical knowledge of programme staff, board members and experts and thus substituted or complemented research needed in many policy areas. This knowledge, in most cases, was not systematic or codified, yet had a subtle impact on the culture of policy thinking. Importantly, this knowledge was shaped in transnational exchanges, in which international expertise was transformed by the diversity of local knowledge. Each programme within the network has a genuinely international staff, whereas the staff members of the local Soros foundations are regularly brought together for 'East–East' sharing of experience, or for undertaking strategic planning and evaluations with the network programmes.

Since the start of policy awakening in the network, knowledge has been sought in areas in which state agencies do not have empirical evidence to make decisions or implement reforms. This evidence might be lacking due to weaknesses of official statistics, insufficient research capacities or knowledge absorption capacities, or due to blindness of decision makers and the uncertainties presented with transition processes. Our examples from the network activities indicate that convincing and credible sets of knowledge – both traditional research as well as local expertise – can be generated when strong methodological underpinnings are developed with transnational cooperation and external review mechanisms, and when reports are written in a style congruent with major international policy debates and their local dialects. The Educational Policy Institute papers, the EUMAP reports, and many IPF research projects were exercises not only in bridging research and policy but also in bridging different traditions of research and policy analysis.

This paper cannot examine the full complexity of changes that occurred in the Soros Foundations Network at the end of the 1990s and the implications of these changes in bridging knowledge generation and policy. Therefore, we have selected the Roma programmes and the policy issues relating to the Roma minority, which, as a cross-cutting field, seems to be an apt choice to highlight the Soros network's involvement in policy research and policy making. The Roma also constitute a cross-border community increasingly subject to international attention and for whom a range of transnational policy responses has been generated. This became most apparent with the Roma conference jointly convened by the OSI and the World Bank in 2003.

Roma programmes in the Soros Foundations Network

The Roma minority is the largest ethnic minority in the region. The Roma minority appears to be a major 'loser' group in the transition to democracy and market economy in the region. This social group generally fares badly along all social and economic indicators: on average its members have a lower level of education, higher rates of unemployment, higher rates of poverty and poorer housing than the majority population. The ongoing residential and educational segregation of Roma is a hard fact. Prejudice against Roma and racism is relatively strong among the majority population (see Ringold, Orenstein and Wilkens 2003; UNDP 2002).

At the start of the transformation processes in the early 1990s, the enormous disadvantages of the Roma community in countries of the region were considered as issues to be handled either by policies related to national or ethnic minorities or by general social policies. Later, however, it became clear that the problems related to Roma communities are complex and also unique so that developing specific policy packages for the social integration of this minority is unavoidable. Most countries in the region made the first, rather precarious steps in this respect at the end of the 1990s, but the refinement of these policies, their implementation and monitoring are lagging behind.

For some time, Soros Foundations Network programmes in Budapest have included issues related to Roma policy among their priorities. Furthermore, the local Soros foundations in all countries with a considerable Roma population have intensified their activities in this particular field of public policy. Some of them have developed Roma programme strategies, others have incorporated important elements of their Roma programmes in different sectoral programmes they pursue. Formulation of Roma policy packages has very strong implications for the field of education, social policy, human and women's rights and public health policies (LGI 2000; 2002a).

The shift in the focus of the network activities towards policy analysis and evaluation is visible in the field of Roma programmes as well. In 1994 the annual report of the network mentions 'support for education and cultural programs, including the training of Roma as teachers, journalists, and human rights advocates' and promotion of tolerance and understanding between Roma and non-Roma. Funding was granted to educational programmes, vocational schools and summer schools, Roma theatres, bilingual newspapers, language courses for teachers of Romanes, for the creation of social bureaus to provide advice to Roma regarding their civil rights, and for stipends supporting Roma students (OSI 1994: 32–3).

176 Andrea Krizsán and Violetta Zentai

In early 1996, OSI-Budapest scaled up its work on Roma issues. A programme officer in Budapest started working with the national foundations to develop Roma-related programmes. Substantial support was made available to the newly established European Roma Rights Centre (ERRC), an independent public interest law organisation based in Budapest that monitors the human rights situation of the Roma and works to promote respect for those rights (OSI 1996: 126).[8] Surveys were conducted in Albania, Bulgaria, Romania, Hungary, Macedonia, Slovakia and Ukraine in order to assess the needs of the Roma. In parallel, discussions were started with representatives of governmental and international bodies (such as Canadian International Development Agency – CIDA, World Bank, UNDP) for improving the assessment of needs of the Roma. Both the appointment of the Roma Programs' Officer and the support provided to the launching of ERRC show that as early as 1996 the network Roma programmes were ready to shift towards a more comprehensive, concerted, and constructive policy oriented thinking. This also meant increasing recognition of the issue as a transnational one, rather than as an issue to be addressed only at the national level.

There is no single cause for this relatively early, and gradually increasing, policy awareness of the network in Roma issues. One may sense here the sensitivity to human rights issues of the critical intellectuals in the region having a significant representation in different local and central boards of the network. Heated public debates on the ethnic division of societies in the region have also cast light on Roma issues. Perhaps, most importantly, government performance is conspicuously lagging behind the promises and elementary democratic requirements in most related countries in the region. By the same token, it became evident that civic action can not exclusively solve those structural problems, which have accumulated in many of the countries over several decades.

In 1997 the Regional Roma Participation Program (RPP) was established at OSI-Budapest. The main goals of the programme were to enable the Roma

> to participate in the majority society in which they live; to open the ways for the Roma leading peaceful lives amidst the general population, while at the same time retaining their identity, to encourage the Roma to take part in the democratization process and to use their own potential to improve their situation in the region; and to empower the Roma to fight for an open society in which they can take part as equal partners.
>
> (OSI 1996: 141–2)

RPP works in coordination with all the other network programmes that have relevance for the issue (Education Program, EUMAP, LGI, Network Woman's Program, etc.) and with the Roma programmes of the national foundations, as well. Through its three subprogrammes, RPP targets the integration of Roma communities in society parallel to their empowerment through capacity building, training and education in different important arenas of life; the improvement of communication between and within Roma communities; the public access to information and thus a better communication between Roma and non-Roma citizens. RPP intends to help the Roma by inviting them to manage the development of their community by themselves, instead of creating programmes outside the Roma community and introducing them to the Roma.

In addition to the Roma Participation Program, other Soros Foundations Network programmes also strengthened the programme components targeting the Roma during the last couple of years. The 1998 Network Report writes

> one area of focus shared by many of these programs [the network programs] in 1998 was an attempt to more effectively integrate the Roma into their activities. The Network Woman's Program invited Roma women to participate in a human rights training program and jointly funded a fellowship with the Roma Participation program. The Media Program supports efforts to build up Roma radio and television channels. The Step by Step Program is reaching out to schools in Roma communities and producing multicultural teaching materials for those schools. In the area of Roma culture, a new program was created late in the year to fund scholarly research and the establishment of cultural centres.
>
> (OSI 1998: 88)

Roma related network programmes are divided into four categories (OSI 2003a): programmes supporting political and civic participation, programmes supporting educational reform, programmes dealing with discrimination, and cultural identity building programmes. Most Roma programmes have some policy relevance, and most use in one way or another research to inform their work. Some of these intend to influence directly policy making processes by advocacy, monitoring, setting up good practices, promoting dialogue with policy makers, promoting policy relevant research. It is more typical however that policy impact is indirect, for example through capacity building, consciousness raising, sensitising public debates, and so forth.

A good example for programmes attempting direct policy impact based on policy research is the educational programmes in different units of the network. In 1999 the Budapest-based Institute for Education Policy released a strategic position paper titled 'Breaking the Spiral: a Roma Education Initiative'. Based on an analysis of the situation of Roma children in education, the paper proposed a series of actions for the Soros Foundations Network centring on the idea of intervention. According to the paper, the Roma Education Initiative should pursue two main purposes: first a 'negative' one, that is the elimination of discriminatory processes, second, a 'positive' one, through proactive interventions the establishment of the conditions that enable Roma children to participate in the teaching–learning process on equal terms.

Programmes addressing ethnic discrimination can also be seen as efforts towards directly influencing the policy process. The advocacy work of the European Roma Rights Centre (ERRC) relies on research results commissioned throughout the network. For example, the work of an International Policy Fellow, David Canek,[9] on educational segregation of Roma in the Czech Republic informed the advocacy work of the ERRC. Research completed for the book *On the Margins. Slovakia* by Ina Zoon (2001) with a grant awarded by the Network Public Health Program and OSI's Human Rights Fund also informed advocacy work of the ERRC, especially in cases dealing with forced sterilisation of Roma women in Slovakia. The European Accession Monitoring Program's activities in the field of discrimination are also very important. ERRC has used several of the country reports produced by the EUMAP for advocacy purposes.

The Managing Multiethnic Communities Project of the Local Government and Public Service Initiative – another OSI Budapest based network programme – illustrates well the network's involvement in Roma policies. Launched in 1996, the Managing Multiethnic Communities Project's initial scope was to identify and disseminate information on good practices in the effective management of multi-ethnic communities. The working premise was that 'the establishment of inclusive systems of local governance in general and from an ethnic perspective in particu-lar, is an important first step towards building participatory systems overall …' (Bíró and Kovács 2001: 12). In its initial stages, the project specifically aimed at analysing good practices, drawing the lessons learned from these practices, and transferring them to other communities, local or regional governments, NGOs, and educational institutions. Cases of innovative local multiethnic policy manage-ment were identified and subsequent case studies were posted on the Internet site of the project.[10] The case-study approach contributed to understanding the need for support of local government capacity-building and multi-disciplinary training of public officials to address problems related to the governance of multiethnic communities.

To condense and learn from the regional case study experiences, the project developed a special curriculum on Management of Multiethnic Communities. A textbook was devised to serve as a teaching material for faculties of public admin-istration and public policy, and for other potential trainers in the region. Published in early 2001, it has been tested in a series of pilot trainings designed for public administrators and other potential users. After a pilot training in Budapest a series of four training sessions were organised in Bosnia, Montenegro and Macedonia within the framework of CIDA and OSI cooperation under the Stability Pact; the kind of official support which demonstrates a quickly gained recognition of this truly new policy developing endeavour.

Some of the Managing Multiethnic Communities Project trainings were also specifically targeting the Roma. In 1999, LGI prepared a training curriculum for Roma elected leaders to improve their expertise in participating more effectively in local governance, and build their capacities for efficient interest-representation.[11] The experience and expertise for this training course came partly from the afore-mentioned good practice project whose collected case studies were carefully studied before the first training. In addition a needs assessment survey was con-ducted among Roma elected leaders in Hungary, which helped the organisers in designing the first pilot training session held in Hungary. The pilot training program resulted in the elaboration of a methodology and the training of 50 Roma leaders. Following the pilot course, in the same year, capacity-building training courses were also organised for other elected Roma leaders in four regional centres in Hungary. After careful local needs assessment the training was replicated in 2000 in Brno in the Czech Republic, and in Bratislava, Slovakia. New versions of the training are under development for Bulgaria and for Ukraine.

The Managing Multiethnic Communities Project of the LGI, Budapest is a good example of a network programme heavily involved in transnational policy processes concerning the Roma in the region. Also evident through the evolution of the projects is how action research and expertise can be generated in network programmes and how the gained expertise can be disseminated or 'exported' to other countries of the region. The project also highlights the potentials of transferring skills and methodology to empower Roma leaders and address the main policy making actor: the state.

An ambitious network-wide initiative in Roma policies was launched at the conference 'Roma in an Expanding Europe: Challenges for the Future' in July 2003.[12] The conference was co-sponsored by the Open Society Institute and the World Bank, and brought together Romani leaders, high-level government officials from eight Central and Eastern European countries, and other international leaders in an attempt to address the need for Roma inclusion in society and in policy making processes. The conference can be seen as recognition of the accumulated knowledge, credibility, and advocacy power of the Soros Foundations Network among the international developmental agencies. At the conference, Soros called for a 'Decade of Roma inclusion'. Spanning from 2005 to 2015, its aim is to provide a framework for governments to set their own goals for Roma integration (World Bank 2003).

The World Bank also plans to initiate a complementary Roma Education Fund, which is planned to scale up successful pilot projects proposed to improve Romani education (OSI 2003b). At the conference, Soros argued that:

> The *Decade* represents a comprehensive approach to address the issues that Romani leaders have identified: education, employment, housing and discrimination. It marks the first time the highest levels of government and international leadership have come together with the Roma to assist them in determining their own future.
>
> (OSI 2003b)

A task force was set up, headed by the Hungarian Prime Minister, to coordinate the actions towards the plan. The Decade plan was endorsed beyond the Soros Foundations Network and the World Bank, by the European Commission, the UNDP, the Council of Europe, the governments of Finland and Sweden, and most importantly, by governments of almost all concerned countries.[13]

The Soros Foundations Network sees itself not only as one of the initiators of the Decade plan but also as one of the central actors taking part in the coordinated action towards its fulfilment. The knowledge and expertise cultivated in the network over the past decade and more are finding outlet in this multi-lateral initiative. By launching this initiative the Soros Foundations Network's role in the region and at the international level as an important actor in the agenda setting concerning the Roma issue is further strengthened.

Regardless of the future successes or failures of the Decade project, it should be noted that the Budapest conference itself, and the initiatives it gave birth to, have made major progress in regional policy thinking on the Roma. They have connected the human rights and the poverty languages in the policy discourses targeting the plight of the Roma in the CEE region. It has been a much-needed step to combine poverty reduction and developmental concepts with an equal opportunity agenda, and in reverse, to enhance the understanding of economic redistribution issues in the human rights debates. This has been the result of collaboration between a transnational NGO with strong open society sensitivity and a major global developmental agency – albeit we are not claiming that these two organisations are the only ones making this conceptual and discursive shift.

From the development described above, one might assume that the Soros Foundations Network treats the Roma issue as one of its priority fields. Yet, due to the shift from 'first-come, first-served' and individual merit-based funding (such as scholarships and grant competition for non-governmental activities) towards supporting an inclusive policy making process, the scope of policy thinking in Roma issues has crucially changed in the network. All Roma programmes in the network, on the one hand, provide state authorities with skills for dealing with the integration of Roma communities in the long term. On the other hand, they promote the development of long lasting and sustainable structures for an equitable and informed involvement of the Roma in the processes of policy making, policy implementation, and monitoring, especially with respect to policies concerning their own group. Roma policies represent a very sensitive policy area for the group of EU accession countries. In this respect, the Soros Foundations Network attempts not only to work together and complement the activities of the respective states, but it also cooperates with the European Commission and other EU institutions in the accession process.

Conclusion

The Soros Foundations Network's role in policy research, debate, and implementation with respect to the Roma in the region is extensive and multiple. The network as a structure allows the integration of various types of research and knowledge generation work into designing more specific policy research, monitoring, and advocacy. Most notably, the International Policy Fellow's research results are often fed into the work of different network programmes, or the grantees themselves become integrated into these programmes. A growing number of instances show that 'white-paper-type' of research reports completed by IPF grantees could move and stir the public debates, and catch significant domestic and international attention. Moreover, when research is conducted together with community capacity building and professional training as 'action research', the utility of the research is greatly enhanced. The coordinated and institutionalised input of the Roma related research and policy analysis work of the network into state and international level policy making processes – as foreseen by the Decade plan for the Roma – also increases the impact of research and other policy work done by the Soros network.

The Roma-related programmes of the Soros Foundations Network expose some major characteristics of the policy process in Central and Eastern Europe. States are not the only actors participating in the formation and implementation of policies. However, cooperation among different stakeholders is often hindered by various weaknesses such as absence of coordination structures and lack of necessary skills in designing and implementing efficient policies. Roma programmes have also uncovered that state capacities in the respective policy fields need to be upgraded both in terms of professional and financial resources. To obtain these resources, states are likely to be reliant on various international actors and networks. Most importantly, the EU accession process provides a strong incentive for state machinery to use the support that EU bodies offer. For example, a relatively large amount of funding is available from the PHARE programme for Roma projects in the region. However, only properly designed programmes will be able to receive this kind of support. Various network units are already prepared to assist governments in the region to design and master major projects suitable for EU support.

In sum, one may argue that the Soros Foundations Network has developed a large and diversified body of knowledge from its first-hand contact, support and monitoring of various projects pursued by its units and grantees. The network is far from having a well-developed framework and practice for processing and sharing all this knowledge within its institutional scheme or with its major partners. But one can find many good examples, especially in the field of minority issues, of a regulated two-way transfer of knowledge within the network. The Decade plan will require coordinated action not only on the CEE regional level between states and public or private international donors, but also within the network.

The approach of the network to the insufficiencies of the communication between knowledge production and policy seems to put the emphasis within network programmes on a supply side approach outlined in the introduction. The assumption underlying most activities of the network reviewed here is that there is no sufficient policy relevant research available in the region. In order to bridge research and policy such research capacities have to be enhanced, relevant research needs to be generated, repackaged and communicated to intervene into the policy process and the policy making community. The network proposes to improve policy research capacities, to commission appropriately designed and focused research (often from researchers who are not related to the network) and to communicate and coordinate such research. Approaching the problem from the demand side so far has been given less emphasis in the activities of the network. This can be explained, on the one hand, by the limited receptivity of policy makers towards cooperation with the Soros Foundations Network and, on the other hand, by the importance of the value of independence for the network and the cautious stance determined by it.

Finally, in Central and Eastern Europe, it is a strange state of affairs that minority policy experts frequently cannot rely on vast sources of empirical findings, analyses, and comparative inquiries that may support policy research and advocacy. At the same time, ethnicity, nationalism, ethnic conflicts, xenophobia, and forms of social exclusion are among the most fashionable and frequented topics in sociological, anthropological, and social history research. It is yet to be analysed why social research has given relatively small intellectual impetus to policy thinkers, and, vice versa, why policy analysts do not translate social knowledge to their own professional language. It should be noted that the network has sponsored social research of crucial policy relevance through its grants and fellowship schemes. However, due to the nature of a traditional and detached academic environment, financial support has not required the promotion and implementation of research results in policy circles. This puzzle is more curious in an organisation that has given tremendous support to improving higher education programmes in the humanities and social sciences. But to unpick this puzzle is a task for another study.

Notes

1 In 1994 the network spent a total of 300 million USD; in 1995, 350 million USD; in 1996, 362 million USD; in 1997, 428 million USD; in 1998, 574 million USD; in 1999, 560 million USD; and in 2000, 494 million USD. See more information on the website of the Soros network at http://www.soros.org.
2 Details can be found at http://lgi.osi.hu/ppi/default.asp.
3 See http://www.soros.org/initiatives/esp.
4 A good example for commissioned research is the Roma Education Research Project which aimed at improving educational programming for Roma children. As a foundation for this effort, the Education Sub-Board (ESB) of the Open Society Institute (OSI) commissioned a focused research project in September 2000 to examine and learn from existing educational programmes serving Roma children. Based on criteria developed and recommendations provided by a Roma Education Working Group, seven Roma education programmes were identified to serve as the focus for this research. Conclusions were drawn across the investigated programmes as well as for each individual programme. Results were aimed to inform among others the future activity of the Education Sub-Board. See http://www.osi.hu/esp/rei/rerp.html (accessed: 29 July 2003).
5 For more information about the program and the work of fellows see the IPF website at http://www.policy.hu. Tsedev's personal website is http://www.policy.hu/tsedev (accessed: 4 August 2003).
6 In some cases EU members' country performance is also monitored. For example the 2002 Monitoring Minority Protection in EU Member States covers minority policies in Germany, France, UK, Italy and Spain. See http://www.eumap.org/reports/2002/content/09 (accessed: 4 August 2003).
7 For more information concerning the methodology see http://www.eumap.org/about (accessed: 29 July 2003).
8 For more information on the European Roma Rights Center see http://www.errc.org. (accessed: 29 July 2003).
9 Concerning Canek's work see http://www.policy.hu/canek (accessed: 10 June 2003).
10 See http://lgi.osi.hu/ethnic.
11 See http://lgi.osi.hu/ethnic/roma/index.html (accessed: 29 July 2003).
12 For more information about the conference see http://www.worldbank.org/roma conference (accessed: 29 July 2003).

13 'In addition to Roma leaders, the event was attended by the Prime Ministers of Hungary, Bulgaria, Macedonia, Montenegro, and Romania as well as Ministers from Croatia, the Czech Republic, Serbia and Montenegro, Slovakia, and Sweden. Ms Anna Diamantopoulou, European Commissioner for Employment and Social Affairs, OSI Chairman George Soros, President James Wolfensohn of the World Bank and UNDP Administrator Mark Malloch Brown also attended the conference' (World Bank, 2003).

References

Bíró, Anna-Mária and Kovács, Petra (eds) (2001) *Diversity in Action. Local Public Management of Multi-Ethnic Communities in Central and Eastern Europe*. LGI Books.

EUMAP (2003) 'Activity and Impact Report November 2002–June 2003' Internal OSI document.

LGI (2000) 'Roma PA Training in Slovakia'. Interim Report No. 2 to the LGI – OSI, Budapest.

LGI (2002a) 'A Postgraduate Program in Public Administration for Roma Representatives in Central and Local State Administration – Bulgaria'. Project proposal submitted to LGI – OSI, Budapest.

LGI (2002b) *Open Society Institute Related Public Policy Centres. Activity Report* 2002. LGI Documents.

Neier, Aryeh (1998) 'The Middle of the Journey', in *Building Open Societies. Soros Foundations Network 1998 Report*, p. 15.

OSI (1994) *Building Open Societies. Soros Foundations Report.*

OSI (1996) *Building Open Societies. Soros Foundations Network 1996 Report.*

OSI (1998) *Building Open Societies. Soros Foundations Network 1998 Report.*

OSI (2003a) 'Roma Programs'. Brief distributed at the conference *Roma in an Expanding Europe.*

OSI (2003b) Press release of July 8. Available online at http://www.soros.org/ news/roma_decade.pdf.

Ringold, D., Orenstein, M. and Wilkens, E. (2003) *Roma in an Expanding Europe: Breaking the Poverty Cycle. World Bank Study.* Available online at http://www.worldbank.org/roma.

Soros, George (1997) 'The Capitalist Threat' *The Atlantic Monthly* 279 (2, February): 45–58.

UNDP (2002) *Avoiding the Dependency Trap. The Roma in Central and Eastern Europe. A Regional Human Development Report.* Bratislava: UNDP RBEC.

World Bank (2003) 'World Bank Supports New Roma Education Fund, Decade Initiative'. News Release. Available online at http://web.worldbank.org/WBSITE/EXTERNAL/ NEWS/0,,contentMDK:20117977~menuPK:34463~pagePK:34370~piPK:34424~theS itePK:4607,00.html.

Zoon, Ina (2001) *On the Margins. Slovakia.* Roma and Public Services in Slovakia. Open Society Institute.

Index

access to global public policy networks 101
Accessible Information on Development Activities (AIDA) 82
accountability 10–11, 19, 22–4, 50
action links 10
advisory committees 6
Africa: developmental issues and institutions 156–8; reconstruction research 156–67; implications for analysis and practice 162–3; security communities 162; track-two diplomacy 163–4
African Centre for the Cooperative Resolution of Disputes (ACCORD) 158
African Economic Research Consortium (AERC) 106, 109, 112, 118
AFSSRN 13, 139, 145–7; capacity building 153; intent 151; key findings 147–53; long-tern commitments 150; national research capacity 148–9; Phase I 146; Phase III 146; Phase IV 147
Agarwal, Bina 111
agenda-setting 61, 168
agents of knowledge 9
agora: as structured space 102; characterisation 90; definition 89–90
Agricultural Policy Research Unit 48
agricultural projection modelling 51
agricultural research and development: rates of return 38
Ahmed, Akhter 49
aid: knowledge-based 72–88
Ain o Sailesh Kendra (ASK) 123
alliance model 14
Alwang, J. 51
Anderson, J.R. 47
Animal Health in Kenya 22, 26
Annan, Kofi 110–11
anti-intellectualism in government 3
ASEAN Institutes of Strategic and International Affairs (ASEAN-ISIS) 91, 97, 103
ASEAN Regional Forum 91

Asia Crisis, 1997 26
Asian Fisheries Social Science Research Network (*see* AFSSRN)
Association for Strengthening Agricultural Research in Eastern and Central Africa (ASARECA) 48
Attacking Poverty 63
attribution 37–56; issue of 53
Aziz, Sartaj 48

Babu, S. 44
Banda, Enric 111
Bangladesh 6, 44–5, 47, 49
Bangladesh Institute of Development Studies 48
bare-foot vets 6
bibliometric indices 42
bilateral development agencies 72
Blacklock, C. 129
blood diamonds 10, 159–60
Blue Bird 92, 98–9
BMZ 73
Botchwey, Kwesi 111
Bourdieau, Pierre 62
Box, Louk de la Rive 66
Brazil: World Bank projects 62
bridging research and policy 8–11, 18–36, 46, 54; comprehensiveness 31; overview 1–8
Bridging Research and Policy programme 119–20
British Petroleum 74
Burfisher, M.E. 39
Byerlee, D. 47

Callaghy, T.M. 161
Campbell, H. 39
Canadian International Development Agency (CIDA) 73, 75, 176, 178
CANDID 9, 57, 69; case studies 59–65
Canek, David 177
capacity building 171
Carden, F. 10, 13
Cassandra problem 40

eBooks – at www.eBookstore.tandf.co.uk

A library at your fingertips!

eBooks are electronic versions of printed books. You can store them on your PC/laptop or browse them online.

They have advantages for anyone needing rapid access to a wide variety of published, copyright information.

eBooks can help your research by enabling you to bookmark chapters, annotate text and use instant searches to find specific words or phrases. Several eBook files would fit on even a small laptop or PDA.

NEW: Save money by eSubscribing: cheap, online access to any eBook for as long as you need it.

Annual subscription packages

We now offer special low-cost bulk subscriptions to packages of eBooks in certain subject areas. These are available to libraries or to individuals.

For more information please contact webmaster.ebooks@tandf.co.uk

We're continually developing the eBook concept, so keep up to date by visiting the website.

www.eBookstore.tandf.co.uk